D1051415

About Island Press

Since 1984, the nonprofit organization Island Press has been stimulating, shaping, and communicating ideas that are essential for solving environmental problems worldwide. With more than 1,000 titles in print and some 30 new releases each year, we are the nation's leading publisher on environmental issues. We identify innovative thinkers and emerging trends in the environmental field. We work with world-renowned experts and authors to develop cross-disciplinary solutions to environmental challenges.

Island Press designs and executes educational campaigns in conjunction with our authors to communicate their critical messages in print, in person, and online using the latest technologies, innovative programs, and the media. Our goal is to reach targeted audiences—scientists, policymakers, environmental advocates, urban planners, the media, and concerned citizens—with information that can be used to create the framework for long-term ecological health and human well-being.

Island Press gratefully acknowledges major support of our work by The Agua Fund, The Andrew W. Mellon Foundation, The Bobolink Foundation, The Curtis and Edith Munson Foundation, Forrest C. and Frances H. Lattner Foundation, The JPB Foundation, The Kresge Foundation, The Oram Foundation, Inc., The Overbrook Foundation, The S.D. Bechtel, Jr. Foundation, The Summit Charitable Foundation, Inc., and many other generous supporters.

The opinions expressed in this book are those of the author(s) and do not necessarily reflect the views of our supporters.

Praise for *Nature's Fortune*

"Mark Tercek presents a timely argument for 'valuing' nature that will be meaningful as much to business as to environmentalists. He demonstrates how this can work and why it is important, whether with water and forests high in the Andes, the floodplains of the Mississippi, fisheries off the California coast, or even in the dense centers of major cities. The result is a compelling 'business case' for investment in nature that is also an agenda for action—and cooperation."

—DANIEL YERGIN, Pulitzer Prize-winning author of *The Quest: Energy, Security, and the Remaking of the Modern World*

"In *Nature's Fortune*, Mark Tercek tackles the environment with a banker's eye and an outdoorsman's heart. He makes a clear case for why protecting nature is the smartest investment we can make."

—TED TURNER, Chairman, Turner Enterprises, Inc.

"[a] very readable book . . . answer[s] the question of why anyone on Wall Street would be interested in green policy . . ."

—*Financial Times*

"This is a critically important book that comes at just the right moment. The business community is coming to understand the value—and the necessity—of protecting the environment. Now, the environmental community needs to talk about nature using the language of business: assets, risks, and innovation. *Nature's Fortune* is the guidebook that can move environmentalism to this next level."

—WALTER ISAACSON, President and CEO, The Aspen Institute, and author of *The Innovators*

"In *Nature's Fortune*, Mark Tercek and Jonathan Adams expertly articulate the interdependence of our economy and nature's economy, and the practiced ways both can be saved in perpetuity."

—EDWARD O. WILSON, Harvard University Research Professor, Emeritus

"The authors convincingly argue that corporate responsibility is not only the right ethical tactic, but the right business move . . . According to this savvy book, both environmentalists and business executives need to understand how nature contributes to economic and ecological well-being."

—*Publishers Weekly*

"Tercek has made it his mission to . . . re–formulate the way we think about economic and environmental issues, and to pursue conservation projects through innovative collaborations around the world."

—RICHARD HERTZBERG, *The Oregonian*

"From renewal of the Mississippi floodplain to the banning of fishing trawlers along our shores to the restoration of prairie and wetlands in urban areas, unlikely allies are coming together to create models of sustainability that serve the interests of both business and environmentalist groups. The authors examine this new kind of conservation and show how it is of utmost economic importance to our farms, fisheries, corporate stakeholders, and communities."

—*Booklist*

"If ever business and nature are going to realize their full potential to grow together, it will come about from the vision and perspectives that are contained in the pages of this book. A case like this could only be made by an author who has led passionately on both sides of the equation."

—ANDREW N. LIVERIS, Chairman and Chief Executive Officer, The Dow Chemical Company

"This book makes plain-as-day why we need to stop taking nature's gifts for granted. Its thoughtful solutions can underpin conservation goals with a powerful business logic. From an alarming premise, we are given reason to hope."

—CHRIS ANDERSON, TED Curator

"In this encouraging, intelligent book that comes none too soon, Mark Tercek and Jonathan Adams show that the corporate world ultimately can't flourish unless the natural world does, too. Through stories equally compelling to entrepreneurs or environmentalists, CEOs or scientists, we see how Nature's Fortune and our own are inextricable. If we conserve and nurture our planet's gifts like any other crucial asset or investment, we profit—or, we squander them at our own peril. Happily, this book shows why we needn't, ever."

—ALAN WEISMAN, author of *The World Without Us* and *Countdown: Our Last, Best Hope on Earth*

"There are probably more important reasons to protect the natural world, but as this book makes clear, it's economic folly to keep wasting our one sweet planet. It's worth infinitely more than economists have traditionally taught—infinitely more!"

—BILL MCKIBBEN, author of *The End of Nature* and founder, 350.org

"The cause of conservation in the twenty-first century desperately needs sharp, sophisticated, practical minds from the world of commerce. Mark Tercek's is clearly among the best of them."

—DAVID QUAMMEN, author of *Spillover* and *The Song of the Dodo*

"Nature is essential for both our human as well as our economic well-being. As someone who has lived in both worlds, Mark Tercek is well positioned to take us on a guided tour of the intersection between business and the environment. With clear examples, this timely book provides a road map for smart investments and new alliances to build a sustainable and prosperous future for people and planet. Bravo!"

—HELENE GAYLE, President and CEO, CARE USA

"Nature has long been recognized as a source of wealth, but we have yet to give natural capital the proper weight in economic decision making. In this timely book, Mark Tercek argues persuasively that investing in conservation and sustainable use can yield huge dividends for both people and the environment."

—LUIS ALBERTO MORENO, President of the Inter-American Development Bank

"In this telling work . . . Mark Tercek reveals how an investment banker becomes a conservationist and brings two seemingly incompatible worlds together with amazing grace and immense success."

—MARSHALL GOLDSMITH, author of *What Got You Here Won't Get You There*, *MOJO*, and *Succession*

"In the 1970s, environmentalists and business despised each other. In this century, they are often close partners. The change was brought about by leaders like Mark Tercek. His book shows how prosperity is as dependent on clean rivers as on strong bridges (both are infrastructure). GMO crops can be as welcome as restoring wildlands, since they both contribute to a healthier planet."

—STEWART BRAND, author of *Whole Earth Discipline*

"Mark Tercek argues with refreshing clarity and persuasiveness that we must recognize the substantial economic value in our scarce natural resources. I agree wholeheartedly that the ultimate allocation and use of these resources must be market-based, backed by wise regulation. Tercek makes his point with wonderful real-life examples and prodigious logic."

—JOHN FAHEY, Chairman and CEO, National Geographic Society

"This is an important book for environmentalists, investment bankers, and everyone else. It presents a compelling case that investing in nature is a great deal—not just morally but economically as well. It is in all of our enlightened self-interest to take this book very seriously."

—MORTON SCHAPIRO, Professor of Economics and President, Northwestern University

Nature's Fortune

Nature's Fortune

How Business and Society Thrive by Investing in Nature

MARK R. TERCEK
JONATHAN S. ADAMS

ISLANDPRESS

Washington | Covelo | London

For Amy, Alison, Margo, Luke, and Rex.
For Susan, Madeleine, and Joseph.

Contents

A Note to Readers

As President and CEO of The Nature Conservancy, I always advocate for greater investments in protecting nature. Many people encouraged me to put my ideas about such investments in writing in order to reach a broader audience. I'd never written a book before so I knew I would need help. I turned to Jonathan Adams—a great science writer whose books I very much admire. Jonathan has been a strong and full partner in this project. This is how we worked: I came up with the original argument for the book. Thereafter, Jonathan and I together developed the stories, did the necessary research, talked with experts, wrote draft after draft, and refined the argument. I've really enjoyed the partnership. Jonathan has been a great coauthor. To capture the spirit of the talks that inspired this book, we've written the book together in my voice.

Mark R. Tercek

Introduction

WHAT IS AN INVESTMENT BANKER DOING TRYING TO SAVE NATURE?
At one of my first big events after I joined The Nature Conservancy
(TNC), I was in a room filled with giants from the field—environmental
thought leaders, major philanthropists, and leaders of other conservation
organizations.

One guest in particular stood out from the crowd: a gentleman in
his nineties, still fit and sharp. His manners were impeccable, even
courtly, yet he was also clearly not a man to trifle with. Something
about him said, "Don't waste my time."

I quickly realized that this must be Russell E. Train, a legend in the
conservation movement: second administrator of the Environmental
Protection Agency, first chairman of the President's Council on Environmental Quality, and founding director of the World Wildlife
Fund. I was the new kid on the block and I was way out of my league.

"Who are you?" Mr. Train said, gruffly but not unkindly. I explained
that I was the new president and CEO of TNC and added some details about my Wall Street background.

He was unimpressed. "How did you get from Wall Street to become the head of TNC?"

I fumbled for the right words but did not find them. We moved on to other topics. Russell Train passed away while I was writing this book. Here is what I wish I had told him.

How I Got Here

Unlike many conservationists, especially leaders of environmental non-profits, I didn't spend my childhood in the late 1960s and early 1970s roaming the great outdoors. I wasn't a backpacker, hiker, kayaker, tree climber, or bug collector. I didn't bale hay or herd sheep. I was a city boy. Born and raised in a working-class area of Cleveland, I spent plenty of time outside — shooting baskets, delivering the *Cleveland Plain Dealer*, shoveling snow, mowing lawns — but not in contemplating "nature" in the grand sense of the word.

In college, I majored in English and busied myself with acting or trying to write poetry, not spending time outdoors or immersed in environmental causes. After I graduated in 1979 I moved to Japan, where I taught English and studied martial arts, then worked for Bank of America. From there, it was on to Harvard Business School and then to a twenty-four-year career at the rapidly growing investment firm Goldman Sachs.

My evolution into a conservationist began as I worked as an investment banker for Goldman Sachs — and, more tellingly, when I became a parent. Like many, I struggled to pry my kids away from their computers and televisions. Hiking and camping were my tools. I found that I enjoyed nature in ways I never had when I was young.

I read *The New Economy of Nature: The Quest to Make Conservation Profitable*, the 2002 book by Stanford University's Gretchen Daily, a professor of environmental science. The book explained the workings of ecosystems and how they delivered goods and services to people. This scientific examination of nature delivering value began to build my appreciation for nature and prompted me to reflect on opportunities and price tags.

After reading Gretchen's book, I called her. Our first conversation, with Gretchen talking biology and me talking finance, was a bit awkward, but it had a lasting impact on me. I started asking the same questions about ecology as my MBA training had taught me to apply to corporate finance: What is nature's value? Who invests in it, when and why? What rates of return can an investment in nature produce? When is protecting nature a good investment? Isn't conservation really about building natural capital?

Toward the end of my Wall Street career, I was fortunate to have the opportunity to find some answers. I was on the verge of leaving Goldman Sachs in 2005, but then-CEO Henry M. Paulson, a committed conservationist who would later serve as Treasury Secretary under President George W. Bush, persuaded me to stay on to build an environmental effort for the firm.

Our idea was simple: it made great commercial sense to employ a group of environmental experts to explore business opportunities for Goldman Sachs. Our primary motivation was not philanthropy or corporate social responsibility, important as those are, but purely business.

We pursued opportunities that produced two kinds of benefits: good commercial results for Goldman Sachs and good environmental outcomes. The more we pursued these win-win opportunities, the more we found. For example, we pushed our investment research division to evaluate companies on their environmental record as well as their financial bottom line. We asked our private equity colleagues to prioritize investments in renewable energy companies. In advisory roles with corporate clients, we showed companies how improving their environmental behavior would bolster their business results. The firm even created a magnificent protected area in rugged Tierra del Fuego in far southern Chile—an investment that produced big returns by inspiring staff and recruits, intriguing clients, and pleasing government partners.

As we pursued these environmental initiatives, we began to collaborate with environmental nonprofit organizations such as TNC, the Wildlife Conservation Society, the World Resources Institute, Resources for the Future, and others. We were surprised and impressed by how much we learned from these partners. We also thought they learned a lot from us. I became excited about the world of environmental organizations and how they might productively partner with the private sector.

I was a late bloomer but protecting nature became my cause and my passion.

The Idea of Natural Capital

I left Goldman Sachs in 2008 to become president and CEO of TNC. When my cellphone rang with the news that I might get the job, I was so excited that I backed my car right into a tree. My back window was shattered. The tree was fine.

TNC seemed to be a perfect fit for me. A sixty-year-old organization with some 4000 staff members pursuing conservation in all fifty states and thirty-five countries around the world, TNC has a reputation for getting things done in a pragmatic, science-based, and no-nonsense style. TNC reminded me of an investment bank—but one whose client was nature itself. I thought TNC was the ideal organization to champion the idea of natural capital, putting a value on nature as an asset.

Putting a value on nature is a tricky and even controversial task. Environmentalists tend to love nature for its own sake, love being outdoors, and believe their children and generations beyond should inherit a world as vibrant and as diverse as the one they experienced. These are all enormously important reasons to protect nature. A business perspective, however, reveals other, perhaps less lofty but no less important reasons to do so—for example, securing the clean water nature provides, and the timber people need to manufacture houses and furniture. Valuing nature does not mean replacing one set of compelling arguments for conservation with another, but it provides an additional and important rationale for supporting the environment.

I BEGAN TO THINK SYSTEMATICALLY ABOUT BUSINESS, BUSINESS PRINCIPLES, and what nature really means. *Nature* is a complicated word—more complicated than I knew. People often speak about human nature, or Mother Nature. But in thinking about this word, I realized that people generally also consider nature as something separate from themselves—something distant, out there in national parks and in the wilderness.

I want to get away from that simple dichotomy. Nature is not just something to preserve in a few special places and degrade in others. Nature is everywhere. Yet nature is also not just a source of practical, tangible benefits to people. It has a deeper meaning to people around the world. By my definition, nature means all species of animals and plants, their habitats and the ecological processes that support them. This broad definition includes human beings but does not include all the things that humans have built, often in a misguided attempt to control nature. Trying to dominate nature will likely fail, but bringing nature back into how people organize society, run businesses, design cities, and even how we live our daily lives can give us reason to hope.

Business as an Environmental Partner

Thinking about the value of nature leads to other ways of thinking familiar to business analysts. For example, concepts such as *maximize returns, invest in your assets, manage your risks, diversify,* and *promote innovation* are the common parlance of business and banking. These are rarely applied to nature, but they should be.

Viewing nature through these basic business principles focuses more attention on the benefits of conservation. You may not become a conservationist, but you will realize that conservation—protection of nature—is a central and important driver of economic activity, every bit as important as manufacturing, finance, agriculture, and so on.

My experience as an environmentalist at Goldman Sachs revealed new possibilities, but I recognize that relationships with businesses can be complicated and risky for environmental organizations. Hardcore environmentalists can be quick to criticize organizations such as TNC when they build alliances with companies. They sometimes see such collaborations as consorting with the enemy. Nevertheless, in my view, seizing the opportunity to work with companies as they pursue environmental strategies to strengthen their business provides the chance to create significant conservation gains.

Companies can be good partners for environmentalists in other ways as well. Large businesses control huge amounts of natural resources, often more than governments. Contrary to popular opinion, companies can be better at making long-term plans for those resources than governments, which often get hamstrung by political divides and the short-term thinking driven by the next election cycle. Companies that have short time horizons and neglect long-term planning and investing generally lose out in the marketplace. Most companies also do a good job of dealing with reality. For example, they tend to accept rather than deny the conclusions of science; otherwise, again, they get punished in the marketplace. There are exceptions—some bad actors in the business community seek to exploit loopholes, break regulations, or mislead the public—usually in misguided pursuit of short-term gain. But in an era of increasing transparency, more companies understand that it is ultimately going to be in their own best interest to follow the rules and to try to do the right thing. They also increasingly understand that investments in nature can produce big financial returns.

Still, nothing is free from risk. Critics sometimes challenge me— "Are you sure working with business will produce environmental benefits?" Of course I'm not sure. But I believe we should try. If other organizations have alternative strategies, I say that's great, too. Let's see what works best. We need more environmental strategies, and we need to pursue them with vigor and confidence, as well as a receptivity to critiques and ideas about how to improve them.

A Three-Legged Stool

All of these considerations lead to an important question. How should environmentalists work with business? I believe the best way forward is to think of business as one of the legs of a three-legged stool. The other two are governments and individuals. Saving the world from environmental degradation requires all three.

Governments and individuals should encourage and welcome voluntary environmental initiatives by business. But to scale such initiatives up in a meaningful way, governments will need to enact strong and effective policies. The role of government goes even further than this regulatory responsibility. Think of the billions of dollars governments invest in infrastructure every year. More of these investments should be made in natural capital.

In turn, to get governments and businesses to do the right thing, individuals need to motivate them as voters and consumers, respectively. These three actors—businesses, governments, and individuals—now have the opportunity to come together to create new practices in pursuit of conservation as a means to invest in and benefit from natural capital. Conservation organizations should do all they can to make this happen.

Environmentalists generally believe in nature's inherent value. That idea is the bedrock of the environmental movement. However, environmentalists cannot persuade everyone to think along the same lines. Focusing only on the innate wonders of nature risks alienating potential supporters and limits the environmental community's ability to reach a broader audience and to mine sources of new ideas. The "Isn't nature wonderful?" argument can leave the impression that nature offers solely aesthetic benefits, or worse, that nature is a luxury only rich people or rich countries can afford. We need to get business, government, and individuals to understand that nature is not only wonderful, it is also economically valuable. Indeed, nature is the fundamental underpinning to human well-being.

One way is to connect nature to what concerns people most—how to make lives better, protect health, create jobs, and strengthen the economy. Whether they grew up in the city or the country, in the United States, Brazil, or Indonesia, and no matter what they've studied or read, every person shares these concerns. In many places around the world people believe they have more pressing concerns than conserving nature, and those concerns will take precedence unless they better understand what nature provides.

The Way Forward

I'm an optimist. I see nature as remarkably resilient and ready to rally if we make smart investments. Optimism notwithstanding, finding workable, science-driven solutions means looking unflinchingly at the facts. And the facts are troubling. Despite the best efforts of the world's passionate and hardworking conservationists, we are simply not getting the job done. We need to move fast to set things on the right path.

To be sure, conservation has won some crucial victories. Over the past half century in the United States alone, the government banned DDT, created the Environmental Protection Agency, and passed the Endangered Species, Clean Water, and Clean Air Acts. Deforestation in the Amazon has slowed and new marine-protected areas have been created across the Pacific. Scientists and activists have worked with government agencies to bring species back from the brink of extinction and to protect some of the world's greatest places.

Still, nearly every precious bit of nature—teeming coral reefs, sweeping grasslands, lush forests, the rich diversity of life itself—is in decline. Everything humanity should reduce—suburban sprawl, deforestation, overfishing, carbon emissions—has increased. The thirteen warmest years for the entire planet have all occurred since 1998, and 2012 was the warmest year on record for the United States. Although daily weather fluctuations cannot be definitively linked to climate change, the collection of droughts, floods, heat waves, enormous storms, and record rainfalls unmistakably signals the need for action.

Communities and nations have made conservation breakthroughs before, and they can do so again. This time, instead of the towering figures of conservation history such as Theodore Roosevelt and Rachel Carson, the catalyst may be newly emerging and highly innovative environmentalists—innovators like Kenya's Wangari Maathai, who passed away too soon, in 2011. Wangari successfully and courageously brought together conservation, economic development, human rights, and democracy goals as a way to make substantial environmental progress, first in Kenya and later around the world. Looking ahead, we need more people to challenge convention, take risks, and tackle the world's big environmental challenges. Unlikely alliances should emerge—businesses, investors, and governments joining farmers, ranchers, students, and urbanites—to pursue strategies based on a shared understanding that we all depend on nature.

These new alliances will enable us to conserve nature at a scale never before achieved. The point is not just to help businesses and governments do less harm, but to make them become part of something far bigger. Saving nature means saving wild species and wild places, but it also means saving ourselves. This opportunity is real, it may not come again, and it should be humankind's priority to achieve it fully and achieve it now.

1

Maybe It's Not *Chinatown* After All

I FIRST MET CARLOS SALAZAR AT A LUNCHEON GATHERING OF conservation scientists and business leaders in Cartagena, Colombia in October 2011. A savvy and successful businessman, Salazar is not an environmentalist. His business, however, depends almost entirely on water. Over the past few years, he began to take seriously the possibility that the growing global water scarcity may soon be at his doorstep.

Salazar runs Coca-Cola FEMSA, the largest independent Coke bottler in the world. His business sprawls across nine countries in Latin America. Running such an enormous organization has not in the past required expertise in ecology or biology, climate change or habitat loss. That may be changing. Salazar and people like him are now asking some of the toughest questions about water, business, and the value of nature.

Coca-Cola FEMSA does not own or have guaranteed access to the water at the core of its business. The key to a reliable water supply lies

1

far from the bottling plants themselves, in forested hills far upstream. Those forests hold rainwater and recharge aquifers, ensuring that water flows steadily to the valley below. Even though the company pays little for water, Salazar increasingly sees the forests as assets to be managed in his business plan. For that to happen, Salazar needs some hard numbers.

Salazar, intense and focused as CEOs often are, sought answers from me and the conservation scientists he had invited to join the lunch. "Tell me this," Salazar said. "If I want to produce water, should I protect an existing forest, or restore a forest that has been cut?" Salazar continued grilling us: "Are more diverse forests better at conserving water than single-species forests? How much water will I get from one versus the other? Where are the most important places to conserve to secure a reliable water supply?" Most important, at least from the business perspective, Salazar wanted to know this: "How much water will I get from each dollar I spend on conservation"?

Salazar has a simple goal: protect his water supply. If the best way to do that also results in saving more plants and more animals, so much the better. He also recognizes that other people depend on the same water resources. Were he to damage the resource he would also damage the company's image and its ability to operate. Whatever his goals, providing water for Coke bottling plants can go hand in hand with maintaining the forests in all their richness.

That may not always be the case—the win-win scenario may not always be available. Ecosystems produce a range of benefits, depending on how they are managed, and there are usually tradeoffs among the benefits. More trees in an ecosystem often means less water in streams in wet seasons, for example, because trees take up water. The flip side is that planting trees helps a landscape soak up and store rainfall, thus controlling floods and providing stream flow even during dry seasons. So each circumstance will need to be examined on its own merits, the trade-offs weighed and balanced. But it is encouraging to see that Coke and other water-dependent companies recognize that their success increasingly depends on where they get their water, how much it will cost, and the impact Coke's water use will have on other people and communities dependent on the same resources.

During my conversation with Salazar, I was struck by how his focus on protecting forests as an investment, and his concern for knowing the return on that investment, challenged the thinking of the conservationists at the table who too rarely frame questions in such business terms. Business executives and conservationists alike should follow Salazar's lead and fully consider the role of natural capital in all of their business planning.

We know the alarming reason why Salazar and others are asking such questions: the growing global scarcity of clean, fresh water. Our current water situation illustrates how properly valuing nature's services can provide important benefits to our environment, communities, and economies. Long a topic of interest for economists and prognosticators, scarcity has recently moved to the top of the agenda for corporate leaders.

Between now and 2050, the world's population will likely grow by an additional 2 billion people or more. Over the same period, billions of people will also join the middle class. By 2030, nearly two-thirds of the global population—as opposed to today's one-quarter—will be middle-class consumers. Seeing people lifted out of poverty is a welcome development. But a rapidly growing and more affluent population will also mean much more demand for food, energy, space, and water—putting strains on the natural systems that sustain natural diversity, human health, and prosperity.

Too Little Water

Whoever controls resources such as water also controls development. Just ask William Mulholland.

As head of the Los Angeles Department of Water and Power for over a quarter century, Mulholland bought huge swaths of the Owens Valley, a few hundred miles northeast of the city. He wasn't after the land. He really wanted the rights to the water that ran through or underneath it. By 1913, Mulholland had accumulated those rights, sometimes with furtive, unscrupulous tactics, and he built an aqueduct to bring water to Los Angeles. That water helped build the city, and the massive infrastructure carrying it still powers the economy of California. Owens Lake ran dry as a result.

Thus began the California Water Wars. Farmers in the valley tried to blow up the aqueduct. They opened sluice gates to fill the Owens River and water their orchards. The armed rebellion was ultimately unsuccessful. Agriculture in the Owens Valley region was decimated as Mulholland's aqueduct rerouted water to Los Angeles. Mulholland quipped that he regretted so many trees had died, because that meant fewer limbs from which to hang the troublemakers.

Mulholland left a decidedly mixed legacy: part visionary engineer, part Machiavelli. Those two faces of Mulholland were embodied in two characters in *Chinatown*, Roman Polanski's classic film noir; Hollis Mulwray, the city engineer whose murder opens the story, and Noah Cross, the unscrupulous land baron who was behind both the murder and the water grab. John Huston played the part of Noah Cross with delicious menace, and it's hard to argue with the portrayal. After all, Mulholland/Cross stole water from beneath California's farmers and sent it to L.A.

That might not be viewed as evil anymore. Removing water from agriculture to use it elsewhere — in cities, or simply leaving it in rivers and estuaries for fish and birds — may be beneficial. These are the kinds of trade-offs that communities, governments, and businesses will face with increasingly regularity. A market-based approach, guided by science and ethics, can provide a basis for making these hard choices. Buying and selling water or other parts of nature such as flood control or access to fisheries can be a force for good, if the laws governing the transactions make sense and people think broadly about who gains and who loses from them. Private gain from ownership of what have historically been public goods can work for both people and nature.

The challenge of water scarcity and distribution is global, with hardly any country protected from its impact, not even economically booming China. Everyone knows of China's astonishing economic successes, but few realize that water troubles now endanger continued growth. Almost half of China's rivers are severely polluted; more than 450 of its cities have water shortages; and 300 million of its people lack access to safe drinking water. More than a fifth of China's surface water is unfit even for agriculture. The amount of water available per person in China is about a quarter of the world average, yet the amount of water consumed per unit of gross domestic product in China is three times the world's average. China does not have enough water and it is using its water inefficiently.

China recognizes the threat water scarcity poses, but its proposed solution reflects the challenges of working at such a massive scale. In 2011, China's "No. 1 Document," which states the government's top priorities, proposed spending $635 billion over the next decade to solve the water problem. That is a lot of money to spend in so short a period, so it comes as no surprise that this plan has a serious drawback: it relies almost entirely on engineering solutions rather than investing in natural ecosystems to meet the water scarcity challenge.

THE UNITED STATES FACES SIMILAR CHALLENGES: SAN DIEGO, FOR example, may soon run dry. This growing city depends on the Colorado River for more than half of its water. Many users upstream from San Diego also claim rights to the river—to irrigate farms, fill Las Vegas fountains, or water suburban lawns and golf courses. To use the perfectly bland bureaucratic term, the Colorado is "oversubscribed"— frequently becoming just a sad trickle some seventy miles north of where it once entered the Gulf of California. In a year such as 2012, when rain and snowfall are well below normal, the Colorado runs out of water. With a changing climate, every year may soon be a bad year.

The Colorado River Basin includes seven states and a complex, contentious series of agreements dating back nearly a century determines who gets how much of the river's water. The latest turn in this long-running drama came in 2003, when the federal government reduced and capped Southern California's share. This accord sent San Diego scrambling to find water. The solution the local government implemented was a more aboveboard and equitable—though still controversial—version of William Mulholland's idea: moving water away from orchards and vegetable farms in the Imperial Valley and into the city. Instead of stealing the water, the city pays farmers in the Valley to consume less water. The city then uses the water saved to augment its water supply. This has given farmers the incentive to line irrigation canals to prevent water loss, to use more efficient irrigation techniques such as drip irrigation or microsprinklers, and to measure soil moisture with highly advanced technology so they know exactly when and where to irrigate. Some farmers have stopped growing crops on some land altogether. This is the largest farm-to-city water transfer ever. In 2011 alone, the farmers sent the city 80,000 acre-feet of water (one acre-foot is the amount of water needed to cover one acre to a depth of one foot, or just under 326,000 gallons), and this amount will increase to 200,000 acre-feet by 2021.

So far, so good. Other aspects of the deal, however, spark public controversy as well as lawsuits among water management agencies in Southern California. First, the farmers in the Imperial Valley buy water at federally subsidized agricultural rates, but sell their surplus to San Diego for far more. This means that this group of farmers can make a profit at taxpayer expense, while other farmers closer to San Diego pay some of the highest water rates in the state and often cannot afford the water they need. Second, the Salton Sea—the largest lake in California—depends on water from the Colorado River. If the Imperial Valley farmers did not sell the water but instead let whatever they did not use run off their fields, it would drain into the Salton Sea. Without that runoff, the Salton Sea, like Owens Lake before it, may go dry.

REBALANCING WATER CONSUMPTION TO SUSTAIN THE COMPETING needs of agriculture, cities, rivers, and lakes requires changing ingrained patterns of behavior. That includes changing who uses water, for what, and how much they pay for the privilege.

A popular view among economists places the last part, price, above all other considerations. Indeed, some who study the problem believe that getting the price right would magically solve our water problems and all sorts of other natural resources problems as well. If only it were that easy.

People around the world have been buying and selling oil for 150 years but have yet to figure out an economically and environmentally sensible way to do the same with water. When the price of oil goes up, people drive less and turn down the heat in their homes, and businesses seek efficiencies or alternative energy sources. Get the price of water wrong, on the other hand, and the consequences are dramatic. Raise the price of water and yes, some people will use less—but rising prices might also force farmers out of business and cause food shortages.

The controversy over sharing water between farms and cities in Southern California has a simple cause: not enough water to go around. The contentious issues are allocation and value. Should farmers use water in the Imperial Valley to grow vegetables or should the residents of San Diego use it for drinking, cooking, and household needs? Elsewhere, the issue is not scarcity but access, moving small amounts of water at high cost by building new pipes and treatment plants, to get water to poor urban areas. In either case, the underlying

principle is clear: water, like all earth's goods and services, should not—
or at least not always—be free.

What Parts of Nature Can People Own?

That principle is far easier to state than to enforce. Basic necessities
such as water, fish, timber, or land safe from floods have to be afford-
able, even to the poorest people who may be unable to pay anything
at all, but at the same time not so inexpensive overall that no one has
any incentive to conserve the resource. Markets offer one obvious way
to approach the problem.

To have a market, you first need to have property; after all, you
cannot rightly sell what you do not own. But what parts of nature can
people own?

People own coal deposits and oilfields, forests of valuable timber,
and pastures for grazing. Can they also own all the water underneath
that pasture, or in the river that runs by it? Can anyone—a government, a business, or an individual—own the diversity of a forest, or the
flood protection that a coral reef provides?

Unease over private ownership of an important part of nature can be
seen in a global context. In June 2010, the United Nations General Assembly declared, without one dissenting vote, that water was a human
right. The vote was not unanimous: forty-one countries, including the
United States, Canada, the United Kingdom, and Australia, abstained
over concerns about sovereignty. That not one country voted against
the resolution suggests that not even the worst despots would take the
public stand that they have a right to deny someone water. Ownership
of water, unlike oil, has an unmistakable moral component.

THE WIDESPREAD ASSUMPTION THAT WATER AND SOME OF NATURE'S
other gifts are and should always be free has deep roots and is thus difficult to upend. In the developed world at least, just about everyone
knows two things for certain: when they turn the tap for their morning

shower, the water will be clean; and when they get the bill, it will be small. Even in Santa Fe, which in 2011 was the US city with the most expensive water, an eight-ounce glass of tap water costs about a dime.

Even that may overstate the case, as Santa Fe is an outlier. The city faced water shortages, so in 2008 it began building a huge, costly project to divert water from the Rio Grande—a project that residents pay for on their water bills. Most everywhere else, even bone-dry Phoenix, a glass of water costs a fraction of a penny. The scarcity of water thus bears almost no relation to its price. Water in the desert is inexpensive, while rainy Seattle has among the highest water prices in the United States. That's due partially to Seattle's need to pay off debt on water treatment plants, as well a conscious decision by Seattle lawmakers to keep rates high to encourage conservation.

In fact, most of us hardly even pay for water at all. The water bills we receive are not for the water itself, but instead for the pipes that bring water to the house and the people who keep the system working. The price of water does not reflect its importance—a lapse that has hidden the risks of water shortages for decades.

For example, consider the Federal Bureau of Reclamation, the Department of the Interior office that oversees US water resources in seventeen western states. Starting in the early twentieth century, the Bureau initiated enormous projects to control water in the West. However, the people who use water or hydropower from projects such as the Hoover Dam or California's Central Valley Project don't pay the full cost of construction. The very name of the Bureau of Reclamation reveals its founding bias; water left in a river for fish was "wasted" and had to be "reclaimed" for use by people. As Marc Reisner points out in his 1986 classic *Cadillac Desert*, in the western United States the lack of water is the central fact of existence, and people will get behind most any plan to get around that problem, regardless of engineering hurdles. In the West, writes Reisner, "water flows uphill toward money."

Selling Water

Markets for water can certainly work on a local scale, something people have known for millenia. In the deserts of Oman, for example, systems called *aflaj* grant each farmer in a village a share—an hour, a day, a week—of the water coming out of commonly built and maintained irrigation channels. What they do not use they can rent or sell to other farmers. This system, in place for at least 2,500 years, creates a market price among the farmers, and has helped secure sustainable water supplies in one of the driest places on Earth.

In Texas, water users living above the Edwards Aquifer hold permits to pump groundwater. They have been vigorously selling them to interested buyers since the mid-1990s. Farmers, for example, have been selling their permits to San Antonio, giving the city rights to approximately 50,000 acre-feet of water. This water market has driven investment in more efficient irrigation, and has shifted water from low-value benefits such as irrigating hay to more valuable urban or industrial uses.

National-scale efforts to create water markets flourish elsewhere, though not without controversy. In Australia, a flexible water market helped the country deal with a devastating drought that affected the entire country for over a decade and is still ongoing in some places. Water rights in Australia now can be sold, traded, or leased. The system led to dramatic increases in efficiency during the drought, and was a factor in the survival of most Australian farms.

The Australian environment, however, particularly the Murray-Darling River Basin, did not fare as well. As surface water became valuable, farmers began using more groundwater and capturing what little rain fell on their property, thus depriving the river of water. "The more efficient you become, the less the river flows," writes Australian economist Michael Young. The challenge for conservationists is not to abandon the market, which works well in many other respects, but how to tweak such a sophisticated tool to ensure environmental benefits are valued appropriately.

But the few national markets are exceptions. In most places, water is free for all practical purposes. This leads to some absurd results, as journalist Charles Fishman details in his book *The Big Thirst: The Secret Life and Turbulent Future of Water*. Consider, for example, that Napoleon, Ohio's Campbell Soup factory, the largest in the world, gets all of its water from the Maumee River for free. Or that in 2008, the state of Florida gave Nestlé, the world's largest food company, the rights to water from Blue Springs State Park for ten years for a $230 permit fee. For what amounts to pin money, and despite protests from local water managers who warned that drought was stressing the spring, Nestlé can pump unlimited water from public land, bottle it, and sell it under the Deer Park brand.

To some economists and policymakers, creating markets for natural resources that currently have none makes perfect sense. These theorists feel that once everything has a price, the price creates an incentive to conserve. The theory seems clear enough—if Nestlé had to pay more for that water from Blue Spring, then the company would likely use less water to keep its costs down. In the right circumstances, markets can help determine the value of nature, and help conserve it as well, as is happening in the Edwards Aquifer in Texas.

Questions on the ownership and price of water remain to some extent issues of philosophy and ethics, with unmistakable political overtones, but the use of water is very much a question of law. Water law can be complex, particularly in the United States, where regional differences in climate and politics have led to widely disparate approaches. In Texas, for example, the state Supreme Court ruled in 2011 that people who own land above groundwater supplies own the water in the aquifer as well. Thus, in Texas law, water is exactly like oil; if you own land above an aquifer and you have a big enough pump, you can drain the aquifer regardless of whoever else wants or needs that water. One consequence could be that a law or regulation that seeks to conserve water by limiting how much of that water the landowners can use constitutes a taking of private property and the landowners would have to be compensated.

The question comes down not to who owns water, but to who has the rights to water: how much, for how long, and what they can do with it. Yet big businesses did not realize the urgency of the issues of ownership, usage, price, and scarcity until 2004, when conflict erupted in the southern Indian state of Kerala.

Companies, Water, and Risk

The people of Kerala survive largely on subsistence agriculture, growing rice and coconuts. Residents of a tiny hamlet called Plachimada eked out a humble living until 1999, when a subsidiary of Coca-Cola opened a forty-acre bottling plant nearby to produce soft drinks and bottled mineral water. Trouble arose in 2004 when Plachimada's wells went dry and farmers could not irrigate their crops.

The community blamed Coke for the water shortages. The outcry forced the company to shut down the Plachimada plant, one of its largest in India, in March 2004. Coke's main rival, PepsiCo, has faced similar complaints in India. Though a high court ruled in June 2005 that Coke was only a small contributor to the water shortage in Kerala—agriculture was the biggest culprit—and allowed the plant to reopen, the company's reputation took a beating. Underscoring the visceral value of water, Plachimada's government in 2010 recommended that residents be allowed to seek compensation from Coke for damage allegedly caused by groundwater depletion between 1999 and 2004.

The problems for businesses extended far beyond Kerala. When activists there launched a boycott, the issue attracted global attention and became a cause on college campuses in the United States and in

Europe. Coke took another public relations hit—this time a global one. Nearly every company that uses water took notice. Though few if any companies will say so in public, Kerala was heard around the world, a turning point in the effort of these companies to understand how much water they use, who else will be using the same supply, and how reliable that supply is.

When you think about it, making Coke by mixing sugar and water, two cheap and plentiful ingredients, could be the stuff of grade-schoolers on the sidewalk, not likely a ticket to great riches. Yet Coke—through its energetic efforts to create one of the world's most revered brands—has built a multinational empire on exactly that. The company's market value, the number of Coke shares multiplied by the stock market's price per share, is many times its book value, that is, the value of its tangible assets, what shareholders would receive if the company was liquidated. Apart from their fabled secret recipe, Coke is a corporate titan because of branding and more than a century of goodwill from consumers.

The same holds for other global, water-dependent businesses such as Nestlé and brewing giant SABMiller. Take away the water and the brand names, and not much would be left. But as Coke learned in Kerala, goodwill can be fragile. Companies must nurture it or, in the long term, risk their very existence. Not only do these companies use huge amounts of water, they do so in hundreds of communities. While no one can predict where the next water crisis will be, there certainly will be one and wherever it is, people will still want to buy beer and soda, so Coke, SABMiller, and Nestlé likely do business there, or want to. Leaders of businesses like these have begun to realize that they must be concerned about water wherever they work, and must also be concerned about the communities with whom they share that water.

Water-dependent companies are ahead of the curve in valuing nature in meaningful ways. They understand that they will prosper or not based on the availability of the one ingredient for which there is no possible substitute. And they know that they are also directly dependent on consumers who are increasingly willing to choose products based on a manufacturer's environmental record.

Coke clearly got the message of Kerala. Charles Fishman notes that in Coke's 2002 annual filing with the Securities and Exchange Commission, under the heading "Raw Materials," the word water does not appear. By 2010, the Raw Materials section opened: "Water is a main ingredient in substantially all our products. . . . Our Company recognizes water availability, quality, and sustainability . . . as one of the key challenges facing our business."

In 2007, Coke vowed that they will "safely return to nature and communities an amount of water equivalent to what we use in our beverages and their production by 2020." They initially called this being "water neutral," but now the company calls the idea "replenishment." Pepsi, evidently eager to outdo its rival, announced in 2010 that it would be "water positive"—that is, putting back more water than it uses.

No one, least of all Coke, wants another Kerala. Coke, Pepsi, and the rest have not fundamentally changed their stripes. They still seek value for their investors on the basis of rational calculations and smart business tactics. Not one of these companies has adopted conservation as its primary motivation. However, especially within the last decade, all of them have begun to think differently about the value of nature, and all understand that investing in nature can sharply improve their business outcomes.

Increased efficiency in using and managing water involves more than just fine-tuning production methods. More important, and more challenging, will be looking past factory walls and kitchen faucets and seeing how all the pieces of the broader system—factories, farms, forests, communities, governments—fit together.

That broad view matters because most of the water that Coke uses to make soft drinks, or that SABMiller uses to brew beer, goes into growing crops like sugarcane, barley, and wheat, not into the factory production lines. The change in perspective also shifts the calculus for both businesses and conservation. Now conservation includes not just the dynamics of the forest but also the specific business decisions that people like Carlos Salazar make up and down their supply chain.

Water Footprints

Water conservation depends not just on how companies such as Coke make their products but also on changing how consumers make purchases. Most people are now familiar with the term "carbon footprint"—a phrase that has become common as concern about global warming has become widespread. Likewise, consumers can now also consider their "water footprint," a concept that a Dutch scholar named Arjen Hoekstra pioneered in 2002. The water footprint of a product is the total amount of water needed to make it, from the very first step in the process to the packaged item on a store shelf.

The numbers can be dizzying. According to Hoekstra, a professor at the University of Twente, a liter of Coke in a plastic bottle requires 1 liter of water for the drink itself, 1 liter for production and washing, 10 liters to make the bottle, and a whopping 200 liters to grow the sugar—a total of 212 liters (56 gallons) of water for every liter of Coke.

Many common products have surprising footprints: 660 gallons of water for one cotton shirt, about 120 gallons for one pound of wheat, and nearly 2,000 gallons for one pound of beef. A typical American breakfast of two eggs, toast, and coffee requires 120 gallons of water—and even more if you put butter on your toast or milk in your coffee. The numbers become positively scary once you look beyond all the products, food, and drinks we consume and add everything else we use water for—watering the lawn, flushing the toilet, brushing our teeth, and washing ourselves, our clothes, our dishes, and our cars. In 2004, Americans had the highest total annual water footprint in the world—over 655,000 gallons per person on average, nearly enough to fill an Olympic-size swimming pool.

When confronted with these data, most people are shocked. Educating consumers on how much water—or energy, or oil, or any other resource—is used in the production of everyday products is the first step in enabling them to make informed decisions on what to buy and how much to consume. Neither carbon footprints nor water footprints have had enormous impact yet. The hope is that they eventually will factor into dozens of routine consumer choices, but that remains just a hope for now.

Consumers generally deal with their direct water footprint, the water they use at home and thus see every day, by installing water-saving toilets or showerheads, or abiding by local ordinances and restrictions during times of drought. Yet, a consumer's total water footprint—that Olympic-size swimming pool—is much larger than the direct one and they are woefully unaware of it.

Now, by promoting the concept of a water footprint with the goal of including it on product labels, researchers and water activists are hoping to draw attention to how drastically we're draining our most precious resource. In 2008, Hoekstra helped found the Water Footprint Network to accomplish exactly that. Some companies are making a virtue of the necessity to use less water. In 2010, Levi Strauss introduced a line of jeans called Water<Less. Manufacturing the average pair of blue jeans requires eleven gallons of water in multiple washings to get the perfect texture. Levi-Strauss says its new line will reduce water consumption in the manufacturing process by an average of 28 percent, and as much as 96 percent in some products. The initial response was positive: Levi's said in 2011 that its Water<Less jeans were outselling regular jeans with the same price.

Water shortages are not simply risks for companies like Levi-Strauss or Coke, nor opportunities for investors buying and selling water rights in Texas. They also have profound impacts on all life. Efforts to reduce those impacts can be enormously beneficial. The way people choose to use or conserve water and nature's other gifts will have deep and lasting effects on us all.

All of these issues were at the heart of the questions Carlos Salazar asked in Cartagena in 2011. Big cities and big businesses depend on rivers once they reach a valley or a coastline. It is what happens far upstream, however, that determines how those rivers flow. Protecting the water that feeds Salazar's business as well as countless human and natural communities means protecting those forests. Conservationists are finding new ways to do that across Latin America, and have found some surprising allies in Colombia's Cauca Valley, but the roots of the idea go back much further, to an even more unlikely source of inspiration for saving nature: New York City.

2

Not a Drop to Drink

In October 2011 I met with a group of sugarcane growers in Bogota, Colombia. They were warm and gracious hosts, affable dinner companions, and extremely proud of their beautiful lands and their booming business. They are folks who don't see the world exactly the same way I do, and they certainly don't consider themselves environmentalists. But they agree with me on one simple point—it makes great sense to invest in nature to protect water supplies.

Over the past decade, Colombia's sugarcane growers have become increasingly concerned that the Cauca Valley, near the country's Pacific coast and one of the richest cane growing regions in the world, will not always have enough water to irrigate their enormous fields. Their solution draws on the same basic ecology and economics that brought Carlos Salazar and FEMSA to the table: protect the water supply by protecting the forested watersheds that feed the Cauca River. The cane growers of the Cauca Valley are helping to ensure that the forests remain intact through an investment strategy called a water fund—an endowment for water conservation.

This ingenious solution provides concrete answers to some of the questions Carlos Salazar asked. Those upstream forests are natural capital. The idea is simple: make a relatively small investment in nature now to obtain plentiful clean water in the future and avoid the prospect of spending far more later on expensive filtration plants and equipment. Not only does it cost less to protect the forests compared to the engineered alternative, the investment also produces a host of additional benefits.

The notion of natural capital is not new. Scholars and writers as different as E. F. Schumacher, Herman Daly, Paul Hawken, Walt Reid, and Gretchen Daily have been writing about it for decades. While the idea may be familiar, putting it to work in real-life situations is new and opens new doors. As more businesses and governments come onboard, the potential grows for solving two pressing challenges currently facing the conservation movement.

First, for more than a century, conservationists have been enormously dependent on and grateful for the help of generous philanthropists. That support remains vital. Nevertheless, no organization or group of organizations can ever raise enough philanthropic capital to purchase land large, connected, or resilient enough to save the world's natural areas and the species they support. However, persuading government and business leaders that investing in nature will secure important benefits should provide a powerful new source of capital for conservation.

Second, many people today seem disconnected from nature and don't understand why they should care about protecting it. But these same people do care about what they need to survive—clean water and air, fertile soil, timber to build homes, protection from floods and other natural hazards. Natural capital can be a powerful concept for spreading the word on why everyone should care about maintaining a diverse and resilient environment.

By making the connection between nature and basic human and business needs, conservation becomes more meaningful to millions of people around the globe. That includes not only the sugarcane growers of the Cauca Valley, who now fully understand their dependence on nature, but also city dwellers seemingly more removed from it.

When I lived in New York, like many of my neighbors, I was only dimly aware of where the city got its water. Despite the abundance of clean, drinkable water available from any tap, nearly every day I bought bottled water from a vendor in my office lobby. Little did I know that more than a century ago New Yorkers found a way to provide clean water at low cost, and that a variation on that solution is now taking root in the Cauca Valley and elsewhere in Latin America.

New York's Water

Eddie & Sam's Pizza in downtown Tampa, Florida boasts "Real New York Pizza." The distinguishing characteristic of real New York Pizza? Not the crust, the cheese, the sauce, the toppings, or even the giant, floppy slices. It's the water. Every few months, Eddie & Sam's brings in one thousand gallons of water from the same Catskill springs that feed New York City's reservoirs. Another company, the Brooklyn Water Bagel Co., with about twenty locations across the country, has gone even further. Rather than import water from Brooklyn, the company seeks to re-create the precise chemistry of New York water through a patented fourteen-step filtration process, and that only then can the water be used to make their bagels.

All that time, money, and technology to get just the right water for pizza and bagels may seem excessive, but New Yorkers take justifiable pride in their water. Most of New York's supply never passes through a filter and receives comparatively small doses of chlorine and fluoride.

For their high-quality and lightly-treated water, today's New Yorkers can thank quite a few forested hillsides and a handful of foresighted city planners. Though they did not put it in these terms, those planners invested in nature, and generations of New Yorkers have reaped the benefits ever since.

The city planners' investment had particular urgency. Cholera outbreaks that spread through the city's water in the early nineteenth century killed thousands of New Yorkers. These epidemics, along with water pollution and a quickly growing population, forced city officials to search the countryside for cleaner and more reliable sources than surface water and local wells. Even in 1837, New York officials, anticipating the city's growth, invested in a system of aqueducts to bring water from the Croton River, east of the Hudson River and some twenty-five miles north of the city line.

By the end of the nineteenth century, population growth outstripped the capacity of the aqueducts from the Croton River. To supplement this supply, officials turned their attention to the Catskills, 2,000 square miles of hills and valleys west of the Hudson and three times as far from the city as the Croton. The region was still almost entirely rural. There were some farms, but forests were largely intact and streams clean-running. Construction of a system of reservoirs, tunnels, and conduits from this ideal water supply began in 1905.

The system grew beyond the Catskills to include the Delaware River watershed, and by 1964, the entire system, the largest waterworks in the country, was complete. An engineering marvel, New York's waterworks rely on gravity and little else to deliver 1.2 billion gallons of water every day through nine reservoirs, three lakes, 300 miles of tunnels, and 6,000 miles of distribution mains.

The system has worked well for decades, teaching us an invaluable lesson: with care, and absent catastrophic changes in climate, this system can provide clean water forever. Clever engineers have not discovered how to build dams and pipes that will never decay. Instead, they knew to rely on services that nature provides. Soil and tree roots filter water, microorganisms break down contaminants, plants in streams absorb nitrogen from automobile emissions and fertilizer runoff, and cattails and other wetland plants suck up nutrients while trapping sediments and heavy metals. Protect those services—which improve with age—and everything else is merely maintenance.

THE CATSKILLS WATERSHED IS A TEXTBOOK EXAMPLE OF WHAT HAS become known as green infrastructure. In contrast to built or gray infrastructure, such as pipes and treatment plants, green infrastructure consists of woodlands and grasslands, wetlands and rivers. Networks of these natural lands, together with working landscapes such as farms, woodlots, and other open spaces, keep ecosystems functioning, provide wildlife habitats, and contribute to the well-being of human communities by filtering water, controlling floods, cooling and cleaning the air, and providing areas for recreation, among many other benefits.

In the choice between building new gray infrastructure and conserving the green kind, the latter option is often less expensive and more efficient. Consider the example of New York's Croton River and Catskill watersheds. The largely suburban Croton lies within an easy drive of the city. The roads, parking lots, lawns, golf courses, and other elements of suburbia mean more pollution washing into reservoirs—fertilizers and other chemicals, trash, motor oil, tiny particles spewing from the exhausts of cars and trucks. This so-called nonpoint source pollution, the bane of freshwater ecosystems everywhere, is notoriously difficult to control.

By the late 1980s, New York officials gave up on fully controlling the pollution through such measures as improving septic systems and reducing erosion and accepted that they would eventually need a filtration plant for the 10 percent or so of the city's water that flows through the Croton system. Construction took eight years and cost $3.4 billion; the plant began operations in 2012, and will cost millions more each year to operate.

Pollution remained far less of an issue in the Catskills throughout the 1980s and 1990s, but risks were growing as a result of changing economics of the region. Owners of small family farms and woodlots struggled to stay in business. Many turned to intensive agriculture in smaller areas, which increased runoff and soil erosion, or they built more roads to get more timber to sawmills. Others chose to sell their land to vacation-home developers, jump-starting even more road construction and the salting necessary to keep those roads open in winter. Pollution began to spike, with a risk of worse to come if development overwhelmed rural septic systems.

Many New Yorkers began to see a new filtration plant as inevitable. When the US Environmental Protection Agency (EPA) issued strict new rules for surface water in 1989, the city faced the daunting prospect of building an even larger filtration plant than that on the Croton River, at a cost of perhaps $8 billion.

The owners of more than 800,000 buildings in New York City would end up footing the bill through increased water and sewer fees. The economic cost to the city overall would be enormous. City officials, led by Al Appleton, commissioner of the New York City Department of Environmental Protection and director of the city water and sewer system, had another idea. Maybe instead of building a filtration plant, protecting the watershed would cost less and achieve the same, or better, results. To put a complex political, economic, and scientific argument in its simplest terms: if you can prevent pollution in the first place, then you won't have to spend huge sums of money to clean it up later. Appleton and other city officials recognized that investing in nature, specifically the Catskills watershed, would pay a huge dividend: decades of clean water for New York City.

No one had tried this before—not at this scale. But with a multibillion-dollar project on the horizon, New York's leaders made the leap. Through much of the 1990s, New York City, sixty towns, ten villages, seven counties, the state of New York, the EPA, and environmental groups negotiated the terms under which the EPA would waive its filtration requirement and allow the city to avoid building the new plant.

They finally reached an agreement in 1997. That agreement limited growth in the watershed and committed the city to spend $1.5 billion to buy land, build storm sewers and septic systems, and upgrade existing sewage plants.

The brilliance of New York's solution was that Al Appleton and other officials did not try to take on just one problem. They thought big. Rather than attempting to plug one source of pollution at a time—an approach that has failed repeatedly—the city worked with farmers to help them manage their land in ways that would allow them to meet their own economic needs while providing clean water downstream.

While the city has the power under state law to manage development in the Catskills, most land there remains in private hands. Conservation would have to be a cooperative venture. Unless the residents of the Catskills were behind this, New York City knew that enforcement of pollution standards from one hundred miles away would never work.

The city began to pay for pollution control investments on each farm as an incentive for farmers to join. Instead of selecting a top-down menu of best management practices, farmers worked with city and state agencies to custom-design pollution control measures—such as building fences and bridges to keep livestock away from waterways—to maximize their effectiveness and minimize their cost. The resulting solutions were not only better and less costly at controlling pollution than previous efforts, they also saved farmers both time and money.

This realization turned the usual pollution dynamic upside down. Businesses and communities tend to resist new regulations, seeing them, rightly or wrongly, as burdensome. Far better, then, to engage these businesses and communities as providers of a valuable service to a willing market. Farmers now had a new crop to sell: water.

The city needs periodic approvals from the EPA, the latest issued in 2007 and lasting for ten years. As part of that agreement, New York also committed to spend another $241 million for land acquisition over ten years. In early 2011, the state issued New York City a permit to acquire 105,000 more acres in the watershed.

New York City has spent billions of dollars in the Catskills, a huge transfer of wealth from the city to the countryside. Those investments boosted the upstate economy with more jobs and businesses, from contractors to install septic systems and upgrade wastewater treatment plants, to jobs with the city and state, to new tourism enterprises. Catskills farmers, who had previously thought of the environment as something that forced them to spend money to solve somebody else's problems, now made money by becoming environmentalists. For some, that extra income was the difference between selling out and staying on the land. More than 90 percent of the farms in the watershed participate in the program, putting about 75,000 acres under improved management.

The combination of protected lands and improved management of working farms enables New York to pull off a neat trick—a win-win-win. People in New York City get cleaner, more secure water; residents of the Catskills get paid for a benefit they have long supplied for free; plants, animals, and people benefit from more conservation. That last one can be tangible, too. Gretchen Daily sums it up in a question, and only partly in jest: "Would you rather spend a romantic weekend at a filtration plant or in the Catskills"?

An Endowment for Water

The lessons from New York City offer great promise when we consider supplying water to booming cities outside the United States. Take Quito, the capital city of Ecuador, which stretches through a long valley high in the Andes. Nearly half a million hectares of parks consisting of forest and unique high-altitude grasslands called páramo protect the city's watershed.

The parks provide habitat for some of the signature species of Latin America, including the rare Andean condor. Unlike their cousin the California condor, Andean condors still soar in most of their historic range. The birds nest in inaccessible cliffs but the animals they depend on for food live in forests that cover slopes lower down the mountains, closer to farms and towns and therefore far less secure than the enormous winged scavengers.

More than 2 million people live near the parks. Fortunately, people understand that they depend on those forests just as much as bears and cougars do. And these people are willing to pay for the forests, too. Providing clean water for people may be essential to saving the condors as well.

The people who live in and around the parks have few roads or schools and little medical care or economic opportunity. They have no choice but to convert forest and grassland into farms and pastures. That leads to some of the same problems seen in the Catskills — erosion, hence sedimentation that lowers both water quality and quantity as it fills reservoirs, plus pollution from farm animals and fertilizer runoff into streams.

In Ecuador the key factor in supplying water for people downstream is the páramo, which exists only high in the mountains, nearly 10,000 feet above sea level. Walking across páramo feels like walking on a giant sponge, sinking slightly into the soft ground with each step. The sponginess accounts for a central ecological role of páramo; soaking up rainfall and slowly releasing it into countless rivulets and streams.

Páramo works like a sponge only when intact. But it does not remain intact for long once people start growing potatoes or grazing livestock on it. In the usual pattern, farmers burn the grass, which releases an intense but short-lived burst of nutrients, and then let their animals loose on it. This process quickly compacts the squishy páramo into rock-hard ground, and water runs right off it.

Keeping sheep and cows off the páramo is the first step in maintaining Quito's water supply. That means facilitating cooperation among groups not used to working together: city- and national-level government agencies, rural communities, local water utilities, water-intensive businesses, and conservation organizations. As in the Catskills, together they must find better ways for people to run their farms or to find new sources of income. Also as in New York, the challenge is moving some wealth from the city to the countryside, bearing in mind that Quito has far less wealth than New York to begin with.

QUITO LEARNED OTHER LESSONS FROM NEW YORK: KEEP THE grasslands and forests intact and work with farmers to minimize pollution rather than fix problems at the other end of the pipeline. But with the city's rapid growth and the expansion of settlements and agriculture into the surrounding hillsides, by the late 1990s a water crisis appeared inevitable. As settlers cleared the forest, dirtier water would reach Quito. A new water filtration plant would be prohibitively expensive and would be only a stopgap measure if deforestation continued apace.

New York's big step was making some private land public, which allowed the government to dictate land use. In Quito, most of the watershed was already in public hands, but there was a bigger problem: neither the city nor the national government had enough money to manage all that land.

The city chose a beautifully simple solution: an endowment for conservation called a water fund. This financial mechanism brings together the general public, local and national governments, utilities, businesses, and international organizations to capitalize an investment fund. The interest pays for forest conservation and management along rivers, streams, and lakes to ensure that safe drinking water flows out of faucets in Quito every time someone turns on the tap.

The Quito Water Fund began in 2000 with a small investment from Quito's public water authority and The Nature Conservancy. A board of directors composed of representatives from public and private water users, local communities, indigenous groups, and nonprofits oversees the fund and determines how to disburse earnings. Quito's power authority joined the fund in 2001, and local beer company Cervecería Nacional signed on in 2003, followed by water bottler Tesalia Springs, all of them recognizing the dependence of their businesses on a reliable supply of inexpensive, clean water.

The fund received an enormous boost in 2006 when the city of Quito convinced the public water company to contribute 1 percent of the fees it collected each year from water users into the fund. Those fees would have been even higher if they had to pay off the cost of building a new filtration plant.

The water utility saw investing in watershed protection as an inexpensive way to manage its risks. Less pollution and erosion means less risk of having to shut down the water supply—as has happened elsewhere in Latin America when landslides foul aqueducts—plus the obvious bottom-line benefit of avoiding the need to build additional filtration capacity. The water fund also provides a means for the water company and all other stakeholders to agree on a common agenda. Motivating the private sector to talk to the public sector, no small feat anywhere, looms particularly large in developing countries, where people often lack trust in public institutions. Without such trust, good governance of both built and natural environments becomes nearly impossible.

The initial investment for the water fund grew to nearly $10 million in capital by the end of 2011. The water fund can now use about $800,000 in annual interest from the endowment to mobilize matching grants and cofinancing of up to $3 million per year for projects to reduce damage to the páramo, the forests, and the water. Money from the fund goes to dozens of small-scale efforts, such as adding park guards, supporting community-based reforestation, and building fences to keep cattle and crops a safe distance from streams and rivers. The fund also provides for microenterprises run by women who would otherwise have to farm or run sheep—for example, by providing the capital for sewing machines to make traditional dresses for other Andean communities farther away from Quito. The fund also pays for taps to be installed in the indigenous communities themselves.

Ecological evidence suggests that the efforts of the water fund are having an impact in the páramo. While they have not returned to their original condition, areas with ongoing conservation projects are healthier than areas that have been burned. In an ideal world, most páramo would be untouched, and all the people living nearby would meet their needs without degrading it. The real world demands trade-offs; a less-than-pristine páramo that still provides a vital ecological service to people while retaining most of its diverse species may be the best anyone can do. While imperfect, if that approach has ecological, social, and economic staying power, it may be enough.

Not all the water fund's efforts are as promising. With cutting-edge conservation sometimes the experiments don't work out as expected. In several places, the fund pays villagers to reforest areas that had been cleared for cattle grazing. The idea is intuitively attractive, and it's also popular with people in Ecuador. But reforestation is expensive, especially compared to conserving the páramo, so it may not pay off, at least not in the short term. Reforesting a few dozen acres can cost roughly as much as restoring a few thousand acres of páramo.

Despite these issues, water funds have caught on. One reason is the simplicity of the model: everyone needs water, and the connection between upstream forests and páramo and downstream water supply is apparent. Most people already pay fees for maintaining grey infrastructure to supply water, so it seems appropriate for water users to pay as well for the natural systems best suited to delivering it. As a result, Latin America now has thirty-two water funds in various stages of operation or design.

Getting the payoff from those efforts to match the potential requires good science, committed financial investment, and increased collaboration across various levels of government. To that end, a public-private partnership of TNC, the FEMSA Foundation (the social investment instrument of FEMSA), the Inter-American Development Bank, and the Global Environment Facility in 2011 pledged $27 million to establish forty new water funds serving major cities across Latin America, including Bogotá, São Paulo, and Lima. The Latin American Water Funds Partnership offers the hope of scaling up water funds from just a few locations to something that shifts how people use and pay for water across vast areas. The projects the partnership supports have the potential to secure sufficient supplies of clean water for as many as 50 million people.

With the popularity of water funds growing, scientists, economists, conservationists, and business owners are asking a central question: What is the ideal water fund? If we were to take the best available information and to use the best tools, what would it look like?

The long-term payoff for answering these questions is clearly worth the effort. The success of water funds will guide us in creating incentives and laws that change how people value water, forests, and oceans, and all the wild species these resources support. This is no longer about just water and water funds, but about all of nature.

Raising Cane

The Cauca Valley is a test case for building the ideal water fund, and its results will yield the hard data necessary to prove how useful these funds can be. All who live and work in the valley now recognize that if they destroy the watersheds that feed the Cauca River—six hundred square miles of tropical forests and páramo, still wild and home to spectacled bear and mountain tapir—the flow of water necessary to grow and process sugarcane will slow. The farmers and mill operators are making hard-nosed calculations on the future of their business interests and concluding that their best investment is nature.

More sugarcane grows in the Cauca Valley than just about anywhere else on the planet. Nearly the entire valley, some half-million acres, is devoted to this one crop, which grows year-round in the wet and warm climate. The deep, alluvial soil yields fifty tons of sugar per acre—a larger crop than in Florida or Brazil.

The sugarcane growers and the government of Colombia first became concerned about water in the Cauca Valley in the 1950s, and sugar became the first Colombian industry to feature an explicitly environmental component. In 1954, the government created the Corporación Autónoma Regional del Valle del Cauca (CVC) to promote development of the Cauca River Valley and to protect its natural resources.

Despite anticipating problems with water supply, the CVC was unable to avoid them. By the mid-2000s, with nearly 80 percent of the water used in the valley already devoted to sugarcane, population growth began to push the resource to its limits. Water for human consumption gets top priority, and if current usage holds, cane farmers may have to cut back from five irrigation cycles per year to four over the next few years, leading to about a 9 percent reduction in their crop, about four tons less cane per acre. With cane selling at about $4 per ton, if they continue as they always have, the cane growers across the nearly 350,000 harvested acres in the Valley are looking at a loss of about $6 million of revenue per year.

The prospect of losing that much revenue tends to focus the mind of any business owner. Getting support for a water fund, however, still demands clear proof of the fund's economic potential. Doing that means getting down to pesos and centavos: the potential costs are clear, and the benefits need to be as well. The growers and mill owners want to see the numbers, not colorful pictures of the dramatic vistas and interesting creatures in the mountains above the cane fields—accurate as those may be.

The data need to be both economic and ecological, delineating precisely where in the watershed the fund should invest. Some water funds work on a general subscription basis. Anyone living in a watershed the fund covers who wants to participate can, and the fund pays some money to all the participants. This can be important politically because it ensures the widest distribution of benefits, but it is likely not the most efficient way to improve the water supply. The groups behind the Cauca Valley water fund sought instead to specify where the highest returns would be found.

Their first step, in the summer of 2009, was to gather representatives from all interested parties: cane growers, mill owners, local communities, government agencies, the CVC, conservation organizations, and grassroots organizations from nine watersheds in the valley. In a series of meetings they gathered around maps to identify all the places they thought were ecologically, economically, or socially important, and what needed to be done to conserve them. The places included the headwaters and courses of streams and rivers, areas of páramo or grazing land, and steep slopes prone to erosion.

Once these key places were identified, the participants had to decide what to do there and how much it would cost. The possible conservation interventions included isolating headwaters and river courses by installing fences to keep cattle out, restoring degraded forests, reforesting areas that had been cut down, converting to sustainable production systems and agroforestry systems, and improving management of existing conservation areas or creating new ones. From this mapping project came plans for each of the nine watersheds. The plans identified different activities in different parts of the basins that all the local experts could agree on, with estimates of the cost for each.

This resembles a standard planning exercise, common to conservation and rural development projects, but there was an important

difference. Among the participants in the mapping effort were economists and ecologists from a Colombia-based research center, the International Center for Tropical Agriculture, and the Natural Capital
Project (NatCap). NatCap, a joint effort of Stanford, the University
of Minnesota, The Nature Conservancy, and the World Wildlife
Fund (WWF), was established to provide innovative economic and
ecological analyses and tools to help incorporate natural capital into
decision-making. Among the tools was computer-modeling software
used to assess a host of biophysical variables from each basin in the
Cauca Valley.

The data the scientists fed into the computers included rainfall intensity, slope, soil depth, land use, distance to the river, and altitude.
The output was a model that showed which investments at which sites
would yield the greatest return in terms of reduced sedimentation or
improved water quality. The scientists could thus identify which
places in the valley were important, feasible, and cost-effective to conserve. By repeating this process across all the watersheds, the scientists
essentially developed an investment portfolio for the water fund.

The model also allowed scientists to predict how climate change
would affect those sites and the services they provide. The current
best estimate reveals that the region may become wetter as the climate
changes, so water supply may not be as much of a concern; however,
erosion may become significantly worse.

When the analysis was done, the business case was clear: investing
$1 million to $3 million per year for eight years to conserve the watershed may halve the sedimentation rate. In that scenario, sugarcane
growers would not have to cut back on their growing season. In short,
as little as $8 million invested in conservation could yield over $45
million in savings.

These numbers have not yet been proven, but the potential is clear.
As in New York, and as in Quito, so it should be the case in the Cauca
Valley. If these benefits pan out—and monitoring is already in place to

see if they will—they will go a long way toward proving how an investment in conservation can work economically and can provide benefits for people and wildlife, and for the ecosystems that support both.

When the sugarcane growers and mill owners saw the potential return on their conservation investment, they decided on the spot to join the water fund. The mill owners have other incentives to participate as well. The broad-based, inclusive approach of the fund provides a way for these parties to become more involved in the management of the watershed. Not only do they get a seat at the table with the government and other stakeholders, they get increased visibility and a public-relations boost as well.

The same business owners who demand hard numbers to justify their investment also demand proof that the investment is paying off. Projects are underway, and the systems are in place to generate the needed data, but the precise impact of the efforts funded by the water fund will take years to appear. Results from water-fund investments should be visible in the next few years at the scale of individual plots of land, but benefits at the scale of an entire watershed will take longer to appear, perhaps five to ten years. Nevertheless, people are onboard.

WATER FUNDS PROVIDE FINANCIAL INCENTIVES FOR CONTINUED engagement in conservation. For the first time, water users, communities, governments, and conservationists have access to the same information and the same standards for determining the impact of management efforts in the Cauca Valley.

The concepts behind the water fund are clear and compelling, but it is too easy to assume that everyone will benefit in the end. This is likely too rosy a scenario. More realistically, everyone involved will need to compromise. Some landowners may have to forgo potentially lucrative opportunities, and some natural areas may be transformed. The questions in the Cauca Valley—and in many other places—will be which trade-offs are worth making, who will benefit, and who will bear the costs.

Simply having better information is the first step, and even that can be transformative. In the early stages of the fund's implementation the mill owners, for example, began to see that they could manage not only their water supply, but their water usage as well. They began to explore how much water each mill uses and where that water goes. This reflects the owners' desire to be part of the broader vision for the future of the valley and its people. The cane growers now seem to be well on their way to becoming full-fledged environmentalists.

3

Let Floodplains Be Floodplains

FARMERS SUCH AS THE CANE GROWERS IN THE CAUCA VALLEY AND city planners in Quito focus their conservation efforts on the challenge of too little water. Climate change, however, leads others to face exactly the opposite problem.

In autumn 2010, I traveled to Iowa, a state that knows all too well the devastation that too much water can cause. The Missouri River forms Iowa's western border and the Mississippi its eastern, with many tributaries in between. In most years, at least one and often more of these rivers flood. In bad years the floods wash out roads and bridges, inundate cities and small towns, and drown crops and livestock. A coalition of unlikely collaborators—sportsmen, farmers, conservation organizations, business leaders, and elected officials—had come together to advocate for the largest conservation ballot initiative in the country. If passed, the amendment would fund restoration of Iowa's floodplains, not only protecting important wildlife habitats, but also reducing water pollution; shielding communities, businesses, and

farmlands from floods; and protecting the fertile soil on which farmers rely.

The challenge: Iowans had to pass the amendment in a statewide
election. Convincing voters in a conservative state in the midst of a
deep recession to allow the state to invest tax dollars in conservation
would be tough. I headed to Des Moines for a press conference before the vote. My role as opening speaker was to convince Iowans—
not often thought of as typical environmentalists—of the multiple
benefits of investing in nature. That on its own would be hard
enough, but to make matters worse my plane was delayed. I missed
the start of the press conference and was moved to the final speak-
ing slot.

As it turned out, my remarks weren't even needed. As I waited for
my turn at the podium, one speaker after another championed the
idea of investing in nature. Floods had changed the conversation and
turned many Iowans into passionate conservationists. Each speaker
described the devastation caused by Iowa's recurring floods. The
speakers also explained that levees, dams, and reservoirs are not always the best solutions for floods. As one city engineer at the press
conference put it, "It's time to let floodplains be floodplains again."
That was supposed to be *my* line!

A few months later the amendment passed with more than two-
thirds of the vote. The bill provides for a permanent fund to restore
wetlands and improve water quality. The fund will generate $150 mil-
lion in new annual funding for Iowa's natural resources. It was a great
victory for conservation.

Of course, Iowa is just a drop in the bucket when considering
global freshwater resources. But the lessons of Iowa apply to other important floodplains around the world. One of those lessons—perhaps
the most important of all—is that wise investments in the natural services of floodplains can provide huge social, economic, and environmental benefits.

Flashy Weather

The world is becoming increasingly "flashy." Any given place will receive more of its annual rainfall in fewer but more intense downpours compared to the past century, with longer stretches of dry weather between the deluges. This problem is already so severe that some regions experience both extremes in consecutive years. In Memphis, Tennessee, for example, 2011 brought record floods, but by summer 2012 so little water flowed down the Mississippi that barges ran aground. In Pakistan in 2010 heavy monsoon rains caused the worst floods in the country's history. However, in 2012, Pakistan's monsoon failed, and water was in short supply.

Nature offers solutions to the problems of both too little and too much water. And again, by comparison, man-made infrastructure is often less efficient and riskier than the natural alternatives.

Consider, for example, our traditional method of flood prevention: the construction and maintenance of levees. From the Mississippi to the Yangtze, levees defend cities around the world from floods. Many people who grow up near water take levees for granted, and may even see them as natural: places to walk along or to fish from, the way things have always been and should always be along riverbanks.

Nature provides another method of flood control: floodplains. Floodplains are flat expanses near rivers where water goes when rivers cannot hold any more. Floodplains relieve pressure on levee systems downstream, lessening flood risks, and filtering harmful agricultural runoff. Unlike permanent levees, floodplains adapt to changing river patterns.

Structures such as levees, dams, and canals are often not sufficient to suppress rising water. In fact, levees often exacerbate flood risks for downstream communities, speeding up the flow of rising water. Floodplains, on the other hand, slow down this flow. Letting rivers do as they always have—spill over their banks and onto floodplains—will be an important part of protecting both rivers and the people who live alongside them. Scientists and engineers are looking for ways to conserve or possibly re-create this natural infrastructure.

The Ouachita

Floods define Louisiana even more than they do Iowa, and not just along the Gulf Coast. The city of Monroe, for example, about thirty miles south of the Arkansas border, sits not on just one floodplain, but two. The Ouachita River—pronounced WASH-i-tah, Choctaw for "country of large buffaloes"—marks the far western edge of the historic Mississippi alluvial plain. Up until the early twentieth century, by the time the Mississippi reached Louisiana, it gathered so much water from such a large swath of North America that its floodwaters occasionally spilled into the Ouachita, some 60 miles to the west.

Once upon a time, that is—not anymore. Today, levees, dams, and floodwalls line nearly the entire stretch of the lower Mississippi, from Cairo, Illinois, where it joins the Ohio River, to the Gulf of Mexico.

The levees have for the most part done their job. Each stretch of levee has a constituency and a story of lives saved or fortunes made. The levee system also offers a testament to undervalued nature: all the engineering genius and mechanized muscle in the world cannot control the Mississippi forever. In fact, all the construction in the name of making people safer and wealthier, and not just along the Mississippi, has increased risk and may in the long run make people poorer by degrading our natural capital.

Floodplains remain an essential tool for dealing with floods. While many have been built on or otherwise transformed beyond recognition, many can still be restored and there are dozens of ongoing efforts, ranging from a handful of acres to thousands of acres along the Willamette River in Oregon and even more ambitious efforts along China's Yangtze. From one perspective, floodplains provide a service in the same way the Catskills serve New Yorkers, as green infrastructure at a grand scale. From another perspective, floodplains tell a far broader story beyond simply protecting a watershed. The prospect of restoring floodplains changes the way people think about their relationship to rivers. From there it is a small step to reconsider all the values of nature.

Nature is not always benign. Sometimes rivers flood and forests burn. Those processes are as essential as those that nourish and support human communities. Our relationship with rivers has long been about control, but communities may need to relinquish some control if they want to thrive, both ecologically and economically.

FAR SMALLER THAN THE MISSISSIPPI, THE OUACHITA IS STILL A MAJOR river in its own right. It rises some 175 miles to the northwest of Monroe, in Arkansas's Ouachita Mountains. By the time it reaches Monroe, it is more than 500 feet across and 30 feet deep. The Army Corps of Engineers built levees in the 1970s, designing the system to protect Monroe when the flood stage reaches 53 feet above sea level.

These days, city officials get anxious whenever a flood crest seems headed for 45 feet or higher. That level of water triggers emergency steps, such as closing lower elevation floodwall gaps in southern Monroe, monitoring the levees twenty-four hours a day, and ultimately raising a unique, folding floodwall that in calmer times serves as a riverside promenade.

Such big floods rarely hit Monroe, with blessedly little need to unfold that ingenious wall. In 2009, however, spring rains fell in torrents across Arkansas and Louisiana; the Ouachita gathered strength in the mountains in late April and May, and as it neared the city, it passed flood stage at forty feet and kept rising.

Then, suddenly, the river level fell.

An official from the local levee district said it was like pulling the plug from a bathtub drain. The floodwaters just upriver from the city dropped six inches in a matter of hours. That might not sound like much, but if you are measuring your life in sandbags, a few inches can mean everything. Less than twenty-four hours later, farther up-river from Monroe at the Felthensal Dam in Arkansas, the Ouachita dropped almost one and a half feet.

What happened? Nature, as it occasionally does, put a problem in stark relief; in this case, people had seen the solution but nature beat them to the punch. A levee about twenty miles upstream from Monroe had failed in two places. When it did, water poured from the swollen Ouachita River into 16,000 acres of abandoned soybean fields. In bursting through the levee, the Ouachita reconnected with its floodplain.

Instead of creating a disaster, this failed levee indicated a way forward. The floods of 2009 made the case for investing in nature to the people of Monroe more effectively than any public service message or publicity effort.

Made permanent, such a reconnection would ultimately benefit the Louisiana hardwood forest that once thrived on the floodplain, as well as the fish and wildlife that live there. It would also benefit the people who live downstream. As the residents of Monroe know, by taking in water, the floodplain relieves pressure on other parts of the Ouachita River levee system.

Even though removing levees makes evident sense, it remains a daring idea for populations alongside major rivers. For Louisianans, still haunted by images of the devastation in New Orleans following Hurricane Katrina's levee failures, such a step would be a stand against history, culture, even law. As economies change, however, so can the perception of the value of nature. When agriculture drove the economy of the lower Mississippi, the value of the floodplain as farm-land overwhelmed any other consideration. Now the region's more diverse economy provides opportunities to reconsider some of the trade-offs made long ago.

Bullying the Mississippi

The campaign to control the Mississippi River began almost as soon as Europeans arrived on its banks. Floodplains have rich soil, and the Mississippi Valley had one of the great floodplain forests on earth, covering about 25 million acres. Early settlers immediately began clearing higher ground and building earthen embankments; in many places, the law required such "improvements" to establish home-steading claims. As towns grew along the river and its tributaries, so did the need to protect them, and a haphazard network of levees — some sturdy, some not — began to appear.

Over the past 150 years or so in the United States, levees have se-cured, or so it seems, hundreds of thousands of acres of farmland and subdivisions. Whether levees alone would suffice has been a question for almost as long. Mark Twain saw the risks clearly in 1883:

> One who knows the Mississippi will promptly aver — not aloud, but to himself — that ten thousand River Commissions, with the mines of the world at their back, cannot tame that lawless stream, cannot curb it or confine it, cannot say to it, Go here, or Go there, and make it obey; cannot save a shore which it has sentenced; can-not bar its path with an obstruction which it will not tear down, dance over, and laugh at . . . the Commission might as well bully the comets in their courses and undertake to make them behave, as try to bully the Mississippi into right and reasonable conduct.

Yet floods came and went, and the levees held. They held, that is, until 1927. Then the fragility of the system and the folly of rely-ing so heavily on levees became clear. In 1927 the Mississippi broke free, bursting out of its levee system in 145 places and flooding 27,000 square miles. The waters covered an area more than 50 miles wide and 100 miles long with up to thirty feet of water, causing more than $400 million in damage and killing thousands of people in seven states. As John M. Barry documents in *Rising Tide*, his definitive history of the flood, official records never accounted for many victims because they were poor, African American farmers.

In New Orleans, residents worried the flood would fill to the rim the bowl in which the city sits, consuming it entirely. New Orleans businessmen persuaded the Army Corps of Engineers to dynamite the levees in nearby St. Bernard Parish and to lower the river level enough to spare the city. Hydrologists and other experts knew the flood would burst levees hundreds of miles north and never reach New Orleans, but they either stayed silent or were ignored. Dynamiting began, destroying nearly all of St. Bernard and Plaquemines Parishes and leaving nearly 10,000 people homeless. Levees to the north began to burst the next day.

The response to this crisis was a revitalized, decades-long effort to tame the Mississippi. Congress turned to the Army Corps of Engineers to carry out this monumental and unprecedented endeavor.

The disastrous 1927 Mississippi flood destroyed scores of levees, in addition to those blown up on purpose near New Orleans. With them went the assumption that levees alone sufficed to manage that or any other substantial river. Congress solicited alternative ideas and settled on one offered by the chief of engineers, Major General Edgar Jadwin. He may not have been the best man for the job; for example, he told a Congressional hearing that, under natural conditions, the Mississippi delta did not flood. The incredulity of the delta delegations notwithstanding, Congress adopted the Jadwin Plan and with it a comprehensive approach to flood management.

The plan included the first acknowledgment that perhaps cutting off rivers from their floodplains was not such a great idea. True to their mission and their name, the Corps chose an engineered solution: keep the levees in place, but install colossal gates and other structures on the floodplains themselves, renaming them floodways or spillways. They could then open the gates during major floods to send millions of gallons of water away from the river, and the floodway would guide it around developed areas and take pressure off levees downstream.

Generally, this system has been effective. The 2011 Mississippi flood carried more water than the 1927 flood, but no levees failed. Still, the current system sees floodplains narrowly and as something to be redesigned with a single goal in mind: managing extreme floods. It doesn't allow for the changing dynamics of rivers that course and move around, or for the unpredictability of enormous floods and unprecedented weather trends. A simpler yet radical step would be to re-create the floodplains as permanent parts of the river system, not places to be kept dry except in the direst circumstances. When the Corps developed the Jadwin Plan, the value of agriculture obscured all other values of floodplains, while scientists knew relatively little about how they functioned, or how they could be restored.

Under the Flood Control Act of 1928, the Corps embarked on the epic Mississippi River and Tributaries Project, building ever sturdier and technically sophisticated levees along the Mississippi and its major tributaries. The result was more than 1,600 miles of levees and floodwalls, the world's longest system, just along the mainstem of the river, with hundreds more miles lining its tributaries. Across the country, the Corps oversees 2,000 levee systems that together include some 14,000 miles of levees.

The levees prevent floods, but more broadly they control rivers in many different ways for human benefit, including navigation, hydropower, and drinking water. Local and national governments build one sophisticated structure after another and hope for the best, patching levees up as necessary and putting faith in stone, rebar, and concrete. The process has gone so far that they can never go back entirely, nor would they want to. But they do need to go partway back. Humankind simply cannot win a battle against the geological processes of the planet.

The lower Mississippi, for example, has not always run down the channel lined with so much concrete. The river swings back and forth across the delta every thousand years or so as it constantly searches for the shortest route to the Gulf. Around 1953, hydrologists and engineers realized that the Atchafalaya River, which parallels the Mississippi south of the small Louisiana town of Simmesport, was on the verge of capturing the mainstem of the river near Baton Rouge. Had that happened, the major ports of Baton Rouge and New Orleans, and the many industrial plants between them, would have been left dry.

In perhaps a unique exercise of legislative authority, Congress passed a law declaring that the Atchafalaya would do no such thing. It decreed how much of the Mississippi's water the Atchafalaya could have in a given year. The river paid no heed to such things, and it was again left to the Corps of Engineers to build yet another masterful device to make it so.

The result, memorably described by John McPhee in *The Control of Nature*, is a tale of human skill and folly. The floodgate system the Corps constructed, the Old River Control Structure, is meant to keep the Mississippi from its inevitable shift to the west. The structure nearly failed in 1973, and the Corps worried it would fail in 2011. Eventually, it will fail. Nature will out. The Mississippi's conduct will be neither right nor reasonable. In a sense, that too is a value of nature, though not one with many obvious economic benefits.

The Old River Control Structure, mainline Mississippi levees, and others maintained by the Corps and numerous levee boards account for a fraction of the thousands of miles of concrete and earthen embankments that hold back water across the country. No one knows exactly how many miles of levees exist in the United States—the best guess is about 100,000—or where all those levees are located, or what condition they are in.

Today, the country's levee system is showing signs of severe strain. The American Society of Civil Engineers gave the US levee system a grade of D- in 2009. At the same time, the pressure on those levees grows every year. Along the Mississippi in 1993 there was a flood so severe hydrologists expect its likely to occur just once every 500 years — hence they label it a 500-year flood. The Mississippi saw a 70-year-flood in 2001, and a 200-year flood in 2008. Hydrologists such as Robert E. Criss of Washington University in St. Louis posit that the assumptions that the Corps made in designing flood projects all over the country look less reliable every year. Climate change, among other factors, has shuffled the deck.

No surprise, then, that levee failures have been both more frequent and more dramatic in recent decades. The surprise is that the levee systems themselves are partly responsible. As engineers box rivers into their channels, the rivers become deeper and faster. The levees may contribute to the very problems they were intended to solve.

Levees have other environmental costs. The deeper, faster Mississippi now rushes topsoil past New Orleans and Gulf Coast marshes, finally depositing it in deep water somewhere off the continental shelf. Deprived of regular infusions of sediment, the marshes are quickly losing ground to the Gulf. An area of marsh the size of a football field disappears every thirty minutes.

The only part of the Louisiana coast where river sediment still accumulates and the marshes slowly grow, as once happened everywhere around the Gulf, is in the Atchafalaya basin. The Atchafalaya delta remains relatively intact. That is a bit ironic: the Corps has walled off large stretches of the basin so it can be used as an emergency floodway, as envisioned in the original Jadwin plan and as was done in 2011 to protect Baton Rouge and New Orleans.

Just as the Atchafalaya protects those cities, large-scale reconnection of floodplains can reduce flood risk to nearby towns and cities. Restored floodplains would store and convey floodwaters, reducing the risk of levees failing. Restoring floodplains on large rivers like the Mississippi will require thousands of acres, many of which are now farmed; so the process demands hard choices and many trade-offs. But climate-change forecasts indicate the likelihood of increasingly severe storms. Data show that rainfall has already increased significantly in both amount and intensity. Some mechanism will be necessary to release pressure as more water is pushed down constrained rivers.

Intact floodplains combined with levees provide better protection for communities than levees alone. We need fewer levees than we have now, but instead our infatuation with building bigger and more sophisticated ways to control floods has convinced us, against evidence to the contrary, that engineering skill can protect us no matter what. As a result, people continue to build and live in places we should not.

Mollicy Bayou

It is one thing to think about taking out levees, but quite another to figure out where and when and how. The Ouachita River north of Monroe provides a perfect opportunity to show the benefits of restoring floodplains.

The effort centers on a small stream called Mollicy Bayou in the northwest corner of Morehouse Parish. The bayou fed the Ouachita from about twenty-five square miles of bottomland forest on the river's east side. Thomas Jefferson sent surveyors to the area in 1804, after the Louisiana Purchase added the land to US territory. Low-lying and wet, dotted with sloughs and lakes, settlers found the area less than ideal for farming, so they cleared other areas first for their small farms and later for the larger cotton plantations.

The land remained wild and for a time was a state game preserve. Not until the late 1960s, with growing demand for soybeans, did anyone try to farm the land around Mollicy Bayou. Private investors bought and cleared a neat rectangle about eight miles long and three miles wide, piling the cut trees in heaps and burning them in enormous bonfires. The new owners quickly realized they would need levees and pumps to keep the land anything close to dry enough to plant. They built some seventeen miles of levees that nearly surrounded the property.

The levees, 30 feet tall and 150 feet wide at the bottom, kept the Ouachita floodwaters off the soybean fields, now called Mollicy Farms. Unfortunately, they also kept rainwater on them. Where the farmers had dug up the soil needed to build the levee, they left behind an enormous borrow ditch and every time it rained hard, a common event in northeastern Louisiana, first the ditch and then the rest of the land would start to fill like a vast bathtub. The land managers had to turn on the pumps and dump tons of water laden with fertilizer and topsoil back into the river.

Making the land suitable for crops required more than just the levees. Ironically, once the connection to the river had been severed and the land had dried enough to be tillable, the floodplain had to be irrigated. In place of winding bayous, the farmers built a lattice of straight irrigation ditches. The mainlines were deep—so deep that the entire parcel could be irrigated from a single pump atop the levee at the spot where Mollicy Bayou once joined the Ouachita.

Despite the impressive engineering, after several farmers went bankrupt in the 1960s it became clear that the soggy bank of the Ouachita was not the best place to grow soybeans. Not easily deterred, and still looking to recoup the investment in miles of levees, the owners decided to try growing rice instead. This enabled them to focus on keeping the crop wet instead of dry, but it was still a hard slog. More farmers went under. By the mid-1990s, the only economically sensible option was to sell, and the only buyer ready to pony up cash for unfarmable land was the US Fish and Wildlife Service.

The service already owned a large piece of land just across the river from Mollicy Farms, the Upper Ouachita National Wildlife Refuge. Here you can still see how Mollicy Farms, and indeed thousands of square miles of the Lower Mississippi River Alluvial Valley, once looked. Even today, despite dams and levees along the Ouachita, floods regularly sweep in among the trees of the wildlife refuge, in places climbing twenty feet or more up the trunks.

The floodwaters deposit silt, thus renewing the soil and forests, and then recede quickly enough to avoid killing the established trees. The water also allows fish to leave the mainstem of the river to search for rich sources of food; wade into the forest in a low flood and you will be tempted to scoop the fish up in your hands. People in the region understand how the ecosystem should function, the give-and-take between the Ouachita and the bottomland forest, a rich and complicated relationship that supports ducks and wading birds, cottonmouths and alligators, wild turkeys, deer, and black bears.

The Fish and Wildlife Service began buying up parcels of Mollicy Farms in the 1990s and adding them to the refuge. But the new acreage bore hardly any resemblance to the land across the river—a fact not lost on two brothers, Kelby and Keith Ouchley, who grew up near Monroe and knew the woods and waters around Mollicy Farms well. Both had strong conservationist streaks. Kelby, the older of the two, eventually became manager of the wildlife refuge, while Keith got a doctorate in wildlife ecology from LSU and took over the Louisiana Chapter of The Nature Conservancy in 2001.

In those roles, the Ouchley brothers were in a unique position to take on a grand experiment. Kelby managed wetlands projects for the Fish and Wildlife Service and had been instrumental in purchasing Mollicy Farms. The agency initially had in mind not a full-blown restoration of the floodplain but instead a more straightforward though still ambitious reforestation effort: replanting 3 million native trees, such as cypress, water tupelo, willow oaks, green ash, and mayhaws.

By 2007, that effort yielded tangible and impressive results. Huge swaths of old farmland now boasted the first suggestion of a new bottomland forest. The best place to admire the progress was from atop the levee, but as the Ouchley brothers turned west to look over the intact forest of the refuge, they knew they were standing on the most important obstacle to a functioning floodplain—for people and for natural communities alike.

The levee would have to go.

Taking out a levee is a complicated business, especially at this scale. Tearing down all seventeen miles of levee was out of the question; the expense of moving so much earth would be astronomical. But even punching holes in something that large is daunting. Keith Ouchley, a gifted raconteur, says he and his brother considered dynamite until they realized that the blasts might shatter windows from Shreveport, Louisiana to Jackson, Mississippi. Ouchley's genial manner does not hide a sharp mind, and he knew that the resulting display would have been an entertaining *MythBusters* episode, but it also might have changed the very course of the Ouachita. Although the Corps of Engineers does not own the levee around Mollicy Farms, it is responsible for the levees that guard Monroe, and would have been most unhappy with the Ouchleys had they put those at risk. Since the goal was quite the opposite, a less dramatic but not less effective method was needed.

Once the Ouchleys moved past the dynamite idea, their only option was to bring in dump trucks, backhoes, and scrapers like those used to grade roads, and gradually to whittle the levee down in spots until it was level with the river. A more difficult question then arose: where to breach the levee. Getting the answer falls in the domain of a highly specialized field called fluvial biogeomorphology. That mouthful requires computer models, topographic data, and aerial survey maps, along with an understanding of the ecology of the bayous.

The result of all the science was a plan for four cuts in the levee, each about 1,000 feet long, at the points where existing or historic streams entered or exited the property. The Fish and Wildlife Service supplied the muscle. The project was eminently shovel-ready, so the

Federal government chipped in $2.6 million in stimulus money to complete the work.

The breach was scheduled for June 2009, but the Ouachita had its own plans. By mid-May, the river reached the top of the levee and the Fish and Wildlife Service closed the entire Mollicy tract to the public. The Ouachita then began flowing across the top of the levee and ultimately burst through in two locations, blowing out two 150-foot gashes. Knowing nothing of fluvial biogeomorphology, the Ouachita made the cuts where it pleased, not where the scientists selected. The river also dug a new lake sixty feet deep and uprooted many of the newly planted trees.

Once the floodwaters receded, work on the planned breaches (the natural ones remained in place, too) began in the summer of 2009. Heavy machinery pushed the earth back into the borrow ditch whence it came, reconnecting the tract's bayous to the Ouachita.

Returning the muddy river to its ancient floodplain would become the biggest levee-busting operation ever in North America. The Ouchley brothers are in the early stages of a plan to coax plants and animals back to flourishing as they had when Jefferson's surveyors measured the landscape in 1804.

With the levees breached, the floodplain began functioning as a natural ecosystem. The full impact won't be known for decades when the forest becomes mature, but already bass can spawn there, and the floodplain is enhancing the health of the trees the Ouchleys helped to plant. In fifty years, visitors to the former Mollicy Farms will see a hardwood bottomland forest with abundant wildlife and flowing water.

Mollicy Farms is already a project with national and perhaps global significance. It may provide a model for other efforts.

From atop what remains of the levee at high water, Mollicy Farms now looks like a large, placid lake. That illusion is easier to maintain if you ignore that it is a lake filled by a raging Ouachita, which at flood stage is a torrent nearly thirty feet deep. You can imagine where Mollicy

Bayou runs and how it empties through the breached levee into the river, but it is invisible beneath the flood. The tops of the replanted trees rise forlornly over the floodwaters, impatient for them to recede.

This is how a floodplain should work. Opening up the levee is just the first step in this investment in nature. Mollicy Farms now stores floodwater and takes pressure off the downstream levees, but in other ways the system still operates as it did when the fields held soybeans instead of water. When the levees were intact, farmers pumped sediment- and nutrient-laden water over the top and into the river. It was visible from the opposite bank, a distinct tendril of muddy water from the farm pushing through the clear water of the river, a stream within a stream. This still happens as floodwaters recede and drain off Mollicy, bringing bits of the farm with it, along with remnants of fertilizer spread over the land for two decades.

Now, fluvial biogeomorphologists, ecologists, and construction crews have another task: replumb the rest of Mollicy Farms to bring back the streams and the natural communities they once supported. This means breaking up and filling in the lattice of straight-line irrigation ditches, rehabilitating the creeks that remain and re-creating those that were destroyed. As with the levee breaches, this is an experiment. No one knows exactly where and how to build a sinuous ditch that looks and acts like the streams that once ran through this bottomland forest.

The return on this investment will not be just in the local environment's improved health, but in the lessons it has for other places as well. Kelby Ouchley likened the whole process, from replanting trees to removing the levee to replumbing the floodplain, to angioplasty. Opening Mollicy's clogged arteries will not only reduce strain on downstream levees and thus lower maintenance costs, as the residents of Monroe can attest. The forest will also sequester carbon and help mitigate climate change, provide recreation such as duck hunting and fishing, and improve water quality in the Gulf of Mexico.

Scientists from Duke University have added up how much all this could be worth — carbon sequestration, recreation, flood protection, and so on — both to the people living nearby and to those on the Gulf Coast and even farther away. Breaching the levees and restoring the forest may make more economic sense than eking out marginal row-crop agriculture. In a 2009 study the researchers totaled all these values across the Mississippi Alluvial Valley and found that wetlands could be worth up to two-and-half times more intact than they would bring if converted to soybeans or cotton.

It will take some time before all those arteries are clear and the patient is healthy again. *Healthy* here is also a relative term. Given how the land around Mollicy Farms was transformed, bringing it back to be indistinguishable from its twin across the river may be too much to ask, at least for now. That may not be the point. A living floodplain may be enough.

There truly are no losers in the restoration of Mollicy Farms. Private landowners had tried and failed to farm the land, sold it, and it is now in public hands. The levees themselves were built not by the Army Corps of Engineers but by the investors, and removing them increased the risk for no one and decreased it for many thousands of people in Monroe. A better example of a win-win would be hard to find. So it is not surprising that no one in the area objected to the plan to breach the levees. Most people were all for it. In part, this simply reflects the near-universal popularity of hunting and fishing in northern Louisiana. Who could object to twenty-five square miles or so of new hunting and fishing grounds?

That no one in northern Louisiana objects to taking out a levee and flooding an old farm is important. The public response to removing the levees may represent a deeper and more profound shift. Over the past decade, dramatic floods in many places, not just in the United States but around the world, have forced us to rethink our relationship with rivers and to realize that our control over them is tenuous and may indeed be slipping. Scientists now know much more about how rivers and floodplains work. That knowledge enables people to work with nature to enhance both human well-being and the health of rivers at the same time. There is no clearer example of this new thinking than Iowa.

Restoring Iowa's Floodplains

Iowa's 2010 conservation ballot initiative was a success, receiving more votes than that year's victorious Republican candidate for governor. The initiative created a permanent and dedicated fund to protect Iowa's water quality and reduce water pollution, to shield communities, businesses, and farmlands from floods, and to protect fertile soils.

The supporters of the ballot initiative, known formally as Iowa's Water and Land Legacy, understand that their lives and livelihoods are dependent on healthy natural systems. They also know that investing in natural resources will bring huge returns for local economies and communities.

Iowa's Water and Land Legacy offers one model of how to pay for these solutions and could provide $150 million in new funding for Iowa's natural resources each year. The tricky part is that the constitutional amendment only built the coffers; filling them requires that voters approve an increase in the state sales tax, a less popular step they have yet to take. That gap highlights a crucial fact: good science and innovative solutions will only go so far without broader changes in law and policy to replicate the best ideas and bring them to a scale sufficient to make a lasting difference for people and nature.

Nevertheless, the initiative provides a compelling example of a state-based project that will have an impact far beyond state borders. Iowa is the center of a watershed that drains 41 percent of the United States into the Gulf of Mexico. Clean water in Iowa means cleaner water in the Gulf.

Many Iowans have firsthand knowledge of the damage floods can do. Iowa has suffered three 500-year floods since 1993. These severe floods turned many Iowans into passionate conservationists. These same Iowans now focus on climate change, fearing that global warming will make flooding risks still worse. The farmers pushing to restore the floodplains are also distressed by the lack of progress in curbing greenhouse gas emissions.

Floods in Iowa and elsewhere are a result not just of changing climate. More immediate human actions compound the problem. In the absence of perennial vegetation, a few inches of extra rain every year manifests itself in much higher stream flows. The loss of natural wetlands and the elimination of floodplains have reduced water-storage capacity in countless landscapes—not just in Iowa, but worldwide.

Now, areas that always flooded regularly and for which floods were a defining characteristic—the Mississippi and the Ouachita, and also the Yangtze and the Zambezi—experience not only bigger and more frequent floods, but floods that come and go more quickly. This may sound appealing, but keep in mind that seasonal floods provide a host of benefits. Where floods benefit people, longer-lasting floods are better—more time for fish to feed on the floodplain and spawn, for sediment to renew the soils, for water to recharge aquifers, among other things. Reopening stretches of historic floodplain will return the usual rhythm of these rivers and provide benefits to people who live downstream.

Even doing this will not restore the rivers to what they once were. The way people use the land around the rivers has changed too much and places too many competing demands on both land and water to go back, and a changing climate means entirely new hydrology for countless rivers. Given the extent of the flooding problem, no single group has the budget, workforce, or broad political clout to address the challenge by itself. Unnatural flooding results from multiple causes, and multiple causes require multiple solutions. A flood-management plan that focuses solely on levees and reservoirs may provide a degree of flood protection for some communities, but that approach will worsen flooding, degrade fish and wildlife habitats, and lower water quality elsewhere. Governments, communities, and conservationists can do better.

People in vulnerable areas can help by supporting efforts to restore floodplains and by changing how they manage rivers. Local-scale efforts, however, are not enough; change has to happen at the scale of entire river basins. Protecting small pieces of nature—wetlands, seasonal floodplains, native forests—remains important, but such remnants are terribly vulnerable and in isolation often cease to function. A more lasting solution will be networks of natural areas that together provide valuable services. Developing these networks is far more difficult than employing the opportunistic land acquisition strategies conservation often followed in the past, but the payoff is also far greater. This solution requires science, policy, and the support of local communities.

Some levees must remain, while others, such as the one around Mollicy Farms, can be breached. Levees could also be pushed farther off rivers to allow some flooding, or breached in extreme floods, with farmers compensated for lost crops. Compensating farmers will allow for more and bigger levee-alteration projects, and many farmers would participate in such a program because they know their farmland is relatively poor. In 2009, for example, the US Department of Agriculture made available $145 million of economic stimulus funds to buy floodplain easements on frequently flooded land. That means taking farmland out of production, something farmers are often loath to do. But the department received applications for 474,000 acres, ten times the acreage for which it had funding available.

Making good use of floodplains without disrupting the economic and social lives of the people who live there will be challenging, but it can be done. The goal is to determine the balance between the various values of floodplains and the communities that benefit from them. Part of the solution is to engage nontraditional stakeholders such as farmers and ranchers, as well as urban planners and community groups. Conservationists must form ties to agricultural interests, government agencies, and both rural and urban communities. This collaboration with residents and public agencies at all levels can lead to changes in how people use their lands and waters—changes that make them more secure ecologically and economically.

Communities facing the growing risk of floods understandably want answers now, along with guarantees that they will be protected. Also understandably, that desire leads to a narrow focus on the local stretch of river and on more levees, more walls, more of the kinds of control people have built for a century or more. The lasting solution requires big investments in nature and a greater appreciation of how communities, be they farmers or fishermen, can define for themselves what those investments should be.

4

The New Fishing

FISH ARE AN EXCELLENT EXAMPLE OF NATURE'S VALUE. THE FISHING industry drives coastal economies worldwide and provides the main source of protein for more than 1 billion people. Yet more than 80 percent of fisheries operate at or beyond sustainable limits. With expanding populations and growing demand for food, business as usual guarantees that this problem will only get worse.

Like farmers, fishing communities understand that their livelihoods depend on nature; as fish disappear, so do their businesses. Those same communities may provide the solution to overfishing.

In 2009, Elinor Ostrom became the first and only woman to win the Nobel Prize in Economics. Not an economist but rather a political scientist who worked at Indiana University for more than thirty-five years until her death in 2012, Ostrom won for her studies of how people who share resources such as fish, timber, or pastureland manage them for the good of all. In addition to being a woman in a field dominated by men and a political scientist to boot, one more characteristic set Ostrom apart from nearly all economists, especially Nobel laureates; her data came not from highly abstract mathematical models of human behavior, but from actual people. Working almost like an anthropologist, Ostrom talked to Nepalese farmers, Maine lobstermen, and many others in between and asked how they worked, how they lived. She found that when communities band together, trust one another, and have clear property rights, they can innovate and overcome shortsighted self-interest, and instead manage forests and fisheries for future generations.

The kind of collaboration Ostrom documented is also saving fisheries on California's Central Coast. In this region, the environmental community had been making little progress toward more sustainable fishing practices. Rather than giving up, some environmentalists joined with the fishing community to create innovative solutions that produce both profits and benefits for nature.

Not long ago, the idea that diehard environmentalists and flinty, weathered fishermen would find common ground seemed unlikely, even absurd. The divide between those communities over questions about the status and conditions of fish stocks was growing, a reflection of deeper economic and political trends. But new thinking about the value of nature spawns new alliances, and in Morro Bay, California, and other many other places, the tide has turned. When both sides are willing to drop old assumptions and experiment with new methods, results can be dramatic.

More Fishing, Less Fish

Morro Bay, a small fishing community 175 miles south of San Francisco, gets its name from Morro Rock, a remnant of a long-dead volcano and one of the most dramatic features of the Pacific Coast. The westernmost of a chain of volcanic peaks called the Nine Sisters, Morro Rock looms almost 600 feet over the bay.

In the 1980s Morro Bay sheltered dozens of fishing trawlers, most of which pursued bottom-dwelling fish called groundfish—petrale sole, sand dabs, thornyhead, several rockfish species, and one known locally as black cod, although it bears almost no relation to the famous New England fish.

West Coast fishing communities such as Morro Bay also depend on Dungeness crab, swordfish, albacore, and salmon, but groundfish have been the most reliable source of locally harvested seafood for decades because of their year-round availability. But the Pacific groundfish fishery began a long, steady decline in the mid-1980s. By the early 2000s, it seemed about to shut down completely. Fishermen (women in the industry in the United States and Canada call themselves "fishermen" as well and recoil at the gender neutral "fishers"; out of respect for their preference I do the same here) held permits but catches had declined so drastically that the gas needed to get to the fishing grounds cost more than the trip itself would bring in.

The pattern is now global. According to the UN's Food and Agriculture Organization, more than 80 percent of the earth's fisheries are either fully exploited, meaning no growth is possible, or overexploited, being pushed to their limits. Larger fleets go out and stay out longer, but they often come back with empty nets; more fishing, less fish. The story is as old as civilization itself, retold through ancient ruins of cultures like the Anasazi or the Maya, whose environmental destruction contributed significantly to their ultimate collapse, as Jared Diamond has masterfully described. Off some coastlines, people kept fishing until little was left except rocks and sand.

In Morro Bay, overfishing drove several groundfish species and the industry itself toward collapse. More than half the boat owners wanted out. The next generation had little interest in fishing and parents encouraged their children to find other careers.

Repairing this situation requires resilient human and ecological communities. For many generations, people assumed that taking fish from the sea was simple (if laborious) and limitless. That assumption remained largely unchallenged even as the science of managing an

increasingly industrial process matured. Over the past two decades
the complexity of marine environments has become clear, as has the
need for far more sophisticated means of managing them. Diverse
oceans require diverse institutions—law, community, and science
among them.

The days of the lone boat captain doing as she pleases based
solely on long knowledge of fishing grounds may be numbered. The
alternative, a collaborative effort of conservationists, scientists, fishermen, businessmen, and governments, may be more lasting. One
such collaboration in Morro Bay demonstrates how communities that
understand the value of nature can work together, overcome mutual
mistrust, and build new economies based on new models.

THE CALIFORNIA CURRENT FLOWS SOUTH ALONG THE COAST FROM
British Columbia to Baja. This upwelling brings up cold, nutrient
rich water from the deep ocean. The remarkable productivity of the
current accounts largely for the rich waters off Central California. In
addition to many species of groundfish, the Current supports schools
of anchovies and sardines, which in turn feed tuna, marlin, and salmon;
vast quantities of krill, the staple food source of great whales; and
seals, sea otters, and many species of seabirds.

This diversity of life is more than a statistic for the Morro Bay fishing community. The more diverse a fishery, it turns out, the more
stable and productive it is. In one influential study, Canadian ecologist
Boris Worm and his colleagues found that with declining diversity,
rates of resource collapse increase, while recovery potential, stability,
and water quality decrease exponentially. Restoration of species and
ecosystems, in contrast, can increase productivity and decrease variability. Natural capital thus refers not just to single stocks of commercially valuable fish, but also to the enormous diversity of marine life,
the loss of which diminishes the ocean's capacity to provide food and
maintain water quality.

Diversity and productivity are linked in complex ways. The question scientists are now asking: what does that relationship look like in particular places and at particular times? Sometimes, providing a service like water retention or flood protection can come at the cost of biological diversity. Other times, the two go together. Balancing them depends on the social and economic context—how much human demand exists for the suite of services potentially supplied by a given ecosystem like a forest or a floodplain or a fishing ground? Such systems can be tuned to produce different suites of benefits, but to complicate matters further, the answer to the question of which benefits are most important depends on whom you ask. Not only water, but services from nature more generally flow toward money and power.

Untangling these knotty issues is one of the greatest challenges in emphasizing the services from nature as a conservation tool. Imagine replacing a natural forest with a tree plantation. The plantation does certain things effectively; it holds onto rainfall, cools the air, provides timber, and so on, but it has none of the ecological richness of the forest it replaced. More dramatically, if a farmer's short-term goal is to optimize the production of, say, soy beans, then diversity will just get in the way.

The bottom line is that over the range of benefits people need and over the long run, favoring diversity over uniformity looks like a good way to go. The trick then is how to broaden the business objectives of farmers, fishermen, and others to promote a longer-term view.

A diverse fishery may also offer a form of insurance—a buffer against shocks to the system such as climate change. Investing in the ability of fishing communities to adapt and find new ways of operating, as well as controlling pollution and creating marine reserves, increases the production and reliability of the goods and services that the ocean provides to humanity. Staying on the current path, on the other hand, will threaten global food supplies, coastal water quality, and marine ecosystems.

Unfortunately, fishing in many places across the planet seems to be proceeding along the lines laid out in one of the founding allegories of the environmental movement: the tragedy of the commons. Coined in a 1968 essay by the ecologist Garrett Hardin, the tragedy of the commons describes how the rational pursuit of self-interest can lead to calamity. Hardin took "tragedy" to mean the "remorseless working of things," describing how herders sharing a common pasture may reap the benefits of adding to their herds because no individual bears the costs of the damage the collectively larger herd does to the land. Its single most famous passage has become almost a mantra:

> Therein is the tragedy. Each man is locked into a system that compels him to increase his herd without limit—in a world that is limited. Ruin is the destination toward which all men rush, each pursuing his own best interest in a society that believes in the freedom of the commons. Freedom in a commons brings ruin to all.

Fishing can follow the same pattern, Hardin warned, with each boat captain pursuing one more netful of fish for private gain but to the collective loss. Hardin's preferred solution was to place common resources under government ownership, or, failing that, to make them private. Hardin's allegory and its notions about the role of government were enormously influential. "The Tragedy of the Commons" remains one of the most cited works in the history of ecology.

Hardin's prophecy of ruin helped set the tone for the environmental movement, but it is deeply flawed. Hardin's biggest mistake, and the mistake of many of his readers, was to misinterpret a rare circumstance as the rule rather than the exception. The tragedy that Hardin described can and does occur, but only where a resource is open to anyone, with no rules to govern it. So-called open-access resources in effect belong to no one. A commons, in contrast, has rules and belongs to everyone, and that distinction can make all the difference.

Hardin recognized the error, but by the time he corrected it the original idea had already taken firm hold of the collective imagination. Only in the past two decades, due in large part to the work of Elinor Ostrom, has there been a broader appreciation for the many ways people can govern a commons. These methods do not necessarily involve the state. Communities, Ostrom found, can organize themselves and, through private agreements set the rules for using and conserving common resources in defiance of traditional economic arguments that such problems of common ownership are unsolvable. In such circumstances, trust trumps contracts. That is beginning to happen in Morro Bay and may be the single best idea for saving fisheries worldwide.

Is Fishing Good for Fish?

For decades, fishing along the central California Coast, from Point Conception in the south to San Francisco in the north, meant bottom trawling—dragging large, heavy nets across the seafloor and scooping up whatever was around. This had the virtues of being inexpensive and reasonably efficient, at least from the fishermen's perspective. The hard lessons would come later. In addition to bringing up tons of whatever fish the captains were after, the nets also tore up the bottom and snared piles of other sea creatures such as starfish, sponges, sharks, and rays, which were deemed worthless and tossed back, often dead. In addition, many depleted species of fish live side by side with more abundant target fish—and the trawl nets' indiscriminate harvest method captures both—eventually leading to severe overfishing of the weaker stocks. As such, in the roster of environmental evils, bottom trawling is often lumped with clear-cutting forests and ripping off mountaintops to get at the coal beneath.

The fishing industry also treated fish as a commodity, with one kind interchangeable for another. If, for example, all fish living on the seafloor are basically the same—a fish is a fish is a fish—then they can all be caught with the same methods and at the same rate. The word *groundfish* itself, a generic, colorless, and slightly odd collision of words, reveals the problem; it's called a groundfish fishery, not a rockfish or sole or bocaccio fishery. The waters off the Pacific coast throng with nearly ninety different species of fish that spend all or part of their lives on the bottom, and the seafloor itself is full of diverse habitats.

Like hunters, many fishermen are natural conservationists. Nearly all go into the business for love of the sea rather than money, which is hardly commensurate with the effort involved. As fishing has become more mechanized, however, their knowledge of the different habitats or the complex ecology of the fish they pursued became less valued. The goals were simply to optimize production of a commodity and to sell large quantities of inexpensive fish.

Those goals stem in large part from a decision made at the end of World War II, which marked a fateful intersection of politics, economics, and science. Fearful that Japanese and other foreign fishing fleets would move into the fishing grounds off the West Coast, the US government staked territorial claims to its coastal and offshore waters. At the same time, US boats were fishing just off the coast of South America, in waters claimed by Peru, Ecuador, and Chile. To justify the double standard, the government made a scientific assertion: fisheries science had advanced so far, the reasoning went, that managers could determine with precision how many fish the boats could catch without harming the fish population.

Thus a concept known as Maximum Sustainable Yield was born, part science, part economics, part politics. As Carmel Finley points out in her book *All the Fish in the Sea*, the effect was that fishing fleets from the United States and other developed countries could go wherever they wanted unless the government of Peru or Chile or another country could prove scientifically that they were taking too many fish. None were in a position to do so, and none had big enough fleets to fish in US waters. The idea that science was guiding fishing safely into the future took hold.

The idea remains in place today, but like Hardin's tragedy of the commons it has significant flaws. The way fishing has long been managed shows a fundamental misunderstanding of the resource that goes back many generations. This idea, that fish are not wildlife but instead a bottomless source of food and money, is as simple as it is wrong. Even as noted a scientist as Thomas Henry Huxley, an early and vigorous defender of Charles Darwin, endorsed the idea. In his inaugural address to the Fisheries Exhibition in London in 1883, Huxley said:

I believe, then, that the cod fishery, the herring fishery, the pilchard fishery, the mackerel fishery, and probably all the great sea fisheries, are inexhaustible; that is to say, that nothing we do seriously affects the number of the fish. And any attempt to regulate these fisheries seems consequently, from the nature of the case, to be useless.

Huxley knew that salmon and oysters were overfished and advocated for better stewardship of those species, but his belief in the inexhaustible deep sea reflected the broad consensus of the time. Another analogy from the same era lacked Huxley's scientific nuance but also captures an attitude toward nature and the role of people in it that has persisted. After the Civil War, homesteaders pushing past the Mississippi found that the land was increasingly dry. Some of the more optimistic among them, backed up by dubious science, came to believe that farming would change the dry local climate for the better. In 1881, Charles Dana Wilber, a glib, energetic land speculator and journalist who promoted western settlement, coined the phrase that captured the spirit of the time: "Rain follows the plow."

The ideas of fish as an endless resource and human activity as ultimately beneficial to nature combined to shape the modern approach to managing fisheries. The basic approach, promoted most notably by a scientist and government official named Wilbert Chapman in the years after World War II, stems from a seemingly commonsense argument: taking some bigger, older fish from the sea leaves more room and more food for the remaining fish to grow. This makes fish analogous to trees, since foresters have long known that thinning the forest creates more light and space for the remaining trees to flourish.

Fishing is good for fish, or so Chapman and others argued. Combine this with the persistent belief that leaving fish in the sea or water in the rivers is a waste—in 1955, Chapman wrote that "fish resources cannot be stored in the sea. They die."—and you have a situation that encouraged more people to join the fishing industry. Politics played a role, too: a bigger fleet meant more US boats at sea and a greater opportunity to exploit international waters for the benefit of American consumers and the American economy.

The result was an enormous industry with a single goal: to catch as many fish as possible. For fishermen in central California, that meant focusing on just a handful of the dozens of species that live on the seabed, such as petrale sole, several types of rockfish, and black cod, often marketed as sablefish. Here, just twelve species of fish account for more than 60 percent of the fishery's total value.

The idea that fishing is really good for fish is too good to be true. Mathematically minded ecologists may attempt to show how this works on paper, but once countries could build more and bigger boats with bigger nets, careful calculations went out the window. By the mid-1970s, the signs that something had to be done were so obvious even Congress could not ignore them. A Democratic senator, Washington's Warren G. Magnuson, and a Republican from Alaska, Ted Stevens, shepherded a bill called the Magnuson-Stevens Fishery Conservation and Management Act of 1976.

The law created eight regional fishery management councils responsible for setting rules governing how many fish could be caught by how many boats using what kinds of gear. The regional councils were intended to continue refining the science of fisheries management, applying the idea of Maximum Sustainable Yield to its fullest effect.

For a time all seemed well. In Morro Bay in the late 1970s and early 1980s, boat owners could go where they wanted, drop their nets, and bring in big catches. With plenty of fish to go around, they made good money. This last golden age for fishing, such as it was, would not last long. Rather than overseeing thriving fisheries that would harvest the bounty of the seas far into the future, managers watched in horror as fisheries began to fail in dramatic fashion, one after another.

The first to fall was also among the most iconic. A wooden cod carved in 1784, known as the Sacred Cod, hangs in the Massachusetts statehouse, a symbol of how cod fishing supported the New England economy for centuries. In the early 1990s the fishery began to collapse. In 1993 the government of Canada closed the Grand Bank fishery off Newfoundland to cod and groundfish. The United States followed suit the next year when it closed the Georges Bank fishery, perhaps the most famous fishing ground in the world, to the fishing of cod, haddock, and yellowtail flounder. Cod and other species had sunk to less than 10 percent of their peak abundance. In 1994, the US Secretary of Commerce for the first time ever declared a fishery disaster, and another declaration followed just a year later.

The disaster declaration in New England meant millions of dollars in federal aid became available to help struggling fishermen. Some of this money was used to buy back fishing permits and boats from those who wanted out of the industry. This both helped them to move to new jobs and reduced the number of boats that would return once the fishery was reopened—a vital step in rebalancing the system. Federal regulators use a telling phrase to describe their efforts: their goal, they say, is to "rationalize the fishery."

The suggestion that fisheries management is somehow irrational was reinforced just a few months after the first disaster declaration in New England. Another iconic fishery, on the opposite coast, was in deep trouble. Pacific salmon, as much a venerated symbol of the Northwest as cod is for New England, peaked in 1988 but soon crashed, due partly to dams on many rivers that prevented salmon from returning to spawn.

With too few salmon, fishermen shifted to groundfish instead, and some made their way to the California fishing grounds. That provided but a temporary sanctuary. With too many boats in pursuit of too few fish, combined with a still unexplained decline in the productivity of the California Current from 1977 through the late 1990s, the fall came steep and fast. In 1987, the value of the Pacific groundfish fishery, apart from the boats themselves, was $110 million; by 2003, it had dropped to $35 million. In Morro Bay, the commercial fishery brought in more than $8 million in 1995, but less than $2 million in 2003.

By the late 1990s, nine long-lived rockfish species were severely depleted and five of the most economically important species dropped below 10 percent of their historic numbers. Rockfish mature so slowly that rebuilding these populations will require at least fifty years, and more than a century for some species.

In 2000, the bottom fell out for bottom-feeders off the West Coast. Washington, Oregon, and California requested help and the Secretary of Commerce once again declared a fishery disaster. By one estimate, this fishery had twice as many boats as the fish population could support.

The problems now touch nearly every coastline in the country. Since the first disaster declaration for New England cod in 1994, forty-six fisheries from Alaska to the Gulf of Mexico to Long Island Sound have collapsed and been declared disasters. Clearly, more rationalization is needed.

As the enormous scope of the problem came into focus, Congress began to take action. These first steps developed over the next fifteen years into a series of new ideas on valuing the seas and the communities that depend on them. In 1996, spurred by the dramatic depletion of cod and salmon, Congress amended the Magnuson-Stevens Act to greatly increase the use of science for managing fish stocks, and to require regional councils to identify important fish habitats and protect them from damaging trawl nets. The federal fisheries councils, under pressure from the fishing industry, were slow to delineate these areas, called Essential Fish Habitats, and when they did so the plans were often insufficient. Conservation organizations like Washington, DC–based Oceana resorted to an old but effective tool: they repeatedly sued the federal government.

The environmentalists won more than they lost. In one particularly important case in 2001, a federal judge in Washington, DC, ordered the Pacific Fishery Management Council to conduct a thorough analysis of the trawl fishery's impact on marine habitats. In the past, such a decision may well have led to a downward spiral of tension, distrust, litigation, and political grandstanding, the usual battle lines drawn between local economies, the environment, and federal regulations. In Morro Bay the decision provided a crucial opening to partnerships that would have been unthinkable a few years ago but now bring together different ways of valuing nature. That partnership may also lead to new ways of fishing, a stronger community, and a healthier marine environment.

One result of the judge's order was a new study on the effects of trawling on fish and their habitats. The study reflected the dramatic evolution in the sophistication of fisheries science since the early days of Maximum Sustainable Yield and its focus on individual fish stocks rather than the broader marine environment. The study confirmed what conservationists had suspected: far from being good for the fish, trawling can change the physical habitat and biologic structure of ecosystems and can therefore have wide-ranging consequences. Also in keeping with what opponents of trawling had advocated for some time, the study recommended closing some areas to trawling, reducing the number of boats and the days at sea, and using new, less destructive kinds of fishing gear.

While fisheries around the country and the world were collapsing and causing huge economic losses, conservationists were arguing for greater protection of marine environments. That strategy had two parts: identify areas that should be protected, akin to parks on land, and find less destructive ways than trawl nets to catch fish.

Conservation organizations felt they had both new and better science as well as law on their side. TNC and other groups had recently completed a conservation assessment of the Northern California Current that identified the most biologically important areas to conserve, as well as the greatest threats to the habitat and marine life within those sites. This study supported conservationists' understanding that offshore areas of California, particularly the continental shelf off the central coast, harbor globally significant marine life, and that bottom trawling poses a great threat to that diversity.

No surprise, then, that conservation organizations wanted to protect the high-priority seafloor habitats and cut bottom trawling in half. The reality was that those same organizations had unsuccessfully lobbied for years to restrict trawl fishing along the Central Coast. Industry participants—fishermen, buyers, processors, and their government regulators—held the seats on the Pacific Fishery Management Council. Simply talking at the fishermen and telling them to do better was not going to work.

The fishermen understood the sketchy state of the fishery. They had lived through the disaster in 2000 and watched helplessly as a few big companies bought up fishing permits. The federal court's decision meant that federal regulation was inevitable, even from the industry-friendly fishery management council, if they could not agree on areas of habitat that could be protected. The independent, family-owned fishing operation was becoming an endangered species.

A Good Deal for Morro Bay

A breakthrough came when conservationists decided that instead of fighting the fishing industry, they would join it. In 2004, a Nature Conservancy staffer named Chuck Cook met with the owners of twenty-two trawl permits on the docks at Morro Bay, Monterey, Half Moon Bay, and Moss Landing, and offered a deal: TNC would buy trawlers and trawl permits from willing sellers on the conditions that all parties would agree to the protection of 3.8 million acres of fish habitat that would be off-limits to trawlers; and they would jointly recommend that action to federal regulators.

The fishermen who were willing to sell saw the prospect of taking the proceeds and reinvesting in another livelihood. Those who wanted to keep fishing thought they had a better chance of striking a fair deal with TNC that both preserved their critical fishing grounds while protecting fish habitats. They did not exactly trust the conservationists, but they saw an opportunity to have a say in their own future.

In 2004, fishermen and conservation scientists from TNC and the Environmental Defense Fund (EDF) got together around detailed maps of the seafloor and started bargaining. The fishermen knew some areas were going to be closed. Being at the table was better than having the decisions made during a crowded and raucous Pacific Fisheries Management Council meeting in Seattle. Conservation organizations were the devil they knew. Fishermen divulged the trade secrets they had resisted revealing before: where they trawled, how often, and what they caught there. The result was the identification of no-trawl zones encompassing 67 percent of the high-priority conservation areas between Point Conception and Point Sur.

Since the plan had both industry and environmental support, it sailed through the regulatory process—almost unheard-of when it comes to something as controversial as closing off fishing grounds to protect habitat. With the plan approved, TNC paid $7 million to buy all six federal groundfish trawl permits in Morro Bay, along with seven more from nearby Half Moon Bay and Moss Landing, plus six boats, four of which were demolished.

These thirteen permits represented more than half the total for the region. Suddenly, TNC was the second largest single-permit holder on the West Coast with 7 percent of the catch quota for Pacific Coast groundfish. Once the deal was done in June 2006, the organization owned a significant portion of groundfish harvest rights on the West Coast, and began to deliberate the best options to redeploy those harvest rights.

No one had ever tried this approach before, so no one knew what the result would be. The fishing community reacted with disbelief. Who could imagine that a bunch of tree huggers would end up owning such a large share of West Coast harvest rights? Some TNC supporters and even some of its own staff reacted the same way, especially when in 2007 the organization decided to lease the permits back to some of the very fishermen who had just sold out—including one who would keep on using his trawl nets. For some, this seemed a betrayal.

What the organization had on paper was a small slice of a troubled fishery. What it had in mind was a new way to fish.

The fishing permits and the process that landed them gave conservationists leverage and a model for collaboration between groups unaccustomed to working together. If these two groups could find common ground, they might be able to rebuild the fishery and to restore profits to four California fishing communities.

Conservationists also had necessity on their side. Simply holding or retiring the trawling permits would not do enough to conserve marine resources in the long run. Current regulations allow the remaining trawlers operating out of other ports in the West Coast groundfish fleet the right to harvest the catch previously landed by the trawlers that sold out. While those other fishermen were not about to boost their catches immediately, that could change given the state of the fishery. Purchasing the permits is not the end of the story.

Scientists, industry, governments, and fishing communities needed a broader vision of the value of nature and of the willingness and ability to act on it. An industry based on a high-volume, low-value catch, with its strict reliance on bottom trawling, was too narrow and outdated. Changing that means a shift in attitudes, techniques, and government policies. Thus Morro Bay is a microcosm of the changes that can happen as we begin to revalue nature.

Until 2011, regulations prevented trawl permit holders on the West Coast from switching to more selective, less-damaging gear. That locked fishermen into poor harvest practices and created perverse incentives, limiting their ability selectively to harvest abundant species, to find more sustainable ways to fish, and to operate viable fishing businesses.

After two years of often difficult negotiations among fishermen, conservationists, and the government, the fishery council agreed in 2009 to allow seven fishermen who leased trawl permits to use other gear, such as hooks or traps. That may seem the dreary minutiae of government regulations, but it had huge significance for both the people and the environment of Morro Bay. It was the crucial first step in giving the conservation and fishing communities a way to work together at a scale that could improve both the economic and environmental performance of the fishery.

Freed from the requirement to use trawl nets, fishermen and conservationists created an unprecedented "Conservation Fishing Agreement," which functions much like a conservation easement on land. On land, an easement prohibits a landowner from using his land in

particular ways, such as subdividing or developing it. At sea, an easement defines how and where fishermen can work, with limits on
species, catch sizes, and gear. Agreements such as this one allow the
fishermen and the conservation community to test the ecologic and
economic merits of environmentally friendly ways to harvest
groundfish.

As anyone who has bought a house knows, a complex and longstanding legal infrastructure governs all land transactions. It is clear
who owns land and how they can use it. Try running a hog farm in
your suburban backyard and the limits to your rights will immediately be apparent. No such laws govern the sea; a permit to fish is not
the same as owning those fish, and while it is possible to own or lease
portions of the seafloor, no one has done so in the deepwater off California's coastline. An easement can work for fisheries only under a
system that creates something legally resembling a property right to
fish, something the fishermen can then buy and sell. That requires a
system that limits access to fish and fishing grounds.

Crafting that formal legal structure, which did not exist on the
West Coast, would take years. The fisheries council guarded its pre-
rogative to set fishing limits for the entire fleet. If the fleet reached its
limit on an overfished species—say, sole or rockfish—a boat owner
could keep fishing for some other fish such as whiting, and any sole
and rockfish they brought up inadvertently they were required by law
to throw back. Some 20 to 30 percent of the catch, millions of pounds
of fish, was shoveled back into the sea, dead or dying.

Fishermen hated doing this. They considered this the height of regulatory stupidity. The policy deepened their distrust of government and
anyone else who wanted to tell them how to catch fish. The system also
encouraged fishermen to get all they could as fast as they could, lest
other boats beat them to it and then have regulators shut down the fishery. This was fishing as a derby and it encouraged wasteful and even
dangerous behavior. Boats went out in all weather and cut corners. It

also did little for the fishermen's bank accounts, as boats dumped all their fish on the market at once, practically guaranteeing a low price.

Federal regulators decided in 2002 to experiment with a new approach called catch shares. In this system, scientists who work for the fisheries council determine the amount of fish from each species the fleet can catch and then the council divides that amount among the fishermen annually. The boats can then go out at any time during the year and pursue whichever fish are bringing the best prices. They can fish to the market with an economic incentive to fish more carefully and not waste the resource. With the quota-based system, fishermen have much more predictability in their lives and businesses.

However, catch shares have a troubling result: in some places where it has been implemented, big, rich operations accumulate most of the shares. That made fishermen in Morro Bay wary. They wanted to preserve their independence. That catch shares would likely be implemented for groundfish provided yet more motivation for the community to find new ways to fish that reflected all the values of nature, not just the price of the fish.

It took nearly a decade to put catch shares in place for Pacific groundfish. In 2011, the fishery became one of just a dozen or so limited-access programs along US coasts. Fish caught under these programs amount to just 10 percent of the national harvest.

Changes in both the scale of fisheries and their tactics have led to dramatic improvements. The boats bring in far fewer unwanted fish and leave more juveniles in the sea, while sparing corals and sponges from the crushing weight of trawl nets. Even better, the economics of the fishery is in the process of turning right-side up: a high-quality, low-volume market for fish caught on hook and line or in a trap. Both of these methods make it possible to keep the fish alive in tanks onboard, something that was impossible with huge trawl nets.

Demand for local and sustainably harvested seafood continues to grow, providing a market stimulus for changes in fishing behavior. A dead trawl-caught fish such as black cod sells for 90 cents per pound. On the other hand, black cod harvested with traps, a delicacy in Japanese restaurants, sells on the dock for about $3.50 per pound and in upscale groceries for $20 a pound or more. As of 2006, black cod accounted for just 2 percent of the catch but 28 percent of the revenue. Blackgill rockfish, often sold in fish markets under the name Pacific Red Snapper, sells for up to $10 a pound; a few years ago, fishermen would be lucky to get 80 cents per pound for the same fish from a trawl.

Most boat captains in Morro Bay saw the changes coming and finally started to turn a profit after three years. Now, many sell part of their catch to a local processor that supplies high-end retailers and restaurants. It is a broad trend. Between April 2008 and March 2009, the market for fish caught on hooks or in traps grew by more than 50 percent, reaching a value of $1.5 billion. Major fish retailers—including Wal-Mart and Whole Foods—now collaborate with conservation organizations to reshape the market for fish, with an emphasis on environmental standards. Overall, the Morro Bay fishery rebounded to over $4 million in 2010.

The new markets for hook and line and trapped fish are vital but not enough. Trawls remain the best means of harvesting still-abundant populations of flatfish such as petrale and Dover sole. These species remain critical to the economies of Morro Bay, Half Moon Bay, and other communities. Few people even among conservationists foresee the complete elimination of trawling from West Coast fisheries. So in addition to moving some fishermen away from trawling, the challenge is to make the trawlers still in operation less destructive. One approach is to restrict trawling to previously trawled areas of sandy or muddy seafloors. This keeps nets away from rocky or reef habitats, no-trawl zones, and areas that have never been trawled.

BEYOND POLICY CHANGES AND SCIENCE, THE MOST EXCITING development of all in Morro Bay are changes in the community itself. Fishermen in the United States tend to be a proud and independent lot who put a great deal of effort into being as self-reliant as possible. But when a fisherman on his own pursues profit alone, then the other values of the fish he catches—to the community, to the environment—are disregarded.

Communally run fisheries can capture more values of nature. Such fisheries are found around the world, from Australia to South Africa to Chile, but they remain the exception. That may be changing, as dwindling catches force communities to find alternatives to the every-man-for-himself approach.

One unexpected alternative has introduced the fishing industry to the information age. Morro Bay fishermen are using a new tool, developed by TNC, called eCatch to track and share data with one another and with government regulators. This is revolutionary on several levels. For one, nearly all fishermen, from weekend fly enthusiasts on up, hate to reveal their favorite fishing spots. Now, in Morro Bay they share data about what they are catching and where, thus identifying hotspots of overfished species to avoid. They are building an information base that will help all fishermen, and the data goes to the community first, before it goes to government.

This data sharing is also revolutionary in its up-to-the-minute evaluations. The lag between when fishermen reported data to regulators and when the regulators acted on that information used to be measured in months, rarely reflecting what the fishermen were seeing firsthand on the water. Now that lag is measured in days or even hours. This makes a significant difference when some species are so depleted that allowable catches are tiny. Off Morro Bay, the total allowable catch of a fish called the canary rockfish is fifty pounds—not fifty pounds per boat, but total, for everyone. A single boat could bring in fifty pounds on one good day. For fishermen, the ability to report immediately that they have caught a few canary rockfish makes life easier for all boats on the water.

ECatch is another example of a community of fishermen taking responsibility for their shared resource for the first time, rather than simply exploiting it to the fullest extent possible. They are even going so far as to report their own violations. In the past if someone brought up, say, forty pounds of canary rockfish, they might have just slipped it back into the water and hoped for the best. Now, with eCatch and the possibility that they might be able to sell those fish anyway by buying unused quota from another boat, a fisherman is much more likely to report that catch, to everyone's benefit.

This collaborative spirit takes other forms as well. Fishermen and conservationists are working on a new institution called a Community Quota Fund. The Fund holds and manages fishing permits, and brings together the community, conservation organizations, and industry interests to make decisions about the fishery. Learning from the results of leasing experiments, the Fund could reduce the amount of trawling while balancing the needs of the environment, fishermen, and local communities.

The strength of the Morro Bay community matters enormously in the development of this new kind of fishing. Changing seemingly immutable traditions for the better will help fishermen, loggers, and farmers to make sound investments in nature. Leading the way is a new yet vital role for the environmental community.

5

Feeding the World—and Saving It

When I speak with agribusiness executives, I stress that it has never been more important for conservation and agriculture to work together. I also tell them that these two fields are less at odds than some of them might think.

You don't have to be a conservationist or a scientist to understand the demands that the world's growing population makes on our planet. Sometime in 2011, the earth welcomed its 7 billionth person, and by 2050 the population will likely hit 9 billion or more. Furthermore, as noted earlier, the population is not only growing in size, it is also growing in prosperity. Billions of people will lift themselves out of poverty over the next few decades. All of these additional people and additional prosperity will lead to more demands for food, water, energy, and space. The pressure on both the world's natural areas and agricultural lands will be intense.

Environmental organizations, agribusiness companies, farmers, governments, and consumers now face the need to determine how they all might work best together as we pursue both more output and better environmental outcomes from agriculture. Such blurring of roles can make people uncomfortable. Nevertheless, big challenges like this one require bold thinking and courageous action.

Fortunately, history offers valuable lessons on bold thinking in agriculture. Take scientist and Nobel Peace–prizewinner Norman Borlaug, for example. When Borlaug was tapped to head up a research institute in Mexico in 1944, DuPont, his employer at the time, offered to double his salary to keep him onboard. Borlaug declined their offer and headed south.

As director of Mexico's Cooperative Wheat Research and Production Program, funded by the Rockefeller Foundation, Borlaug worked with local farmers to boost wheat production. Where others saw peasant farmers struggling with poor harvests and diseased crops, Borlaug saw potential. Where others saw low returns on investment, long lead-in times, and up-front costs in plant breeding research, Borlaug saw opportunity.

Within twenty years, Borlaug's disease-resistant, high-yield crop varieties helped Mexico double its wheat production. Borlaug later brought these techniques to India and Pakistan, sparking the Green Revolution credited with more than doubling world food production between 1960 and 1990 and saving as many as 1 billion lives in developing countries.

In the 1940s, few experts would have seen the business potential of Mexican wheat farming; and in the 1950s, no bottom-line analysis would have identified wheat farming in Pakistan and the Punjab as good opportunities. Borlaug understood their potential and his discoveries formed the foundation for food security and economic growth around the world.

The children and grandchildren of the farmers with whom Borlaug worked are now achieving yields and returns unimaginable to their grandparents. This is an instructive and encouraging precedent.

The role of agriculture in feeding the world, and saving it, has never been clearer. At the risk of oversimplifying, if agriculture does not effectively increase productivity, farmers will spill into nature reserves and national parks to find their land. If conservation does not protect watersheds and forests, farms will suffer from more destructive floods and more prolonged droughts. If conservation fails to protect habitat for pollinators and natural pest controls, yields will fall.

Food companies also must account for environmental services in agriculture, especially those provided by land, soil, and water. If these companies pursue higher yields without considering these essential resources, then they will run out of all three. Agribusinesses can mine soils for several years by adding more fertilizer but doing so will eventually impoverish both the ecosystem and the farmers.

Already we see a broad consensus on the nature and urgency of the challenge: the world's food supply must double by 2050, not just to feed all the people on the planet, but also to support the more resource-intensive, protein-rich diets of an expanding middle class. Over a few short decades, agriculture must find ways to use less habitat; to use water more efficiently; and to manage land, soil, and water in ways that strengthen rather than degrade the environmental services they provide.

Businesses, conservationists, and governments can benefit by viewing the future as holding as much potential and hope as Norman Borlaug did. Businesses must think of the bottom line more imaginatively, with a focus on long-term results. Conservationists must work with the agriculture industry to intensify food production safely, to minimize the further conversion of land, and to lessen the impact of intensified agriculture on nearby wildlife and natural habitat. Governments must make policies and investments to protect the natural systems that the earth's 7 billion people rely on for their health and well-being.

The stakes are too high to continue with a vision any less ambitious.

Mad Cows and Rainforests

Cargill, an agribusiness titan and the largest privately held company in the United States; McDonald's, the largest fast-food chain in the world; and Greenpeace, the renowned and effective global environmental activist organization: these three may be the most unlikely of partners. Yet in 2006, they formed a successful alliance to stem deforestation and to protect natural capital in the Amazon.

The long road that led to that unexpected alliance began two decades earlier, with a cow—cow number 133, to be precise. Cow 133 lived on Pitsham Farm in Midhurst, England, about forty miles southwest of London. In December 1984, the cow became unsteady on its feet, had tremors, refused to eat, and seemed nervous and aggressive. After it died, no one recognized the significance of its odd behavior or of the lab tests that showed brain tissue with a distinctly spongy appearance. According to *The Telegraph*, it was another two years, as similar cases popped up across the United Kingdom, before scientists realized that Cow 133 had died from the first-known case of what the tabloids labeled Mad Cow Disease, and what scientists called bovine spongiform encephalopathy (BSE).

BSE can kill people who eat contaminated meat, so the discovery of BSE led to a global health scare. More than 220 people worldwide have died from BSE since 1984, most in the United Kingdom, and millions of cows have been slaughtered to control the epidemic.

BSE's biggest impact came from realizing that the root of the problem was what farmers in the United Kingdom and elsewhere in Europe fed their cattle. In most places, soybean meal provides the main protein supplement to animal feed, but because soybeans are difficult to grow in Europe, farmers there turned to animal by-products—the meat and bone left over in slaughterhouses—as a cheaper alternative. Unknown at the time, the misfolded protein that causes BSE survives the rendering process. Once this was discovered, it was clear that feeding offal to farm animals was dangerous and would have to stop.

The result of this finding was a sudden, worldwide surge in the demand for soybeans. Prices soared. In the early 1980s, the United States grew the vast majority of the world's soybeans, but demand soon outstripped the US supply. As a result, in the mid-1990s, major soy producers began to look for places where they could expand production quickly and cheaply. They found Brazil.

Multinational agribusiness giants such as Cargill, Archer Daniels Midland, and Bunge invested heavily in the seeds, fertilizer, and infrastructure necessary to transform Brazil into a soy-exporting powerhouse. Cargill built a shipping terminal, completed in 2003, capable of handling over 60,000 tons of soy every day in the city of Santarém.

Santarém has a history of attracting a wide variety of fortune seekers—miners, loggers, farmers, even Henry Ford. Ford set up two rubber plantations in the region, one rather unfortunately named Fordlândia, and the other, just a few miles outside Santarém, the more lyrical-sounding Belterra. Both plantations failed, defeated by the poor soils of the rainforest, an abundance of insects, and leaf blight. Some combination of those and other tropical hazards kept the human footprint around Santarém relatively small. Not so long ago, jungle surrounded the city.

Santarém lies deep in the rainforest, and when Cargill started planning the terminal, the nearest major soy plantations were hundreds of miles away. Thus, Santarém seemed an odd place to build a soy shipping terminal, especially one as enormous as Cargill's. However, Santarém had a major selling point: its location at the junction of the Amazon and the Rio Tapajós means an easy route to the Atlantic and markets in Europe and, via the Panama Canal, in China, too. Even this far inland, the Amazon is deep and wide enough for oceangoing freighters.

Cargill did not have an explicit goal of drawing farmers to Santarém, but that was the effect of the new terminal. Build it and the farmers will come. When they come it is at the expense of the forest. The reason has much to do with the fact that soy is an agricultural commodity—undifferentiated and bought and sold in huge quantities at a price set on global markets. Since farmers have no way to influence the price they get, they boost their profits only by decreasing how much they spend on getting their crop to market and increasing how much land they plant. Transportation costs are an obvious place to cut. The closer farmers can be to buyers such as Cargill, the better. When Cargill opened its terminal, soy farmers quickly realized the benefits of moving closer to the facility. Farmers flocked to the region. Production of soy around Santarém increased twentyfold in four years, from 1999 to 2003. Annual deforestation rates in the region approximately doubled as well.

By the mid-2000s, Brazil's economy was hurtling forward and deforestation reached record levels. Cattle ranching continued to be the main threat, but clearing land for soy was catching up quickly. Whereas most beef produced in Brazil stays in the country or is sold to its neighbors, Cargill and other exporters shipped Brazilian soy to Europe. Access to global markets, hence global capital, threatened to add even more fuel to the Amazon fires.

Cargill felt the heat early. European press reports on the link between deforestation and the Santarém terminal appeared in 2003. The company responded by setting up a satellite-based monitoring system to try to check forest cover in the farms around the terminal. Then Cargill received a lesson in the new environmental politics of global supply chains. A 2006 Greenpeace report, *Eating Up the Amazon*, documented the link between soy and deforestation in the Amazon in a compelling and dramatic fashion. To make the case in terms readily understandable to the greatest number of consumers, Greenpeace chose one of the highest profile corporate targets available: McDonald's. Greenpeace explained that soy from fields in the rainforest traveled from the terminal in Santarém, down the Amazon, then to Liverpool, and ended up in feed for chickens that were eventually sold as nuggets in McDonald's. Greenpeace sent its ship, the *Arctic Sunrise,* to block the terminal. Protestors in chicken suits invaded McDonald's outlets all over the United Kingdom and chained themselves to chairs. Posters went up across the country featuring Ronald McDonald carrying a chainsaw.

Serving as the poster boy for the destruction of the Amazon was the last thing McDonald's wanted. Company executives had seen this before: in 1981, ecologist Norman Myers coined the phrase "hamburger connection" to describe how the demand for cheap beef drove deforestation in Central America. McDonald's fielded accusations of this sort for decades. By 2006, the economic landscape and public opinion had changed. A reputation as a force driving deforestation was no longer just an annoyance. It could be devastating to the company's brand. That risk, combined with a growing sense of corporate responsibility, pushed McDonald's to join forces with Greenpeace. McDonald's put pressure on Cargill, and threatened to stop buying their soy unless they agreed to new environmental oversights.

To its credit, Cargill had quietly been trying to balance agriculture and conservation for several years prior to the Greenpeace campaign. Cargill had begun that process in Santarém and Henry Ford's old stomping ground of Belterra. Some 90 percent of producers in those areas bring their soy to the Santarém facility, so it became an ideal testing ground for new ways to invest in nature, to grow more soy, and to save the rainforest.

The two-pronged attack from Greenpeace and McDonald's gave those efforts new urgency. Cargill agreed not to buy soy from any land deforested after 2006. The company pushed fellow soy traders to do the same, resulting in an unprecedented moratorium on the purchase of any soy from newly deforested areas. Originally intended to last two years, the moratorium has been extended repeatedly and is still in place as of January 2013.

The moratorium reduces deforestation by channeling agricultural expansion into cleared but abandoned areas rather than into virgin forest. That is vital: the moratorium is not a case of conserving forest at the expense of farmers. The farmers can grow more soy if they wish, they just cannot grow it by pushing back the Amazonian frontier. For soy farmers in Santarém and Belterra, the cost of noncompliance is huge: they cannot sell their crop. Compliance, on the other hand, brings a guarantee of access to a global market and a reliable trader.

That is a landmark achievement, but also a fragile one. The headlines from the campaign against McDonald's have faded. If soy prices continue to rise, so will pressure to lift the moratorium or find ways around it, perhaps by expanding soy cultivation elsewhere. The most likely places for new soy farms are in the unique grasslands of central Brazil called the Cerrado and in the Atlantic forest in the southern part of the country. A campaign there might not work as well as it did in the Amazon. Everyone knew about the Amazon and its multitude of species, but the Cerrado is relatively unknown outside of Brazil and it looks dry and scrubby, not like the green towering jungle. Both the Cerrado and the Atlantic Forest are biologically rich and even more threatened than the Amazon because a much larger percentage of the land has been converted already. The remaining Atlantic forest is the source of water for millions of people in Rio de Janeiro. Pushing farms into those areas would not be a victory for either conservation or people.

Environmental Debt

Cargill's business decisions boil down to a simple matter of ethics. The company would not buy soy from a farmer in Iowa who was violating US law. Likewise, they would not buy soy from a farmer who violates Brazilian law—in this case, the Forest Code.

The government of Brazil recognized as early as the 1920s that unregulated use of forests was transforming the countryside. A series of largely ineffectual laws did little to stem the tide. When the military seized power in 1964, the new government enacted sweeping reforms. Despite its authoritarian roots, the Brazilian Forest Code remains among the most sophisticated conservation laws in the world. The Forest Code applies to far more than forest; it sets environmental obligations for all agricultural producers, including soy farmers. Farmers and ranchers must preserve particularly important ecosystems on their property, such as riparian forest and stream headwaters. Most important, the law requires that producers keep a certain percentage of their land in native vegetation. This percentage varies: in the Cerrado and the Atlantic Forest of southern Brazil it is 20 percent, and in the Amazon it is 80 percent.

Many farms breach the law by logging and burning the native vegetation to below these levels, especially in the Amazon. In the words of the law, the owners of such farms have run up a *passivo ambiental*—an environmental debt. Under the Forest Code, farmers can square their accounts by preserving native habitat elsewhere. Such debts must always be paid, one way or another, either by the farmers themselves in the short term or by Brazil as a whole in the longer term as the consequences of deforestation play out. Only Brazil has built this idea of compensation into its farm legislation. The compensation requirement when enforced has the unexpected effect of creating opportunity from the worst of circumstances. As fires consume the rainforest, the parts of it that are protected elsewhere should grow apace.

Growth in protected areas depends on the law matching in practice what it promises on paper. If farmers actually obeyed the law, then they would be the most responsible agricultural producers in the world. Sadly, the Forest Code is dependent on central authority, and Brazil's government agencies are stretched too thin to police it effectively. Most farmers for years simply ignored the Forest Code and suffered few consequences, although the Code includes provisions for fines or even prison terms.

Complying with Forest Code is no longer just an environmental and ethical issue; it has become an issue of competitive advantage. The government of Brazil is well aware that consumers and markets across the world are increasingly worried about climate change and the impact of industry. As such, Brazil's reputation as a responsible steward of the Amazon matters as its role in the global economy grows. Companies such as Cargill may have initially been drawn to Brazil for its land and resources, but if they now want to take advantage of new markets for Brazilian agricultural products, they need to be partners in the stewardship of the country's environment as well.

Growing more food while cutting less forest is a tall order, beyond the scope of any one company or any one crop. Even making incremental progress toward that goal requires reaching many thousands of farmers. There is no time to do that piecemeal, one farm at a time. The most efficient route is for the government and conservationists to work with the large companies, such as Cargill, that source from and sell to all of those farmers.

This cooperation is also an excellent way to curb deforestation. Despite losses over the past three decades, the Amazon remains the size of India. That matters to more than just Brazil; the Amazon helps drive the global climate. Trees in the rainforest draw water from deep underground and pump it into the sky; about one-third of the rain that falls in the Amazon is first made into clouds by trees. The forests of the Amazon contribute about 8 trillion tons of water to the atmosphere each year, much of which circulates around the world.

For Cargill, other companies, and the government of Brazil, the problem became how to monitor who complied with the Forest Code and who did not. The argument against compliance was that it was impossible to distinguish those who were in from those who were out. Cargill buys from thousands of farmers and was unable to monitor them all.

The advent of cheap access to satellite imagery changed that. Soy farmers can now register their land and record exact boundaries using a GPS system developed by Cargill, conservation organizations, and the government. An annual satellite image now shows clearly whether any new deforestation has occurred. Anyone planting on newly cleared forest goes on a blacklist, and those farmers cannot sell to Cargill. More than 300 farmers participate in the effort around Santarém. This technically advanced but modestly priced solution shaped government thinking on controlling deforestation.

The moratorium has been remarkably effective. Soy farming had been a growing threat to the Amazon just a few years ago, but it now contributes little to deforestation. The moratorium helped to make the industry part of the solution.

As encouraging as success with soy farmers has been, there is another, far larger threat to the rainforest: the cattle industry. Since the early 1980s, when reliable satellite images became available, more than 80 percent of the lost Amazon forest has been replaced by pasture. In the Brazilian Amazon, pasture covers more than 150 million acres, an area roughly the size of France, compared to less than 500,000 acres of soy.

Scale is not the only thing that distinguishes the beef and soy markets. For one thing, cattle ranchers are far more likely to use fire to clear land, and fire poses a huge threat to the Amazon. For another, while a few large companies control the export-oriented soy crop, thousands of ranchers raise cattle and sell their product locally, sometimes illegally. Beef from the Amazon is sold in supermarkets in major cities, but also in tiny shops in remote villages. No one keeps track of where all the beef comes from or how ranchers raised the cows.

Environmentalists can convince companies such as Cargill that avoiding deforestation is in their best interest. Greenpeace did not target the company by accident; they knew it could be swayed. Beef buyers, in contrast, paid little notice when environmentalists came calling and tried to get the industry to change its ways to reduce the amount of deforestation the cattle ranchers were causing. With no pressure from buyers, and no monitoring system such as the one Cargill set up, ranchers felt no need to abide by the Forest Code and continued to clear the rainforest. Greenpeace got involved again, this time joined by another organization called Friends of the Earth, to point the media spotlight at this situation.

In June 2009, the two organizations issued separate reports — Greenpeace called its report *Slaughtering the Amazon*, to bookend its soy report a few years earlier — detailing the role of the beef industry in driving Amazon deforestation. The targets were not the producers themselves, but instead governmental regulators and Brazilian supermarket chains, including international giants such as Wal-Mart and the European retailer Carrefour. These companies are likely powerful enough to spur major Brazilian beef companies to pursue significant change.

As with the soy report, the timing and choice of targets was impeccable. Within days, all the major Brazilian supermarket chains announced new policies banning the purchase of meat linked to deforestation in the Amazon. TNC's director of agriculture, David Cleary, who has worked on agricultural issues in the Amazon for decades, remarked, "Greenpeace and Friends of the Earth achieved in a couple of weeks what others tried to do for years with no success." The campaigns by Greenpeace and Friends of the Earth focused global attention on beef production in the Amazon.

Unfortunately, none of the meat-processing companies have any good way of documenting land-use change in the ranches that supply their Amazon slaughterhouses, and thus cannot guarantee that their meat is "deforestation-free." As such, Wal-Mart and Carrefour may be better off avoiding meat from the Amazon altogether.

Relocating cattle ranching from the Amazon may seem a big win for conservation, but it is not. If big buyers cut out ranchers in one part of Brazil, then the ranchers will simply move their cattle to the nearest approved locations—pastures in the Cerrado savannas and Atlantic Forest. Worse, if Wal-Mart stops buying beef from the rainforest, other customers with few environmental scruples would be more than happy to fill the void. In 2008, the main export markets for Amazon beef were Russia, Venezuela, and Iran, none of which worries much about deforestation. We are left with a delicate balance. Engaging the big multinational companies brings leverage, but driving them out of Brazil leads either to someone else filling the void, or to simply relocating the problem.

Now comes the hard part: transforming the beef market so that it reduces deforestation, instead of allowing shoppers in the United States or Europe to look the other way as beef they refuse is sold in Moscow or Tehran. As with soy, the first step is setting up a system to track who is raising cattle where, and whether they are expanding into the rainforest. Cargill had the capacity to adapt the satellite technology, but that is not true of the beef companies in Brazil, most of which are far smaller and far less technically sophisticated.

Building that capacity is part of the larger effort to minimize the spread of pasture in the rainforest. Part of that process is providing the satellite technology, but a bigger part is finding the right people to use it.

Growing the Economy While Saving the Forest

The soy moratorium did not kill off the Brazilian soy industry. Raising cattle in a way that does not lead to deforestation will not kill the beef industry either. It is no longer a given that a country such as Brazil must trade conservation for economic success. Indeed, the economy can grow while the forests remain standing and both harvests and protected areas can expand.

That may sound like naive optimism, or perhaps a press release from the Brazil's Ministry of Agriculture, but it is true. From 2002 to 2009, the area of legally protected Amazon forest increased by 50 percent, and the Brazilian economy grew by 7.5 percent per year. By mid-2010, deforestation in the Brazilian Amazon had fallen 67 percent below its ten-year average, while agricultural production in Mato Grosso reached an all-time high and soy harvest profitability peaked at levels comparable to those of the 2000–2005 boom.

Still, that is one crop in one part of one country—cause for hope but not for complacency. Brazil faces a host of challenges, not least the risk that powerful interests like cattle ranchers and land developers will seize on the country's success to argue for weakening the very regulations that made it possible. International businesses see that money is to be made in the Amazon. Without continued vigilance on the part of the government, any recent gains could be wiped out in a blink. The stakes are high.

Success may depend on the land that cattle ranchers have already cleared. Directing new farms to that land rather than clearing forest will be essential. Thus far, Brazil has been able to provide incentives to encourage farmers to do that. If we see another boom in demand and a spike in the price for soy or biofuels—which would encourage farmers to clear land for sugarcane—the game may change again.

A rise in prices may bring more farms into cultivation, worsening the loss of forests. On the other hand, paying farmers or cattle ranchers a premium to avoid clearing new fields may be an even greater incentive. Such premiums are the most direct way to push the adoption of improved farming or manufacturing. The biggest barrier to new methods, or at least the one foremost in the minds of farmers, are up-front costs, and the guarantee of a better price pushes down that barrier.

CHANGING THE BEHAVIOR OF THOUSANDS OF FARMERS OR POTENTIALLY millions of consumers will be difficult if not impossible. But there may be a better way. The idea, laid out forcefully by Jason Clay of the World Wildlife Fund (WWF), is to work not with either of those large groups but with a much smaller but hugely influential group of companies that sits in between the producers and the consumers. Clay has pointed out that a relatively small number of commodities companies control the majority of the markets for those commodities. If conservationists can influence these companies by demonstrating the effectiveness of conservation on their own bottom lines, the companies can have a major impact on how sustainably commodities are produced.

We already have evidence to show that this can work when consumers are willing to pay more. Coffee growers have implemented a variety of ways to certify their coffee as organic, shade-grown, and free-trade. Some coffee buyers—though still just a tiny percentage of the market, a pattern repeated for other commodities—gladly pay for those labels. The same holds for certain kinds of tropical hardwoods. Tropical timber is relatively easy to track, and the market for a high-end, forest-friendly product is growing.

Unfortunately, other commodities, such as beef, soy, and palm oil, have been harder to crack. Consumers buy little soy directly; most goes to animal feed or becomes a largely invisible component of processed foods, ink, or other materials. That makes it almost impossible to add a premium to the price a soy farmer gets for his harvest.

Even if paying farmers more to change the way they grow our food and other agricultural products may work only rarely, identifying good producers is still important. As one example, an international organization called the Forest Stewardship Council has emerged to assess timber production in environmental terms and to provide certification to companies that adhere to its guidelines. Such certification, a green stamp of approval, helps consumers identify responsible companies. The real hope for supply-chain initiatives with commodity crops is that major buyers will insist on better standards, forcing producers to move to those practices. This will not happen through corporate action alone. Enlightened buyers can create an added incentive for application of enlightened government conservation policies. Buyers put

pressure on producers and governments change management policies as a result.

Another emerging trend may overshadow such subtle market dynamics. For over a century, businesses have seen commodity prices
fall or at worst remain stable. Now they are becoming more expensive. In 1980, ecologist Paul Ehrlich, along with Berkeley physicists
John Harte and John Holdren, made a bet with Julian Simon, professor of business administration at the University of Maryland, on
whether the prices of a selected group of commodities—copper,
chromium, nickel, tin, and tungsten—would rise or fall over the next
ten years. Ehrlich said they would rise, as growing human population
increased demand, while Simon said they would fall, as technology
improved.

When they settled the bet after ten years, Simon was correct, as
prices of the five metals fell. In the longer term, however, he was
wrong. Another thinker, Jeremy Grantham, points out that if Simon
and Ehrlich had extended the original bet past its arbitrary ten-year
limit to the present day, Ehrlich would have won on all the commodities he chose except for tin. If he had chosen a bigger basket of commodities, he would have been an even bigger winner.

The commodities market, says Grantham, a famed investor with
his own Boston-based firm and a superb long-term investment record,
is finally reflecting the fact that the world is finite. From 1900 to 2002,
the prices of metals, oil, and gas, and agricultural commodities such
as soy, wheat, and cotton, fell steadily after adjusting for inflation.
This trend seems to fly in the face of two other trends: the growing
human population and the increasing use of those commodities.

Basic economics says that as commodities grow scarce, prices must
rise. Improving technology, new reserves of commodities, and more
efficient usage has kept that from happening until now. Now, says
Grantham, the market is giving us "the Mother of all price signals" in
the most important economic event since the Industrial Revolution.

According to analysts at the consulting firm McKinsey & Company, real commodity prices have increased 147 percent since 2000.

If Grantham is correct, then the recent rise in commodity prices is not a temporary surge, something commodities markets have seen in the past, but a permanent change in the value of our natural resources. That shift has profound implications for agriculture, industry, and conservation.

Freezing Agriculture's Footprint

Among the resources that are becoming scarce is agricultural land. Brazil's experience in getting more production from existing agricultural land gives us a glimpse of the future. With agriculture becoming more efficient and less geographically extensive, Brazil is managing to produce more with less. Brazil thus demonstrates how science, innovation, and partnership can develop a smarter world food system.

Consider what this new agricultural system involves. It must produce more food on less land, using less water and fewer chemicals — and that's just to start. Farmers cannot bring more land into production because there is not enough left: farms and ranches already occupy nearly 40 percent of the terrestrial surface, and nearly all of the land that is suited for agriculture. The rest is either in places that should not be farmed, such as the Amazon or Yellowstone, or places that cannot support farms, such as Mollicy Bayou, the Sahara, the Andes, or Paris. There also is no water to spare. Agriculture, mostly irrigation, accounts for 70 percent of global water consumption. Not only does agriculture consume water, it also pollutes water with fertilizers, herbicides, and pesticides.

Agriculture must therefore freeze its footprint and double global food production on existing farmlands while using water and other resources far more efficiently. Jonathan Foley, a leading thinker on this topic at the University of Minnesota, points to two options: boost the productivity of either the best farms or the worst. Yields have room for improvement in highly productive North America, Brazil, and Australia, for example, but even more in Africa, Central America, and Eastern Europe. An analysis by Foley and his colleagues showed that in these regions, better seeds, more effective fertilizer application, and more efficient irrigation could produce 50 to 60 percent more food on the same amount of land without massive amounts of water or chemicals.

Increasing yields will have to be part of any effort to take the pressure off forests. This seems intuitive: if farmers can grow what they need on land they have already cleared, then they have little incentive to clear more. In practice, this becomes more complicated.

More intensive agriculture also often involves more chemical fertilizers and more water, so balancing costs and benefits at various scales is essential. Intensifying agriculture on some land so that other land can be spared tends to divide the landscape into neat sections, as you might see from an airplane: farms here, forests there.

That works particularly well in sensitive areas where increased agricultural productivity creates incentives to convert natural habitat to cropland. Here, the simplest solution—more protected areas at the agricultural frontier—may be best.

Many other landscapes, particularly in the tropics, present tougher choices. There, a variety of owners and managers with conflicting interests often oversee property. Rural people depend on the land more directly than other communities, but intensive farming tends to favor larger landowners with better access to capital.

An alternative to more intensive farming is to farm in ways that support both domesticated and wild species. Such tactics, which go by a variety of names including wildlife-friendly farming and agroforestry, generally follow the same idea: reduce the intensity of agriculture by limiting clearing and plowing, leaving patches of native vegetation scattered throughout the landscape, and using less fertilizer so that native species can survive.

In Indonesia, for example, people grow cacao, the source of cocoa powder and chocolate, beneath the forest canopy. In addition to conserving the larger trees, this approach provides habitat for native flora and fauna. In some cases, this provides the elusive win-win scenario: the biodiversity of these forests does not decrease as the yield of cacao increases. Moreover, these farming landscapes provide a broad array of other benefits in addition to the farm products themselves—climate stability (through carbon sequestration), water purification, flood control, and scenic beauty.

Similarly, and encouragingly, agroforestry does not always necessitate the removal of native species. Again in Indonesia, a surprising number of orangutans have been found on pulp and paper plantations, areas planted with fast-growing exotics intermixed with stands of highly degraded forests and scrublands. This discovery comes with a host of caveats, chief among them that how long these populations of orangutans can survive is unclear. Even so, if such a rare and charismatic creature is more flexible than previously believed, and if other species can coexist with some degree of human use of their habitats, this has important implications for feeding the planet's growing population.

The main argument against wildlife-friendly farming, and indeed organic farming in general, has been that the yields are reported to be much lower, so farmers need more land to grow the same amount of food. Overall, this argument goes, wildlife-friendly farming saves less wild nature than completely converting some land for intensive farming and leaving other places completely alone. Organic farming does often have lower yields, but for some crops, such as fruits and oilseeds, the difference is not great. For others, such as cereals and vegetables, organic methods fare worse. The point, says Jonathan Foley, is to use all approaches, and to apply them in the right places and to the right crops.

Jeremy Grantham points out that organic farming offers a solution to a looming long-term problem, one connected to his observation on commodities: the risk of a fertilizer shortage. Among the commodities Grantham has tracked and whose prices are rising are phosphate and potash (potassium). Phosphorous and potassium are necessary for the growth of all living matter, and organic farming can greatly extend existing reserves by reducing the need for extra doses of the fertilizers to a small fraction of that used in current large-scale agriculture.

One of capitalism's great virtues, says Grantham, is that high price is the best teacher. Rising fertilizer prices may force greater interest and investment in organic farming. Since the best organic practices reduce the use of increasingly expensive fertilizers without huge sacrifices in yield, such farming can be equally profitable also, even without having consumers pay a premium for organic products.

The real challenge is that organic farming requires a great deal of time and effort to fine-tune to each crop and to each type of soil. Farmers need better training and data on how to do organic farming well, so getting them to take the leap now to complex and risky practices will be difficult. As Grantham wrote in his July 2012 newsletter for investors:

> The bad news is that to gear up for 100% organic farming is a herculean task that will take decades of effort, including government participation and considerable research. The worse news is that this is a task for which there is absolutely no alternative in the long run for the status quo will guarantee that we will run out of potash and phosphorus . . . and eventually come to a very bad end. The good news, though, is that this vital job can without doubt be done and when done would guarantee for the first time a sustainable basis of food production.

Smarter Agriculture

New technologies can also help make agriculture smarter. These include both high- and low-tech solutions, from sculpting fields with ridges and ditches to harvest water in Africa to sophisticated sensors that guide where famers should irrigate or add fertilizers based on precise analysis of soil conditions. Foley points out that with fertilizers, farmers face a Goldilocks problem: some places have too few nutrients and therefore poor crop production, whereas others have too much, leading to pollution. Almost nobody uses fertilizers "just right."

Farmers in the United States, Europe, China, and elsewhere could substantially reduce fertilizer use with little or no impact on food production, says Foley. In the United States, an online tool called the Fieldprint Calculator, developed by a consortium led by Colorado-based Keystone Center, can help. A "fieldprint," according to Fieldtomarket.org, is the ratio of output to input, or an estimate of the impact an input has on an output. Assuming a given output, a smaller input means a smaller footprint and greater sustainability because fewer resources are needed to realize the same end result.

The Fieldprint Calculator allows farmers to enter information about their operation—soil crop rotation, management systems, and so on—and to assess whether their energy use, climate impact, soil loss, and water use are smaller or greater than county, state, and national averages. The Calculator enables farmers to evaluate the sustainability of their operations against that of other farmers, and to assess how well they are doing.

Farming is a competitive business. In a test of the Fieldprint Calculator's energy-efficiency metric, Nebraska farmers used the calculator to compare their energy efficiency to that of their neighbors. They can also see how changing their practices can affect the sustainability of their farms. This information will help farmers monitor and manage their inputs more effectively, identifying routes to improving water quality and carbon footprints at the same time as improving bottom lines by maintaining and increasing yields. When farmers compete to be more efficient—hence both more sustainable and more profitable—then both nature and economies will prosper.

The calculator is part of the Keystone Field to Market initiative, a diverse alliance of producers, agribusinesses, food companies, and environmental organizations. Working across the agricultural supply chain, the group is developing collaborative solutions to increase agricultural productivity while minimizing environmental impacts.

THE FIELDPRINT CALCULATOR RELIES ON SOME SOPHISTICATED technology, but the most important technology for agriculture is not new at all. Humans have been modifying plants and animals to suit their needs for millennia. Except for wild fish, most foods people consume in significant quantities have been altered through intensive breeding. Most modern crops bear practically no relation to their wild forebears. The Paleoindians who domesticated corn some ten thousand years ago in Mexico would not recognize the crop farmers grow in Iowa today.

The natural genetic variability that allowed the development of sweet corn and softball-size seedless oranges is a vitally important but often overlooked form of natural capital. Conserving wild relatives of domesticated plants and animals conserves genetic variety as well, and that variety ensures adaptability, especially in the face of shifting weather patterns and an increasingly unpredictable climate.

While everyone agrees that genetic variability is a form of natural capital of tremendous value to plant breeding, there is enormous controversy about genetic engineering—manipulating that variability and moving it between species. Some countries have gone so far as to ban genetically modified crops entirely. Genetic engineering unquestionably has risks that warrant thoughtful examination, but the environmental case against genetically modified organisms (GMOs) is beginning to fracture. Environmentalists who once opposed this technology have begun to speak out in favor of its potential benefits. For example, one-time anti-GMO activist Mark Lynas now writes in support of the technology in his book *The God Species*.

Conservationists should keep an open mind toward GMOs because in some cases they likely can help us solve our biggest challenges. For example, genetically engineered cassava has been developed with resistance to viral diseases that often destroy as much as one-third of the cassava crop. This is significant because cassava is the primary food source for more than 750 million people. This new GMO variety of cassava has been developed by the Danforth Plant Science Center with funding from the Bill and Melinda Gates Foundation and the Howard Buffett Foundation. The Danforth Center is a nonprofit and is not seeking to make money from this discovery, but rather to help address the world's need for more food. From a conservation perspective, cassava is an ideal plant to engineer because it is a low-input crop—able to withstand months of drought and requiring no irrigation.

Some of the anger about GMO crops is in truth about the control of seeds and food trade by large global corporations. When GMO crops are produced by nonprofit organizations such as the Danforth Foundation that charge no royalties for the seeds, then perhaps farmers can see clearly that they can benefit from new plant varieties. Others worry about GMOs because of environmental and health hazards. However, the data concerning human-health hazards are extensive and provide little evidence that GMO foods pose a health risk of any kind. Hundreds of millions of people consume foods containing GMO plant material every day, and as of yet no problems have appeared.

The data on environmental risks are more mixed. Overall, the US National Academy of Science has concluded that the widespread use of GMO crops—80 percent of the soybeans, corn, and cotton grown in the United States—has led to farmers using less insecticides and herbicides that linger in soil and waterways, with likely benefits to water quality. This does not mean that scientists and government regulators can safely ignore new types of GMOs with entirely new traits. As the technology advances and evermore exotic crops are engineered, we will need to be vigilant in assessing environmental risk and also respecting the views of people who as a matter of personal choice seek to avoid GMOs.

Nevertheless, synthetic biology, of which GMOs represent just one dimension, is an exciting new technology that promises to revolutionize our world and that could provide technical solutions for some of our most significant environmental challenges. For example, engineered microbes have been modified so that they produce biodegradeable plastic. Microbes can also be engineered to act as biosensors for trace levels of chemical contaminants, or perhaps to produce energy dense biofuels. Conservationists can be a balanced voice for examining the benefits and costs of these new technologies, and making sure that they are part of the solution and not the problem for our lands and waters.

Conservation and agriculture require, as my colleague Glenn Prickett says, a grand bargain: the private sector putting nature front and center in its thinking, while the environmental organizations do the same with productivity and yields. Everything should be up for discussion: How can GMO product development address conservation and productivity in an integrated way? How can conservation organizations help farmers increase agricultural productivity? How can agribusiness support the creation of more protected areas where critical habitat is threatened by an expanding agricultural frontier?

Throughout history, human ingenuity and technology have broken previous limits and boundaries. If agricultural industry and conservation science work together more broadly, we will have room for those additional 2 billion people. There will also be room for wildlife and nature, for ample water, and for ample food.

6

The Million-Dollar Mile

IN MAY 2010, I FLEW OVER THE GULF OF MEXICO, JUST A FEW WEEKS after the explosion on *Deepwater Horizon*. I was overwhelmed by the size of the slick, hundreds of miles wide and spreading like fingers toward the coast. Cleanup crews lined up oil-blocking booms to keep oil out of estuaries and bayous, and pressed shrimp boats into service as oil skimmers. During my visit, I met many people who depended on healthy Gulf lands and waters to make a living.

In sharp contrast to the fisheries crisis in recent decades and the looming food crisis, both of which usually play out quietly and out of the public eye, the oil spill in the Gulf of Mexico was a global wake-up call. The disaster focused widespread attention on the important benefits and services that healthy ecosystems provide to people.

The visit drove home for me the particular vulnerability but also the resilience of coastal communities. In few other places are people's lives and livelihoods so closely linked to the health of their environment. Coastal waters provide jobs, income, food, and recreation to millions of people worldwide.

The health of our coastal waters is directly linked to the health of our planet's reefs. Oyster reefs, seagrass beds, and coral reefs provide multiple benefits for both nature and people. They produce fish for recreational and commercial harvests, filter water, reduce pollution, and buffer coastal communities from rising sea levels, storm surges, and erosion. They provide as well the foundation for local tourism and recreation economies.

Many of these ecosystems have already been lost. Approximately 30 percent of underwater grasses are gone. Overfishing, dredging, pollution, sedimentation, and disease have destroyed or made unproductive 85 percent of oyster reefs. Without dedicated conservation and restoration, up to 70 percent of coral reefs may disappear by 2050.

Fortunately, scientists and policymakers know how to bring these systems back. In some places, doing so will require sophisticated engineering to rebuild reefs. In others, it may require comprehensive planning across large areas of the ocean. Or it may call for something as simple as declaring certain places, even relatively small ones, off-limits to fishing. In all cases, restoration makes good economic and environmental sense.

Restored oyster reefs, such as those being built in Alabama and Louisiana, cost about $1 million per mile. At that price, a $1 billion investment would essentially fully protect and nurture the Gulf with one thousand miles of reef. That would be conservation and restoration at the scale of the Great Wall of China.

A better investment is hard to imagine, even with a billion-dollar price tag. The design, construction, operation, and monitoring of such large-scale coastal and marine restoration projects directly create jobs. The National Oceanic and Atmospheric Administration (NOAA) says that each $1 million invested in wetland restoration can create more than thirty new jobs, from scientists and engineers to tugboat operators and construction managers—double or triple the number of jobs produced by building levees, dams, roads, and bridges.

These projects also support industries that rely on healthy lands and waters including fishing and tourism. Protecting and restoring the world's oyster and coral reefs is both an economic and ecological imperative—a smart investment that produces significant returns.

Don't Mess With Dakio

In the 1970s, Dakio Paul left his birthplace, the tiny south Pacific Island of Pohnpei, for the larger, more developed island of Saipan, about a thousand miles west. A onetime fisherman, Dakio hoped to find something with better pay and eventually found a job in the tourist industry. Dakio worked on Saipan for some twenty years, got married, and then decided to return to his roots. He wanted to be a fisherman again.

Dakio returned to Pohnpei in 1995. He went straight from the airstrip to his village, got in a boat, and headed out to his old fishing grounds on the coral reef that rings the island, near a place called Black Coral Island. When he was a boy, the spot, known locally as Kehpara, teemed with fish, particularly several species of grouper, as well as turtles and a large seabird colony on small neighboring islets.

Though Dakio likely did not know it at the time, Kehpara is one of the most important sites for grouper in the western Pacific. From February to April, some 20,000 grouper gather along a 200-meter stretch of reef just east of Black Coral Island. Marine biologists call this a spawning aggregation, and fishing communities in the Pacific islands have known about the phenomenon for centuries at least. Since grouper do not spawn until they are five years old, only the largest fish, some six feet long, gather near Black Coral Island. This makes for great fishing, but it also makes grouper particularly vulnerable. If large numbers of boats work the reef during the spawning aggregation, they can remove the individual fish capable of producing the most offspring at the most crucial time in their life history, which can decimate a population.

Dakio's family and his village depended on those fish and on everything else the reef provided. For this reason, the local chiefs who manage village affairs traditionally banned fishing while the grouper gathered to spawn. The longstanding prohibition on fishing during the spawning aggregation near Black Coral Island allowed that remarkable natural dynamic to survive. In other places, intense fishing pressure on spawning aggregations can reduce them to almost nothing in less than five years, and once that happens, they do not recover.

The ban near Black Coral Island epitomizes the community rules that Elinor Ostrom highlights as solutions to the tragedy of the commons. In effect, the community acted as owner of what are otherwise public waters. Creating some form of ownership—whether through the community, or through tradable quotas as in Morro Bay, or through leased oyster beds as in Louisiana—can be crucial to marine conservation. This does not imply that all rights over a resource should be turned over to private interests to do as they see fit, but recognizes that a degree of ownership can bring a willingness to invest time and energy in protecting nature.

When he returned to Pohnpei, Dakio did not realize that the island had changed. Starting in the 1980s, people no longer lived off what they could grow or the fish they could catch but depended on cash to buy food and other necessities. The shifting economy weakened traditional restrictions on fishing. When Dakio put out his nets in 1995, they came back nearly empty. Corals in the area had been heavily damaged by anchors and had been trampled by numerous fishermen working in the area. Dead fish, bird bones, and turtle carapaces littered Black Coral's beaches.

The reef had not passed the point of no return, but it was close. Dakio was angry. He headed to the government offices in Pohnpei's main town of Kolonia, reported on the reef's deterioration, and asked what they were doing about it. Unfortunately, the government was part of the problem. Pohnpei is one of four states in the Federated States of Micronesia, and in the 1990s the government had decided to invest heavily to develop its fishing industry. People fished for themselves, and the government collected license fees from foreign commercial fishing boats, but Pohnpei had no domestic industry to speak of. To change that, the government began giving out boats, motors, and nets so people could catch more fish, built warehouses to store this fish, promoted exports, and so on. Dakio then visited the local TNC office, but it only had three people working at the time and was unable to help.

Dakio's next step will not be found in any list of the best practices of conservation. He got back in his boat with a fifteen-horsepower engine, a spotlight, a bottle of bourbon, and a shotgun. He would defend Black Coral Island himself. Dakio announced to the adjacent communities that Black Coral was now closed to fishing. His neighbors, many of them family, balked. They had become accustomed to fishing wherever and whenever they wanted.

Since neither the government nor the community was willing or able to enforce rules on how the commons should be used, Dakio did so himself. He looked and acted a bit like a drill sergeant but also had something of a royal bearing, descended as he was from the family that ruled the southern kingdom of Pohnpei. No one really wanted to mess with him. He patrolled the waters and enforced his fishing ban twenty-four hours a day. At night, when most fishing took place, he focused his spotlight and fired warning blasts at any boat that came near. The government attempted to remove Dakio from the island, thinking perhaps he had lost his mind, but he took shots at them, too, so they left him alone.

After three years of Dakio's constant vigilance, local fishermen gradually began to notice more and larger fish, not only on the reef Dakio defended, but also along stretches of reef nearby. Kehpara was once again full of fish, and as the population recovered, fish spilled over into adjacent areas. Bill Raynor, who runs the TNC office on Pohnpei, went out to the island—in broad daylight and waving a white flag, just in case—to ask Dakio's permission to bring local chiefs and fishermen to see what was happening. Dakio agreed, and when the guests snorkeled around the reef they were astonished.

The news spread quickly around the island, and soon other communities wanted their own no-fishing areas. These are now known by the unlovely name "no-take marine reserves," but a more telling name would be "fish factories." Local communities now defend them, though few if any people want to grab a shotgun. Instead, in 1999 the Pohnpei legislature declared eleven islands, including Dakio's, to be state-protected sanctuaries under the Pohnpei Sanctuary Act. This act, the first of its kind in Micronesia, prohibited fishing and collecting in these areas, and has since spawned similar legislation in other islands and nations.

Today Pohnpei has twenty marine reserves, and the demand for more outstrips the capacity of the government and private organizations. The grouper spawning aggregation near Black Coral Island has fully recovered and each year the number of returning adults increases. Neighboring islets boast huge colonies of seabirds. Sea turtles again nest on the beaches. Fishermen and conservationists alike continue to flock to Black Coral Island, gaining inspiration to set up their own community marine-protected areas.

In 2006, the presidents of five countries in Micronesia—Palau, Guam, the Northern Marianas, the Federated States of Micronesia, and the Marshall Islands—declared that they would protect 30 percent of their near-shore marine areas and 20 percent of their terrestrial areas by 2020. They called their commitment the Micronesia Challenge.

Dakio's pioneering efforts have fostered widespread support to move forward on a national system of parks and protected areas for the entire Federated States of Micronesia, more than 600 islands spread across 1,500 miles of the Pacific. In 2001, the Pohnpei state government appointed Dakio one of the first State Marine Conservation Officers, and through this position, he trained and motivated a new generation of marine conservationists working to protect and rehabilitate Pohnpei's reefs to their former bounty. In 2006, *Condé Nast Traveler* magazine recognized him as an environmental hero.

Dakio Paul died in 2009. Before he died, he saw the seeds he planted in Pohnpei take root across the entire region.

Investing in Coral and Fish

Many communities now understand that it makes senses to view coral reefs as investment accounts. These coastal communities find that, if they leave the principal untouched, then the interest—that is, the fish—will grow and improve people's health and their economies.

Preserving reefs means protecting their inherent diversity. Ample evidence shows that more diverse reefs are more productive. With reefs, conservation and commerce can be aligned. In many other cases, conservation requires carefully balancing the need for diversity in ecosystem preservation against pressure to simplify these systems for maximum commercial yield. Fortunately, in the cases of coral reefs, the benefits people gain from them depend on maintaining their diversity. In Pohnpei and elsewhere in the Pacific, marine conservation can have direct, tangible effects on reducing poverty and in the process also build new alliances for conservation.

The spillover effect seen in Pohnpei is one way that marine protected areas contribute to the well-being of the local community. The mechanism seems intuitive: no fishing means more fish. The reserve provides space for fish to grow bigger. Big fish generally have many more offspring than small fish. Most reserves fill up with fish after about four years, and after that the fish spill over into the area outside the protected zone.

This spillover can be vital where people are poor and the fishing they have traditionally relied on is in crisis. The impact is most obvious just outside the reserve, no farther than a few hundred yards beyond the boundary. Scientists have documented the spillover dynamic and its consequences in many places. In Fiji, for example, a marine-protected area has substantially increased income and improved nutrition for 600 people living in five nearby villages. Researchers compared villages near reserves with others far away and found that spillover from two community-managed marine areas in Fiji roughly doubled local incomes within five years of establishing the reserve.

On Apo Island in the Philippines, the protected reef attracts so many visitors that tourism now surpasses fishing as a source of income. Fishermen also catch more fish with less effort, meaning children have more time and parents more money for school and school supplies. Incomes are up and housing is better: residents attribute most of the improvements to the protected area. Like Dakio Paul, the fishermen are now fierce advocates for conservation.

In further confirmation of Elinor Ostrom's insights, researchers have found that the spillover mechanism works better when communities help create the rules that govern the fisheries. That community participation has its own spillover as well: once organized to manage a no-take zone, communities often build the cohesion needed to solve other social problems as well, including poverty.

Protecting spawning areas such as Black Coral Island can have widespread benefits, even if that particular reserve covers just a small area. The question of size is tricky. The benefits of no-take marine reserves thus far are seen most clearly at the scale of Black Coral Island— small reserves so close to small communities that residents can see the reefs from their homes. If a no-take zone is too large, spillover will not offset the losses from closing sections of the fishing grounds. Here the art, as well as the economics and politics, of conservation will replace the science. We can both protect the reefs for their own sake and also protect them as a source of fish for poor communities.

National governments and alliances of multiple countries now recognize the value of coral reefs and mangroves as key factors for economic development. These multinational efforts need to determine which parts of the seascape can support fishing or other industry and which cannot.

The need for such an understanding on land has been obvious since the beginning of the Industrial Revolution; no one today would expect to be allowed to build a town or a factory or a road just anywhere. Applying the same rigor to how people use the seas is of far more recent vintage, beginning with the effort to protect Australia's Great Barrier Reef Marine Park in the late 1970s. Governments, communities, conservationists, and businesses can protect areas where fish aggregate to breed as well as the sensitive bottom habitats the fish need. The way to do this is with a new, sophisticated science called marine spatial planning.

Marine spatial planning helps government and industry identify ocean areas where restrictions are appropriate as well as areas where it is not overly destructive to drill for oil, install wind turbines, and operate aquaculture facilities. All of this must be based on sound science and community involvement. Zoning in this way can make it easier for energy companies and the fishing industry to extract valuable resources from our oceans.

MARINE ECOSYSTEMS ARE MORE DYNAMIC AND INTERCONNECTED than grasslands, forests, or deserts. And compared to land-based resources, much more of the ocean is considered common property, open to all comers, from tiny artisanal fishing communities to huge industrial fleets, to tourism, shipping, and energy development.

This complexity leads some experts to question whether zoning the oceans is even possible. But it clearly should be part of any broad effort to balance conservation and development of marine resources.

The Micronesia Challenge—the collaborative effort at regional marine protection—marked one of the first regional political commitments to finding that balance. In 2009, inspired by that effort, six more governments in the western Pacific joined to protect the oldest and richest coral system on earth, the Coral Triangle.

The Coral Triangle covers over 2 million square miles of eastern Indonesia, parts of Malaysia, the Philippines, Papua New Guinea, Timor-Leste, and the Solomon Islands. It is home to more than 150 million people, more than half of whom rely on the sea for food. Located at the intersection of the Indian and Pacific Oceans, the Coral Triangle is a genetic mixing bowl. The region's unique coral reefs draw tourists from around the world. All told, fisheries, tourism, and shoreline protection from coral reefs and mangroves are worth some $2.3 billion annually.

Each of the six governments in the Coral Triangle has made unprecedented conservation commitments under the Coral Triangle Initiative on Coral Reefs, Fisheries and Food Security. Indonesia, for example, created an 8.5-million-acre marine-protected area in the Savu Sea, near the eastern end of the archipelago. The program helps countries in the Coral Triangle expand national Marine Protected Areas and Marine-Managed-Areas Networks, develop strategies for responding to climate change, and find the money to pay for it all.

The Coral Triangle Initiative highlights a crucial fact: while individuals and companies can value nature, sometimes the only investor capable of making a significant difference will be the government. Only governments can establish laws that allow markets to flourish, for example, or that take Ostrom's insights about community-level cooperation and make them work across a nation, a region, or even more. Governments—local, national, and even multinational alliances— now recognize the potential of nature as a source of jobs and economic development. Shovel-ready projects to restore or re-create that capital offer abundant short- and long-term returns in the developed and developing worlds.

Compelling examples of these projects can be found where people rely on the oceans for sustenance. The natural and human communities near shore are rich, resilient, and at risk.

Oil, Oysters, and Communities

Grand Isle, Louisiana bears no resemblance to Pohnpei, and oyster reefs look nothing like coral reefs. Though the natural communities are different, the reefs provide many of the same services, from coastal protection and nurseries for fish to recreation and tourism. Coral reef conservation builds resilient natural and human communities in the Pacific. So, too, oyster reef restoration helps communities on Grand Isle, in Mobile Bay, and across the Gulf of Mexico.

A single narrow road, Louisiana Highway 1 (LA 1), connects Grand Isle with the mainland. The term *mainland* applies only tenuously here, thousands of acres of salt marsh and bayou between the island and New Orleans, about fifty miles due north. Grand Isle itself seems to have just a tenuous existence, a bit of sand less than a mile wide bracing for the next hurricane, a row of modest beachfront houses known locally as camps perched on tall stilts to stay above inevitable storm surges.

The fragility of Grand Isle is something of an illusion. In that way, it is a metaphor for the entire Gulf of Mexico and other watery parts of the world. Both the human and natural communities at land's end are more resilient than they appear.

The community's roots here are deep. Early visitors to Grand Isle included the pirate and privateer Jean Lafitte. The pattern of life on the island was established centuries ago: storms come, do their worst, and people rebuild. Not even the twin hurricanes Katrina and Rita, a month apart in 2005, could keep people away for good. The storm

surge from Katrina breached the island, tearing up houses and hurl-
ing boats five hundred yards inland.

Grand Isle faced perhaps its most difficult challenge in 2010. The
Deepwater Horizon, drilling just off the continental shelf about a
hundred miles southeast of the island, exploded and began to spew
millions of barrels of oil into the Gulf. The bays and marshes behind
Grand Isle and all along the coast support one of the most productive
fisheries in the world. But the largest oil slick in history was headed
their way.

The island became the front line of the fight against the crude.
Thousands of workers arrived in town, swamping the permanent population of roughly 1,500 residents. Fishermen stopped trawling for
shrimp and started laying booms to protect marshes and other habitats, or skimmed the oil off the water and scooped it off the beaches.
Volunteers scrubbed oil from sea turtles, birds, and other wildlife.

All those efforts were essential to the recovery effort and mini-
mized the damage as much as possible. Many were heroic. None, by
themselves, were enough. Like a patient in an emergency room, the
Gulf has passed the immediate crisis, but its health remains uncertain. Ensuring vigorous natural and human communities on Grand
Isle and across the Gulf, indeed wherever people live close to the
border between land and sea, means more than minimizing loss. It
means rebuilding natural capital on a broad scale and understanding how people are entwined with the marshes, the rivers, the forests,
and the reefs.

Despite all that nature and humanity can hurl at it, the Gulf still
offers reasons for hope. During the oil spill, as engineers struggled for
weeks to cap the gusher, the live video from a mile underwater made
many people feel like helpless witnesses to a crime. Ghastly as it was,
that crime did not fulfill our worst fears. The Gulf, though wounded,
survived, and its survival turns a story of fragility and despair into one
of restoration and resilience.

That story is understandable only when read in the context of decades of human activity in the Gulf. The *Deepwater Horizon* disaster drew needed attention to the Gulf, but the ecological and economic trends have been worrisome for many years. Yet prior to the spill, Gulf fisheries, including for oysters, were still good business.

The fisheries should now recover over time. Rather than wait, communities and local and national government recognize it is better to put people to work rebuilding oyster reefs, marshes, beaches, and fish habitat. That work will employ thousands of people in the near term and create even more jobs in fishing and tourism for the long term. This is both ecological and economic restoration.

NOAA, the Federal agency overseeing the coastal projects, was overwhelmed with interest. In 2009, the agency received more than eight hundred project proposals totaling more than $3 billion in habitat restoration needs, almost twenty times the funding they were able to distribute. In Louisiana alone, the Army Corps of Engineers has at least a $2 billion backlog of restoration projects that could put thousands of people to work but that it cannot complete because of budget cuts.

The people of Grand Isle understand this connection. The island's economy is an unusual mix of oil and gas, fishing, and tourism. Offshore drilling rigs in the Gulf dot the horizon, clearly visible from the tops of the dunes, and helicopters shuttling workers back and forth land regularly at a large storage depot just past the center of town. The tight-knit community depends on the industry for jobs. However, Grand Isle's population grows tenfold on summer weekends. Those visitors come for the beaches and the fishing. Grand Isle understands that environmental restoration can be the foundation for lasting economic security.

AMONG THE PROJECTS FUNDED WITH STIMULUS MONEY WAS ONE TO restore some of the Gulf's most vital infrastructure: oyster reefs. Oyster fisheries in the Gulf offer perhaps the last remaining opportunity to achieve both large-scale oyster reef conservation and sustainable fisheries. Maryland's Chesapeake Bay oyster fishery may be the most famous and the most imperiled in the world, but the Gulf's fishery may be even more important.

In a typical year, nearly two-thirds of the US oyster harvest comes from the Gulf. In 2009, the value of the Gulf harvest was nearly $75 million. Restoring Gulf oyster reefs saves this important resource, and there has never been—and quite possibly never will be again—an opportunity like this to restore the Gulf of Mexico.

Oyster reefs once defined estuaries around the world and supported thriving economies. When European settlers first arrived oysters were so abundant in the Chesapeake Bay and even in the Hudson River estuary that they posed a hazard to navigation. New York City was once considered the oyster capital of the world. The productivity of oysters can be staggering. Shell piles from historical harvests in southwest France contain more than 1 trillion shells apiece. In the United States, oyster shells were so abundant they were once used as building material. Even the old back roads along the Gulf are made of oyster shells.

Now things have gone topsy-turvy. Instead of using oyster shells to build roads, Louisiana uses roads to build oyster reefs. The state takes concrete and other road rubble and situates it offshore in carefully designed structures hoping that oysters will settle and grow. Oyster shells are in short supply. Scientists now estimate that 85 percent of oyster reef ecosystems have been destroyed worldwide by fishing, coastal development, dredging of shipping channels, pollution from a variety of sources, and other threats. In most bays, oyster reefs are at less than 10 percent of their prior abundance.

Oyster restoration has been going on for years. Federal and state government agencies have spent many millions of dollars trying to revive oyster industries in the Chesapeake Bay, in the estuaries of North Carolina, and in the Gulf of Mexico. Their goal was commercial, and the success or failure of those efforts was measured in bushels of oysters harvested. In this case, a strictly commercial view is too narrow. Oyster reefs provide so many benefits that the most exciting restoration efforts will not even allow any oyster harvests, at least not for some years. The oysters themselves—at least as most people think of them, on the half-shell with lemon and Tabasco sauce—are just a delicacy we must await.

The restoration underway on Grand Isle includes a new bridge for LA 1 that opened in 2009 and rebuilt fishing camps, some now even higher off the ground. On the north side of the island, facing a stretch of water called Caminada Bay, there is a bit of restoration that is less visible but no less important than either the road or the houses: a new oyster reef is being born.

Restoring the Reefs

An oyster reef, which consists simply of oysters piled one on top of another, is far simpler than a coral reef. A female oyster releases millions of eggs into the water. Once fertilized they become larvae, which drift in the current. If they are not eaten, the larvae seek a hard place to land, preferably atop another oyster. They then begin to form tiny shells, at which point they are called *spat*. That settling process, known by the Vaudevillian-sounding *spatfall*, builds up the reef into a solid structure as the spat adheres to other oysters. In the right conditions, both the reefs and the oysters grow quickly.

Oyster reefs are natural coastal buffers, knocking down the height of waves and absorbing much of their energy as well, thus reducing erosion caused by boat wakes, sea-level rise, and storms. The goal of the restoration effort on Grand Isle is to prevent erosion by protecting the shoreline from wind and waves.

In most bays and estuaries, the seafloor is flat and muddy, with some vegetation such as sea grasses but nothing to break up the topography except for oyster reefs. The importance of the construction work the oysters carry out is clear in Caminada Bay. The water is just a few feet deep near the shore and even the middle of the bay is only about eight feet deep. Save for some small islands and some even smaller manmade breakwaters, there is nothing between Grand Isle and the dense bayous of Jefferson Parish, some fifteen miles away.

Grand Isle's new reefs, like all green infrastructure (and unlike gray), do many things at once. Oysters, along with beavers, coral, and mangroves, are natural engineers; they modify the environment around them in ways that influence the health of other organisms. Oyster reefs provide habitat for other fish and shellfish—so much habitat that the fish that live near restored and protected reefs can be worth more at market than the oysters themselves.

Oysters also filter water—with dramatic results. Time-lapse videos show how a fish tank full of cloudy water becomes clear just hours after the addition of oysters. An adult oyster can filter up to fifty gallons of water a day. In the Chesapeake Bay, scientists estimate that prior to European settlement the oysters filtered the entire volume of the bay—about 19 trillion gallons—every three days. Today, due to over-harvesting and pollution, the same filtering takes more than a year.

When oysters and other shellfish such as clams and mussels filter sediments and algae from the water, it becomes clearer, and more sunlight can reach the bottom, enabling sea grasses to take root. The seagrass beds provide yet more habitat for crabs and nurseries for young fish.

Shellfish can also remove excess nutrients from coastal bays. Those nutrients usually wash into rivers with untreated sewage, or as rain carries excess fertilizer off farms, fields, and lawns, and they can overwhelm coastal waters. Fed by the abundant nutrients, particularly nitrogen, algae blooms extravagantly. When the algae die and sink to the bottom, bacteria decompose the dead plant material and in the process use up most of the oxygen in the water. Without oxygen, everything that cannot move to more hospitable water dies, leaving a dead zone. The dead zone in the Gulf of Mexico, fed by the tons of nutrients gathered across the entire Mississippi Basin, in some years covers as much as 7,000 square miles.

Oyster reefs will not solve the nutrient problem across the entire Gulf. The Mississippi is too big and its basin too filled with farms for oysters to make a significant dent at such a broad scale, even if restored to their historic abundance. But in other, smaller estuaries, such as Mobile Bay, New Hampshire's Great Bay, or even Chesapeake Bay, oysters can significantly reduce the scale of algal blooms.

Engineered structures meant to protect the shoreline do just one thing and not always well. In the United States, the Corps of Engineers builds or issues licenses for seawalls and riprap—the granite or limestone rubble often found along rivers and streams—but such barriers cost millions of dollars to build and even more to maintain. Armored shorelines can also have the adverse effect of redirecting wave energy back into the water, further damaging remaining habitats. Worse, the bottom of Caminada Bay consists of a thick bed of sediments deposited over millennia by the Mississippi. Eventually, large piles of concrete just sink into the mud. A living shoreline is a far better idea.

Recreating a living shoreline won't happen by itself; it will require hard labor and sophisticated engineering of welded steel, plastic, and oyster shells. On Grand Isle, stimulus funding began in 2010 to pay for a reef built from triangular cages made of rebar, each about five feet on a side and two feet tall. The triangular rebar frame, containing mesh bags full of oyster shells, are lowered into the water with a crane and secured to blocks on either side. The top of each cage sits just at the surface of the water at high tide, providing a solid foundation on which new oysters can grow.

Grand Isle's new reef stretches just under a mile, on average about fifty feet from shore. A similar reef in St. Bernard's Parish, about sixty miles northeast on the other side of the Mississippi, brings the total re-stored reef to just under three and a half miles. The reefs began to provide protection from storm surges as soon as they were installed, and oysters are already starting to settle on the reefs.

If experience elsewhere with these kinds of engineered reefs holds, they may begin to reduce erosion just as quickly. In Texas, similar reef blocks now protect an eroding shoreline of a nature preserve in a stretch of the Matagorda Bay's intracoastal waterway. In 2007, the new reef began to reduce damage caused by wakes of the big barges headed for Freeport and Galveston. Sediment deep enough to plant marsh grass has begun to fill the area between the reef and the shore.

The potential to curb the loss of coastal marshes and perhaps be-gin the long process of rebuilding them is hugely significant in the Gulf, especially Louisiana. The state has the most wetlands in the lower forty-eight states, and is losing them at the fastest rate, in part because of the levees along the Mississippi (see "Let Floodplains Be Floodplains"). The US Geological Survey estimates that, if present trends continue, by 2050 the losses will amount to 2,400 square miles of land. The principal cause of the losses is subsidence—river deltas naturally sink if they are not replenished with sediment. A number of other factors exacerbate the problem including the many channels cut through the marshes to facilitate oil and gas operations, changes in land use across the huge Mississippi basin, and of course climate change.

The eroding coastline will have enormous ecological and eco-nomic effects. It threatens to disrupt oil and gas pipelines, force ports to relocate, and destroy habitats that are the basis for commercial and recreational fisheries. Salt marshes are among the most productive ecosystems on earth, and that productivity is a major reason for the vi-tal Gulf fishery. The marshes provide nursery habitats for many species of commercially and recreationally important fish and shellfish, such as striped mullet, anchovies, blue crabs, flounder, and redfish.

Oyster reefs by themselves will not stop the loss of the salt marshes, but they can be part of the solution.

ON GRAND ISLE IN 2011, FISHERMEN ALMOST IMMEDIATELY NOTICED that redfish and spotted sea trout like to lurk near the new reefs. That fact alone has made the reefs popular with permanent residents, as well as those who come just for the fishing.

The same pattern plays out in Alabama, near uninhabited Coffee Island in Portersville Bay, about ten miles west of Mobile Bay. Coffee Island guards the entrance to Bayou La Batre. Made famous as the home port of *Forrest Gump*'s Bubba Gump Shrimp Co., it is Alabama's largest seafood processing harbor. The boats, shipyards, and associated businesses depend on Coffee Island to protect the port, but like Grand Isle and other barrier islands it was at risk from storms and sea-level rise, and its shoreline had been receding for decades.

Stimulus money in 2010 paid for an oyster reef along two stretches of shoreline, protected thirty acres of habitat, and created almost two acres of oyster reef. Both the shoreline and the oysters began a comeback nearly as soon as the workers lowered the last piece of reef into place. The restored reefs are already producing new commercial flounder catches, just two years after the reefs were completed.

Coffee Island falls under the umbrella of 100–1000: Restore Coastal Alabama, the most ambitious reef restoration effort in the world. This project unites more than two dozen community groups, including one church, with universities, scientists, and conservation organizations. Its goal is to build one hundred miles of oyster reef and to restore 1,000 acres of coastal marsh and seagrass beds in and around Mobile Bay. An early effort demonstrated the power of the idea: in January 2011, more than 550 volunteers turned out to help build a quarter-mile oyster reef in the Bay.

Reef restoration in Mobile Bay, on Grand Isle, and in St. Bernard's marsh have grabbed public attention. New Yorkers are even trying to bring back their oyster reefs as well. Perhaps one day oyster reefs will help defend the city against storm surges like the one that devastated parts of the city during Hurricane Sandy in 2012. The new reefs already underway are changing the way that people see oysters, even among policymakers who previously would have paid attention only to the dollar value of the oyster harvest. A similar broadening of perspective is happening other places, too, but the Gulf is further along than anywhere else in the world.

OYSTER REEFS ARE UNLIKELY TO ATTRACT PRIVATE INVESTORS BECAUSE returns come in too slowly. Reefs provide public benefits including coastal protection that justifies public investment.

Conservation scientists and economists are beginning to formulate good estimates of the economic return from oyster reefs. An analysis of three miles of planned oyster reefs on either side of Mobile Bay reveals that the new reefs will add nearly 7,000 pounds to the commercial and recreational fisheries each year. That amounts to as much as $46,000 per year in added benefits for producers and consumers of commercial and recreational fish.

That figure accounts for just the fish—and from just two short stretches of reef. Tally all the benefits of the reefs across wider areas, and the math becomes more compelling: every mile of reef restored would produce more than a thousand additional pounds of fish and crabs per year and would reduce wave energy by at least 75 percent. When Restore Coastal Alabama reaches its goal of one hundred miles of reef, the project will generate more than $1 million in economic benefits every year—not including avoided damages from the control of coastal erosion and flooding.

Unlike the entirely synthetic options, the oyster reef will eventually take care of itself. Once the reef substrate is in place, nothing else needs to be done, except to monitor its progress. The construction jobs may be short-lived, but the other benefits from the reefs will survive as long as the reef, likely decades or beyond.

Perhaps most encouraging, even a $1 billion investment is not out of the question. The RESTORE Act, included as part of Congress's 2012 Federal Transportation Act, directs that 80 percent of the Clean Water Act penalties that could be levied on responsible parties in the *Deepwater Horizon* spill be invested back in the region for long-term restoration and economic development. These penalties could reach as much as $21 billion. Obviously not all of that would be for oyster reef restoration, but even a portion would go a long way.

Oyster restoration in the Gulf, like coral reef restoration in the Pacific, demonstrates how conservation and economic recovery can go hand in hand. Intact coastal habitats deliver tangible, measurable value to people. Those benefits will become even more important as the consequences of climate change emerge.

7

Investing in the Future in the Face of Climate Change

My grandparents immigrated to the United States from Eastern Europe. When they settled in Cleveland, they planted a huge garden with lettuce and pumpkins as well as many fruit trees—apples, cherries, pears, and plums. I spent many childhood hours in the 1960s weeding the garden and picking fruit.

That era did not last long. Even as a grade-schooler, I could tell that air pollution was getting worse, thanks mostly to steel plants and other heavy industry in and around the city. The trees stopped producing good fruit, weakened, and some died. Then, in 1969, the Cuyahoga River caught fire. You don't need to be much of an environmentalist to know that something is terribly wrong when a river bursts into flames. It was embarrassing to Clevelanders. I'll never forget Randy Newman singing "Burn On," and Rowan and Martin cracking jokes about the river on *Laugh In*. Those events opened my eyes and a lot of other people's, too.

Events such as the river fire prompted passage of landmark federal water and air pollution laws, reducing pollution dramatically in many places that had been badly damaged. The transformation in Cleveland has been remarkable. People have been cleaning the Cuyahoga for four decades, and the city's waterfront is at last becoming vibrant.

Air and water pollution are big, complex problems. Even so, governments, businesses, and individuals can still address them within a watershed like the Cuyahoga River basin or by targeting specific industries, such as the steel and electric power plants that contributed to air pollution in the Midwest. Most kinds of pollution have local or at worst regional impacts. Nature at this scale is resilient. Damage can be repaired in a matter of years or decades.

On the other end of this scale, the main environmental threat of our time will bring changes that cover the entire planet, affect everyone, and last for millenia. This threat of course is climate change.

As I travel and speak about conservation and the value of nature, the issue of climate change always comes up, especially as heat waves, storms, floods, and droughts make the issue tangible to everyone. The people who ask me questions about climate change generally break down into two camps. One wants to know why we aren't doing more right now. For them there is no more pressing issue. They believe all conservation organizations should make climate change the top priority. The other group hopes I will say that everything is going to be all right. Unfortunately, given what science tells us, I cannot reassure them. Climate change is an overwhelming threat and the elephant in the room for any conversation about the environment or the economy.

Climate change is real. We know what to do about it. The longer we wait, the more we will lose, and the more it will cost. Every carbon molecule that is emitted today—emissions that could have been avoided at low cost—will be part of the atmosphere for eons. We need strong and effective policies to reduce carbon emissions now. A variety of paths may lead to those reductions, and governments may need to experiment with various methods, but we need to accelerate that process immediately.

Less noted than the need to reduce emissions are the connections between climate change and natural capital, and how investing in that capital is itself a response to the changing climate. Natural capital can help us adapt to the inevitable consequences of a changing climate. As we have seen with floodplains, oyster reefs, and coral reefs, nature provides services that no engineered solutions can match.

Investing in natural capital can also protect our climate and oceans by reducing emissions. Consider, for example, that a significant portion—as much as 15 percent—of greenhouse gas emissions result from the loss of tropical forests. That amount is as much as the output of all cars, trucks, buses, trains, and airplanes combined worldwide. It is also the primary source of emissions in Brazil and Indonesia, two of the top five carbon-emitting countries. This presents a clear win-win opportunity: save the rainforests and all that they contain and help slow climate change at the same time. By the way, saving a ton of carbon in the forest is also often cheaper than reducing a ton of emissions from cars or power plants.

I arrived at The Nature Conservancy in 2008 with the hope and expectation that the US government would join the European Union and others and put a price on carbon pollution. Many of my colleagues in the environmental community also anticipated—too optimistically, it turned out—that forest conservation would be able to attract financial resources through carbon-pricing mechanisms and as a result take our work to a whole new scale. I still believe that will happen. But building carbon markets to protect our climate system depends on government action that seems many years away today. Investors and businesses are ready to make carbon markets that include forest conservation and other investments in natural capital part of the solution. But without government action, business-led voluntary initiatives will fall short of what we need.

Rising Seas and Sinking Marshes

The narrow two-lane road down to Grand Isle reveals one challenge of adapting to climate change. The new, southern part of LA 1 sits on concrete pilings more than twenty feet above the marshes. Good thing, too: the marshes now feature more open water than ever before as the shoreline erodes and the sea rises. The raised road ends at a fork: turn east and you head toward Grand Isle; head southwest and the road leads through the dwindling marsh to Port Fourchon, one of the most important oil and gas shipping terminals in the country, serving 90 percent of deepwater oil production in the Gulf.

The tall pilings protect the road from storms and floods. Unfortunately, the elevated stretch does not go far enough north. Get past the tiny, nearly abandoned settlement of Leeville, and for seven miles the road is only a few feet above sea level and sinking. According to the National Oceanic and Atmospheric Administration, at this rate the road could be underwater more than three weeks per year by 2030. Closing the road even temporarily could cost billions, as no other ports can replace Port Fourchon's unique role in oil and gas production.

Raising these seven miles of road will cost hundreds of millions of dollars. This is the shape of things to come, not just on LA 1 but in coastal communities around the nation. By 2030, the same year that Gulf of Mexico waters start lapping over LA 1, more than 2 million homes in other American communities may also be underwater.

LA 1 reveals the unintended consequences of relying too heavily on gray infrastructure. Not the infrastructure of the road itself—at this point, the only option is to sink the pilings and elevate the roadway. No, the infrastructure causing the marshes to sink are the levees on the Mississippi that redirect tons of sediment that once nourished the marshes in the deepwater of the Gulf. Reconnecting the river to its delta would rebuild the marshes and diminish the need to rebuild miles of road. It may be too late to save LA 1 with natural capital, but we are in for a long battle with rising seas. The lesson that it could have been different if we had paid more attention to nature's role should not be lost on other communities. Engineered solutions can do only so much to help people adapt to climate change. Much of the adaptation will depend on countless natural systems. Such systems— like marshes and oyster reefs—are generally resilient, but the seawalls and levees in which we invest so much money and trust are far more brittle than we care to admit.

LA 1 ALSO ILLUSTRATES A FAR LARGER PROBLEM. MUCH OF OUR infrastructure, from dams to culverts to water mains to levees, was designed on the basis of the once unassailable assumption that the climate would vary only between fairly well-defined boundaries. This idea, *stationarity*, stems specifically from hydrology. Engineers designing flood control systems have for decades based their calculations on a long historical and even geological record of rainfall and floods, and extrapolate from that record the worst flood the system would face over, say, 100 or 500 years. Engineers believe, reasonably enough, that their creations can withstand the worst that nature is likely to throw at them, and can do so for many generations.

That assumption may no longer be viable, at least in part due to climate change. Take Nashville, for example. In an average May, the city gets about five and a half inches of rain. On May 2, 2010, that much fell in *six hours*. The deluge continued for two days, spilling the Cumberland River into downtown and causing millions of dollars in damage. The Army Corps of Engineers estimated this was a 1,000-year flood; other observers judged it to be rarer still, perhaps a 5,000-year flood.

Or consider New England. The region's beloved covered bridges have withstood a century or more of floods, blizzards, and ice storms, even surviving the Great New England Hurricane of 1938, the worst on record for the region. Many of them, sadly, did not withstand Hurricane Irene in 2011. Hurricanes are not becoming more frequent as a result of climate change, but more powerful hurricanes—indeed, more powerful storms of all sorts—are. One analysis of more than 80 million daily precipitation records from the lower forty-eight states showed that intense rain and snowstorms happen 85 percent more often in New England now than in 1948.

The trend is indisputable. Communities everywhere are seeing more of what meteorologists call extreme weather events and more variability in climate generally. While the storms may surprise the residents of Nashville or Vermont, the data should not surprise anyone. They are exactly in-line with predictions that climate scientists such as James Hansen, among the first to warn of the consequences of continuing to burn fossil fuels, made three decades ago.

If what was once extreme becomes routine, then we must reexamine not just roads such as LA 1, but all manner of things people have built, maybe even the location of entire cities. The management of some of our most important natural assets, such as forests, also requires new scrutiny.

Another climate prediction has been borne out dramatically. Scientists have long feared that climate change would bring drier conditions to many areas and that droughts would lead to both food shortages and more intense and more frequent forest fires. In 2012, nearly unprecedented fires in the western United States and punishing droughts across the Corn Belt focused attention on the reality of climate change in a way that no amount of careful data crunching or impassioned advocacy could manage.

There is no more daunting or more important challenge than climate change. While the sight of thousands of acres of ruined crops and forested hills on fire can easily lead to despair, we still have time to make a difference. Sound investments in nature can help us adapt to a new climate and keep the changes from getting much worse.

Tierra y Libertad

When facing a global and seemingly overwhelming challenge, the solution may be to start small. Take, for example, the village of Tierra y Libertad, in the southern Mexican state of Chiapas. As my colleague Frank Lowenstein has documented, here simple shade trees are part of a strategy that aims to protect the lives and livelihoods of poor ranchers in the face of a changing climate, while also helping to sustain Mexico's economy.

The region offers a telling illustration of "flashy" weather (see "Let Floodplains Be Floodplains"). The amount of rain that falls here has not changed significantly but the timing has. Chiapas receives about 140 inches of rain each year making it one of the wettest places in North America. That rain is typically spread over six months, with little or no rain falling during the other half of the year. Now, the dry season can last for eight months, and the rain comes in torrents that rush down mountain slopes and flood the valleys below.

The Grijalva River collects much of the floodwater and eventually deposits it in four large reservoirs, which supply water for turbines that produce nearly 10 percent of Mexico's electricity. The increased risk of flooding means that reservoir managers must keep water levels lower to allow room for the extra water, even when it doesn't come. The floods cause another problem as well: they bring in so much sediment that the reservoirs are filling from the bottom up.

The flooding and the sediment combine to reduce significantly the volume of water behind the dam. The volume of water is the crucial variable in how much electricity the turbines generate. Less water equals less power. Less power could take a bite out of Mexico's economic development.

The longer dry season causes problems, too—both locally and nationally. Pastures throughout the mountains are producing less grass. Traditional grazing practices that were once effective now strip the land down to bare, red dirt. The grass not only feeds the cows and sheep but also holds back rainwater. Less grass means both hungry animals and worsening floods.

A simple but effective solution is to plant drought-tolerant trees in the pastures. The trees produce fruit and forage for the livestock, while the leaves intercept and slow the rain so more of it filters into the ground and also shades the grass so it does not dry out as quickly. Some trees also increase the productivity of the pastures by drawing nitrogen out of the air and fixing it in the soil.

By slowing the rain and keeping grass growing, the trees reduce floods, protecting not only downstream cities and critical reservoirs of the Grijalva but also the ranchers themselves. This should make less likely a recurrence of some recent hardship. For example, one entire village recently had to be moved hundreds of yards uphill and away from the river after severe floods. Looking ahead, perhaps new trees can make moves like this less likely.

Planting trees is one part of an integrated approach to repairing the pastures. The other components are portable water supplies and solar-powered electric fencing that enables farmers to rotate cows through the pasture, giving the grass time to recover. Since they do not have to travel far to find shade and water, the cows can put more energy into milk. Some ranchers have seen milk production double as a result.

CHIAPAS SHOWS US HOW LOCAL PROBLEMS CAN SPREAD AND AFFECT larger areas, and how concentrating on those local problems can begin to repair more global ones. In Chiapas, the changing climate in the form of a longer dry season combines with other complex factors to decrease electricity for Mexico City, more than 400 miles away. The same pattern holds in the American West, where diminished rainfall begins a cascade of events, from insect infestations to intense fires and finally to floods. The idea that drought causes floods seems bizarre, but this is the new world humanity has made.

In other places, diminished water supply is the challenge arising from a changing climate. For example, reduced snowfall is a major problem across the West, particularly in Arizona and the Sierras. Snowpack acts as water storage, holding billions of gallons of water that are released each spring. Water from the snowpack eventually reaches the Colorado River and helps to fill Lake Mead, the massive reservoir that supplies water to Nevada, Arizona, and California. Snowpack effectively transfers water from the relatively wet winter season to the typically dry summers. If what once fell as snow and stayed in the mountains for months now falls as rain or melts away quickly, then the result can be flooding and rapid runoff that doesn't last through the summer.

One response the US Forest Service and independent forest scientists are now investigating is to manage forests specifically to retain snowpack further into the spring. This involves thinning the forest so more snow reaches the ground and trees take up less water. Scientists at the University of California Berkeley call the idea a "water-efficient forest." Not only does this help with the downstream water supply, it also keeps the forest itself from drying out, making forest fires less likely.

So, to all the other values of the forest, you can add one you may not have imagined before: the forest as a snow-capturing service. One day, economists may—indeed, likely must—determine precisely how much such a service is worth to anyone who hikes in the forests, harvests their timber, or drinks their water. For now, precision is less important than recognizing that investing in healthy forests may be the best choice when it comes to adapting to climate change.

Putting a Price on Carbon

It bears repeating that valuing nature does not always mean putting a price on things that never had a price before. Recognizing that nature has value and devising incentives to conserve it are the most important steps, not in every case quantifying that value through a price tag. But in some cases a price is vital.

Chief among the components of nature that currently have no price (in most parts of the world) is carbon. Pumping carbon into the atmosphere, mostly in the form of carbon dioxide, is the primary anthropogenic cause of climate change, and doing so costs the polluter nothing. Fossil-fuel users dump carbon into the atmosphere through our tailpipes and smokestacks. Putting a price on that carbon is the single most important thing to do regarding climate change. Debates now should be about how, not whether, to set that price.

When partisan passions are not at a boil, this idea can cross party lines. Lindsay Graham, Republican Senator from South Carolina, who co-sponsored a climate bill with Senators John Kerry, a Democrat, and Joe Lieberman, an Independent, said in 2010: "The idea of not pricing carbon, in my view, means you're not serious about energy independence. The odd thing is you'll never have energy independence until you clean up the air, and you'll never clean up the air until you price carbon."

Economists generally agree. William Nordhaus, Sterling Professor of Economics at Yale, argues that any proposal dealing with climate change that does not discuss the price of carbon fails to recognize that creating a market incentive to release less carbon into the atmosphere is the central economic message about how to slow climate change. He states, "To a first approximation, raising the price of carbon is a necessary and sufficient step for tackling global warming. The rest is at best rhetoric and may actually be harmful in inducing economic inefficiencies."

The details of setting a price on carbon get complicated, but they boil down to two basic choices: have the government set the price through a tax, or have the market set the price by limiting emissions and allowing supply and demand to set a value for the right to emit. Each option has advocates. Evaluating the strengths and weaknesses of each is beyond the scope of this book; both options, however, depend on new ways of valuing nature, and each has implications for conservation and the economy.

A carbon tax has the virtue of simplicity. Set aside the question of whether anything resembling a new tax could become law in the United States any time soon—but note that the growing focus on the need to reduce fiscal deficits in the United States could lead to political support for additional tax revenue. Also set aside the likely debate about the size of the tax—but again note that the tax initially could be set at a low level and ratcheted up slowly over time so that the economy could adjust to it without too much disruption. The overall idea is simple: by adding a tax, the cost of emitting carbon would rise and all energy users would have an incentive to use less. This is what we mean by "putting a price on carbon."

The incentives associated with a carbon tax rely on common sense and Economics 101. Taxes not only raise revenue but also discourage whatever activity is being taxed. Accordingly, when the government taxes a specific activity—say, smoking cigarettes—you tend to get less of it.

Once the price of carbon is set, it will filter down to increased costs at gas pumps and on electric bills. Other state and national governments have already established a carbon tax. Several northern European countries adopted carbon taxes in the early 1990s and the U.K. joined with its own in 2000. British Colombia instituted a tax in 2008 and Australia did the same in 2012. In the United States, a carbon tax could play a role in comprehensive tax reform or be used to reduce our enormous fiscal deficits.

The United States had a real life experiment in using economic incentives like this to encourage energy conservation. I recall this experiment well from my childhood—do you remember the long lines at gas stations beginning in 1974? That's when OPEC reduced oil supply and prices tripled. (The Iranian revolution had comparable effects in 1979, and prices doubled.) Think of these price increases as taxes—except in this case the revenue went to OPEC. To be sure, the high prices were a shock to the system. But they quickly led to significant reductions in energy consumption and associated reductions in carbon dioxide emissions. In other words, as environmental policy, the tax worked. Of course we could administer such a tax in a carefully designed manner. We could avoid the sudden shock by introducing the tax initially at a moderate rate and then gradually raising it thereafter. This would allow energy users to adjust their behavior and reduce energy use over time. The tax revenue would flow not to OPEC but would stay home.

What might result from a carbon tax and associated higher energy prices? As the OPEC example illustrates, efforts to reduce energy consumption lead to more efficient personal transportation, energy-savvy building codes, and greener cities. Likewise, higher prices for carbon-based energy would make emerging cleaner energy sources much more competitive, encouraging new investment and innovation.

Cap and Trade

Some environmentalists, discouraged by our inability to pass comprehensive energy and climate legislation during the first years of the Obama administration, choose to drop any mention of recent efforts to champion cap-and-trade climate legislation. I view this as a mistake for several reasons. First, we err when we allow opponents of cap-and-trade programs to misrepresent them as an antimarket, big government approach. To the contrary, the whole idea is to let market forces direct emission reductions to where they can be achieved at the lowest cost. Second, cap-and-trade programs are underway in some jurisdictions such as California, the European Union, and Australia and deserve our support. Third, even though environmentalists together with others have not succeeded yet in helping to pass comprehensive climate legislation in the United States, we did make some important progress and now should try to build on it. For example, the US Climate Action Partnership (USCAP)—a coalition of more than twenty multinational companies and five environmental organizations—showed that big business and environmental organizations could work together to develop detailed and comprehensive legislative proposals. USCAP even got its proposed bill through the House. It's time for this group or groups like it to reconvene, perhaps with new and more diverse partners, and get back to work.

Cap-and-trade has been used with great success to combat acid rain. The basic idea was to cap overall sulfur dioxide emissions from power plants—the main culprit behind acid rain—at half their previous levels but allow each utility to decide how to get under that limit. Companies received a certain number of credits representing the amount of sulfur dioxide they could emit. If they reduced their emissions and did not need to use all of their credits, they could sell the extras to other companies unable to reduce their own emissions at as low a cost. Utilities thus had an incentive to get below the cap as inexpensively as possible so they could benefit by selling excess credits.

This approach created a brand-new market: pollution permits. For acid rain at least, cap-and-trade has been effective. Under that approach, written into the 1990 Clean Air Act and signed into law by President George H. W. Bush, sulfur emissions from power plants have been reduced by more than 50 percent and at far lower cost than economists had predicted.

As environmentalists work to put a price on carbon more broadly and in more jurisdictions, governments can take many other steps to address climate change. For example, in the United States new auto-fuel economy standards will lower emissions significantly. Likewise, EPA's recent efforts to tighten regulations on power plants—along with cheap natural gas—has resulted in the closure of older, less efficient facilities. Renewable electricity standards adopted by twenty-nine states and Washington, DC also play an important role in accelerating the transition to cleaner energy sources.

Ultimately, the global-warming crisis requires global solutions. This means that high carbon-emitting countries such as China and India also need to get on with pricing carbon. China is already trying experimental cap-and-trade programs. The United States will be in a much better position to encourage international progress here when it finally takes decisive action at home.

A New Kind of Development

Interest in a carbon market has not disappeared, it has just changed locales. With federal efforts stalled in the United States, action has moved directly to the states. Everyone is watching California, by itself the eighth largest economy in the world. In 2006, frustrated by the inability of Congress to pass a climate bill, California Governor Arnold Schwarzenegger and the state assembly decided the state should create its own cap-and-trade scheme. After various legal and political challenges, the state started auctioning carbon credits in 2012.

Even more interesting, California signed an agreement with the Brazilian state of Acre, in the Amazon. Both California and Acre hope that as the carbon market takes shape, some companies that need to reduce their emissions will—in search of the lowest cost source of reductions—look to the Amazon or the rainforests of Indonesia, or to wetlands and coastal marine habitats such as mangrove forests, seagrass beds, and salt marshes, all of which contain large amounts of what is known as "blue carbon." All of these ecosystems absorb and store carbon. Accordingly, paying to leave forests standing (or paying for new forests) should count toward a corporate or national emission reduction target. Instead of cutting their own emissions, the companies could instead buy carbon credits from Acre or Para, another

Amazonian state in Brazil, or East Kalimantan in Indonesia. Revenue from credit sales could be used to support other kinds of economic development that avoid deforestation.

The good news is that these huge flows of cash to tropical forest countries—helpful to be sure—may not even be necessary. The rainforest countries are changing how they view their own economic development. Instead of an approach counting on carbon markets in which payments flow from developed countries to stop the industries that are deforesting, a more sustainable model is emerging. Low-carbon rural development driven by public funding, forest-country ownership, and pressure from consumers, such as that seen in Brazil regarding soy and beef, is now underway and may in fact be a more successful approach.

Brazil, for example, already shows great interest in that kind of change. Deforestation rates in Brazil have dropped significantly since 2006. Likewise, Indonesia has committed to reducing deforestation by at least 26 percent by 2020. Mexico's new national climate law mandates stopping deforestation by 2020. Other countries are pursuing similar commitments to protect their natural forest capital.

These countries are bucking a historical trend. In nearly every country, deforestation accompanies economic development. This happened in North America and Europe and is happening now at a faster pace—over decades rather than centuries—in the tropics. Fortunately, what economists and development experts call the forest-transition curve shows that eventually deforestation slows and at least partially reverses. So rather than simply transferring money to tropical-forest countries, a better approach would be to help those countries shift to a different model of economic development, one that does not follow an inevitable path of deforestation. The key is to see forests not simply as either a biological or an economic resource, but as both.

That approach means linking climate change, deforestation, and development. Part of that linkage entails not just stopping logging altogether, but making it better. From a conservation perspective, fully protected forests are often better at conserving more plants and animals than forests managed for timber. Why then should conservationists create incentives for cutting down trees?

It's simple: the world's growing population will need timber. Forestry today sustains millions of jobs worldwide and provides wood and paper products. Recycling and development of nontimber alternatives can reduce demand for these goods, but well-managed forests and plantations must still play an important role. They can provide a reliable, sustainable supply of paper and wood while diverting pressure away from pristine lands that contain the highest amount of carbon and that provide homes for endangered species and indigenous communities.

Rather than always fighting logging, a more productive approach in many circumstances is to find responsible ways to provide timber, including keeping logging out of places that cannot sustain it. Destructive logging practices, many of them illegal, are a serious driver of forest loss and resulting carbon emissions. Transitioning from destructive logging to low-impact harvesting practices can reduce damage to forests and can in some cases cut carbon emissions by 40 percent, while delivering the same supply of timber. In well-managed forests loggers harvest the most commercially valuable trees and leave the rest. Instead of using bulldozers that clear wide swaths o forest and require wide roads just to get to the logging sites, loggers can be more selective and use winches to slide the highest value logs out on narrow trails, replacing a 250-horsepower bulldozer with something as small as a 22-horsepower cable winch.

Well-managed forests can also retain much of their biological diversity. Selectively logged tropical forests retain nearly all their plants and animals and about three-quarters of the carbon and can also continue to produce timber for years. Unless entire forests are razed to the ground to plant soybeans or graze cattle, the forests withstand a good deal of use without causing an ecological train wreck. They will not be the same as forests protected from all logging, but they are not a lost cause either. The hard part is determining which places demand the highest level of protection and which represent opportunities to invest in natural capital for both people and the environment.

Logging companies are symbols of environmental destruction, demonized almost as often as Big Oil. Seeing them as potential allies in forest conservation requires a markedly different perspective. In many remote, tropical areas, however, conservationists must ally themselves with logging companies. In those areas, logging companies are often the only game in town—if there even *is* a town. These companies, which include everything from multinational giants to tiny firms operating on a shoestring budget, also often have the most important asset of all: legal tenure over huge swaths of forest or the hope of acquiring it. Governments have already designated more tropical forests for logging than they have set aside in all the tropical-protected areas on earth.

Many communities that depend on forested lands do not have legal rights to that land or do not have rights to the timber or carbon. Without clear legal titles, the communities have little recourse if unscrupulous timber operations move in and start clear-cutting. The same pattern can play out even where governments claim a forest and at least nominally place it under protection. Many forests across Asia and Latin America have been heavily logged over the past three decades even though they are designated national parks.

In Indonesia, much cleared land has been used for oil-palm plantations. A better long-term investment would put those plantations not on virgin forestland but instead on degraded land, of which Indonesia has tens of millions of acres, just as Brazil is directing cattle ranches to already cleared land (see "Feeding the World—and Saving It"). Making this change happen, however, will be difficult. Oil-palm planters cash in a quick profit from selling rainforest timber, and clarifying rights to degraded land can be complex. We will need a variety of policies to change these incentives.

Forest conservation alone will not solve the climate change challenge. Nevertheless, reducing carbon emissions from deforestation is critical and potentially transformative in benefiting communities, ecosystems, biodiversity, and the global climate.

A Way Forward

I remember well the events of 9/11 in Lower Manhattan. Although my colleagues and I were able to get out of Wall Street safely, we witnessed up close scenes of extraordinary suffering and destruction. Since that day I have tried to neither think nor talk about those memories.

All of those images came roaring back for me when Hurricane Sandy pummeled the East Coast. Once again vulnerable people were subjected to shock, loss of life and property, and widepread suffering. And once again, questions arise: Why weren't we better prepared? Shouldn't we have known better? Where was our government? Might this happen again? Most importantly, what should we do now to reduce the liklihood of this happening again and how can we better prepare ourselves in the event that it does?

The truth is we know exactly what to do. First, we must immediately do all we can to reduce carbon emissions. We know how to do this, and we know how to do it a way that is not too disruptive to the economy.

Second, we need to think hard about the infrastructure needed to protect us from such extreme weather events. Gray infrastructure like seawalls and seagates will be important, but barrier islands, reefs, and wetlands also need to be protected and restored on the most urgent basis.

In Cape May, New Jersey, for example, three communities have banded together to restore coastal dunes and wetlands to reduce flooding. While Sandy came ashore just a few miles away, this restored beach and wetland system spared the nearby communities from the kind of flooding they experienced before the restoration was completed. In New York City, the Redesigning the Edge project being supported by the Metropolitan Waterfront Alliance and others is looking at ways to combine built and natural infrastructure to reduce flooding and to create more usable open space along the city's waterways.

Sandy might have been a necessary wake-up call. New York City is the world's financial and media capital. New Yorkers now have no choice: fight for the policies that will address the threats of climate change, or pack up and move away to high ground inland.

Cities hold untapped opportunities for conservation, and not just in adapting to climate change. Urban conservation has not been the main focus for most mainstream conservation organizations. Yet, the best place to appreciate the value of nature may be where it is most lacking.

8

Town and Country

When I lived in New York City, I escaped the pressures of Wall Street by jogging in Central Park, so I know firsthand the value of urban green spaces. But in all my years running through the Park, I rarely thought of its other benefits. Only now are many urbanites starting to understand green infrastructure and its role in improving water quality, reducing air pollution, and generally improving public health.

In my early months at TNC, I was reluctant to reveal my big-city roots. I did my green credentials no favors by sipping from a plastic water bottle during one of my first all-staff town hall meetings. Sure, I had a terrible cold and was losing my voice, but that was no excuse for my new colleagues. When I came to work the next day, they had left me a host of reusable Nalgenes and Klean Kanteens.

I appreciated the thoughtfulness but was also struck by the symbolism. Environmentalists cannot buy reusable water bottles for everyone, yet it sometimes seems as if that has been the retail strategy for saving nature: person by person, special place by special place. That will not be enough—not anymore. Making a difference means showing how nature matters to millions of people who may not have noticed it: people living in big cities.

Mainstream conservation has long neglected cities. The movement's roots in wilderness preservation have kept it focused on lands far from madding crowds. Conservation also draws inspiration from the idea that among unspoiled nature's greatest values is its capacity to renew the human spirit.

Abandoning such ideas would be a great mistake; protecting wild places for their own sake has enormous value. However, making wilderness the sole focus of conservation risks ignoring that human beings are now, for the first time in history, an urban species. Science offers compelling reasons for conservation in urban landscapes. Urban forests, rivers, and estuaries provide huge benefits both locally and farther away. Most need to be restored to some degree. Connecting city dwellers with nature also builds support for conservation of remote areas that many of them may never see. Organizations such as the Trust for Public Land and environmental justice organizations such as Sustainable South Bronx have been doing great work in this arena for years. For many other organizations—TNC among them—urban conservation has been, at best, a low priority.

That must change. More than half the people on earth live in cities. Architects and city planners are now thinking about building materials, city design, and architecture from an environmental perspective. The result will be new ways to build cites that reduce both the amount of land they use and the greenhouse gases they produce.

Among the leaders in the field is the Berkeley-based architect Peter Calthorpe. In his book *Urbanism in the Age of Climate Change*, Calthorpe wrote: "Confronting climate change is a little like the war on drugs: you can go after the supplier—coal fired power plants—or you can pursue the addicts—inefficient buildings and suburban sprawl. Both will be necessary."

In 2011, Calthorpe's firm and the state of California did a study of alternative paths of urbanism in the state. Comparing green urban development with business as usual (just extrapolating the current trend), greenhouse gas emissions fall from 348 million metric tons to 83 million metric tons, land consumption falls from 5,600 square miles to 1,850 square miles, and water usage falls from 147,000 gallons per household to 66,000 per household. This means denser living and smaller lawns and more walking. But this also better serves an aging population that does not want to do yard work or drive very far.

The lesson that conservation can take from the work by Calthorpe and other innovative thinkers is the need to address urban conservation far more broadly. Just as conservationists see the need to look beyond single nature reserves to the larger landscape, so too they should consider the whole urban system and not just open space or pocket parks. Conservation can be a major contributor to protecting the people who live in cities.

Nature is as important in a city as it is in wilderness—perhaps more so, since many cities are defined by an absence of nature. Our task is to make cities function more like natural landscapes.

Reimagining cities through nature's lens will not be easy, but the basic idea and the underlying economics are not that complicated. Making this a reality requires a change in perspective, one that brings nature in close to where people live. Doing so will also unveil the value of nature in places it has been forgotten.

Urban conservation is not an effort to redirect conservation efforts from sparsely inhabited places to densely inhabited ones in the name of simplistic utilitarianism. Building support for conservation means making it relevant to city dwellers, which requires working on parks, waterfronts, and other green spaces that people in cities can see every day. Such a shift will also bring a host of benefits, economic and otherwise—a deeper connection to more diverse nature, cleaner air and water, and a thriving culture.

Urban Wilderness

Stories about the value of nature rarely consider cities, except as places to escape from. Nature lies beyond the sidewalk and the last traffic light, past the end of the last road; there, many of us hope, the wilderness begins. In some important senses, that remains true. Most plants and animals thrive in places with few people or their accessories—roads, houses, farms, and other hallmarks of human ingenuity. Many people in many different cultures prize most highly those rare bits of the earth where human presence fades away almost to nothing, fonts of spiritual renewal and communion.

In focusing our gaze on the far distance, conservation may miss something just as important but closer at hand. As the value of nature in all its forms enters mainstream economics, science, and politics, it may revolutionize our society and our economy in the same way as the automobile or the Internet.

To see that transformation, consider how everyone depends on nature for their most basic needs, whether they live in Manhattan or Montana, in the United States or the farthest corner of the remotest desert. The same dependence binds people whether they see in wildness the preservation of the world, as Henry David Thoreau put it, or see nature as a source of raw materials to be transformed for profit or for the betterment of humankind.

Thoreau sought to turn his back, even briefly, on civilization, though even in 1845 Walden Pond, just two miles from town, hardly qualified as wilderness. Other visionaries of that era sought to bring nature and its many values to the city, planting the seeds of a broader approach to conservation that is coming into full flower only now. Foremost among them in the United States was Frederick Law Olmsted.

Olmsted practically invented the profession of landscape architecture and was without question its most famous American practitioner. Between his own work and that of his firm, which carried on his legacy long after his death, the Olmsted franchise covers hundreds of parks and other public spaces across the United States. New York's Central Park towers above them all in terms of fame, number of visitors, and influence. After more than 150 years, it remains the quintessential urban wilderness.

Olmsted saw the potential, long before nearly anyone else, of linking the ecological and social functions of an area. He deployed natural areas to enhance the lives of human communities nearby. The intertwining of the human with the natural allows at least the possibility of landscapes that have more than one function and fulfill more than one need.

Olmsted also understood the need to think big, beyond the boundaries of any single park. In this, as in many things, he was far ahead of his time. He developed a plan for Staten Island—in his day, a suburb rather than a component of New York City—that would have been the first regional plan in the country, but it was never enacted.

Olmsted's unique approach to investing in nature had greater success elsewhere. Less iconic than Central Park but more ambitious, Olmsted's design of a network of parks and open space around Boston, which he began in the late 1870s, anticipated the ideas of green infrastructure by more than a century. The city had filled in part of the Charles River and created a new and fashionable neighborhood called Back Bay. Unfortunately but not surprisingly, the low-lying area flooded regularly at high tide. The area also gathered sewage overflow from the Muddy River, which formed the boundary between Boston and the small town of Brookline to the west.

Olmsted's plan took an engineering challenge and transformed it into a much greater opportunity. He diverted sewage into underground conduits and solved the flooding problem by creating an artificial salt marsh, which he called the Back Bay Fens. He then placed sluice gates across the Charles, installed boat landings for recreation, and constructed motorways along the edges. As described by biographer Witold Rybczynski, Olmsted's aims were not artistic but pragmatic. He took great care in the design and construction of nearly everything in the Fens, but his goal was to make it appear entirely natural, as if the city had been built around it rather than vice versa.

Olmsted saw two possible futures for the Muddy River. One entailed making it into a several-mile-long stretch of masonry to carry floodwaters to the Charles. That would have been expensive and would have taken many years to round up the necessary funding. The delay, Olmsted said, would leave the river to become "dirty, unhealthy, [and] squalid," in the meantime destroying property values and creating a source of pestilence. Many cities continue to face those precise concerns and nearly all could learn from what Olmsted did instead. He left the river largely intact, but sloped the banks to prevent erosion, and built a parkway connecting Back Bay to other natural areas farther from the river, including Jamaica Pond, the Arnold Arboretum, and West Roxbury Park. Between 1878 and 1896, this became a string of parks now known as the Emerald Necklace.

The six parks Olmsted designed stretch across central and western Boston, from Franklin Park in the south to Back Bay Fens by the river, just a long foul ball away from Fenway Park. Along with Boston Common, the Public Gardens, and Commonwealth Avenue, all of which predated Olmsted, the nine parks of the Emerald Necklace enclose a substantial portion of downtown Boston on three sides, providing green space for more than a million people.

Design with Nature

Modern research has verified much of what Olmsted believed about the benefits of urban parks and green infrastructure more generally, as well as additional benefits he did not foresee. Creating or re-creating green infrastructure such as street trees, private gardens, and city parks in distressed urban neighborhoods—of all urban environments, those most likely to be barren of the green and growing—can contribute to the well-being of the urban poor by improving air and water quality, for example. Green infrastructure such as the Emerald Necklace simply makes cities better looking and more livable.

In the mid-twentieth century, Ian McHarg observed these same qualities in green infrastructure. A gravel-voiced, chain-smoking ex-paratrooper with a rich Scottish brogue, McHarg transformed landscape architecture from the narrow discipline it had become after Olmsted's death in 1903 into a broad-based view of how people can fit into the places they live without destroying them. He took no prisoners: according to the journal *Science,* when an elderly woman asked him what she could do to fight pollution, he said she should seek out the CEO of US Steel and "bite him on the jugular."

In 1962, just at the dawn of a broad environmental consciousness, McHarg wrote:

Cities are probably the most inhumane environments ever made by man for man. It is taking the best efforts of modern medicine and social legislation to ameliorate the abuses which the physical environment imposes upon us.

McHarg founded the University of Pennsylvania's Department of Landscape Architecture and it was far more interdisciplinary than nearly any other of its day. McHarg brought together architects, landscape architects, and city planners with a geologist, an ethnographer, an anthropologist, a geochemist, a medical anthropologist, a hydrologist, a soil scientist, a plant ecologist, a limnologist, and a resource economist to train what McHarg called "applied human ecologists." McHarg described the work that such professionals would do in his

1969 masterpiece *Design with Nature*. Completed with the encouragement and financial support of Russell E. Train, then head of a
small environmental think tank called the Conservation Foundation,
the book remains a landmark in the evolution of how to reintegrate
humanity into the natural landscape.

In *Design with Nature*, McHarg picked up where Olmsted left off
on Staten Island, laying out a plan that revealed and interpreted the
hydrological patterns of the island, which was the least populated and
least developed of New York's five boroughs. It took more than a decade for city planners to put elements of his vision into practice. The
city took advantage of existing green infrastructure, a series of wetlands and creeks in the southwestern part of the island, to deal with
stormwater. It also added man-made wetlands and waterways to
mimic the natural versions, just as Olmsted created the Back Bay
Fens. This so-called Bluebelt, covering sixteen watersheds and 10,000
acres, has saved the city tens of millions of dollars compared to the
cost of building conventional water treatment plants.

At a finer scale and within city limits, the Bluebelt replicates the
lessons of the Catskills: the importance of connectivity, and the potential, when so connected, for landscapes to offer multiple benefits to
people and nature. The Bluebelt was not initially intended to have
such a broad impact; its designers had the simpler goal of providing
clean water. But as it moved from concept to reality, city officials and
local residents realized that investing in nature on Staten Island could
mean more than just clean water. It could mean wildlife habitat, protected wetlands, recreational areas, and a better quality of life in an
often-neglected corner of the city.

THOUGH NEITHER USED THE TERM *GREEN INFRASTRUCTURE*, MCHARG
and Olmsted both understood what makes a city livable: controlling
sprawl, providing green space, and creating a framework for more sensible and ecologically sensitive development. Even cities, the most

transformed landscapes on earth, provide opportunities to create systems in harmony with nature.

With careful thought but not massive investment, cities can devise ways to provide multiple benefits to both people and nature. McHarg showed how this can work for landscape architecture, but the implications run far deeper. It is not just buildings and roads and public plazas that must work with nature, but all human activity—city to countryside, factory floor to grain elevator, executive suite to governor's mansion.

Some theorists, such as Harvard economist Edward Glaeser, view the growth of cities as beneficial for the environment. Better to concentrate people in high-rise living, writes Glaeser in *The Triumph of the City*, than for humans to spread ever farther into the countryside, creating more suburbs, roads, lawns, and strip malls as they expand.

Glaeser's claim is far from outlandish. But New Yorkers will not trade Central Park for high-density housing—a logical extension of Glaeser's argument—because most city residents will gladly relinquish a small slice of liberty in the form of zoning laws in return for Central Park or other urban refuges. People have been making similar trade-offs for generations, according to historian Jon Christensen and sociologist Carrie Denning. They argue that history provides examples of how to protect nature and provide for people in an urban setting.

Christensen and Denning point to what they call "the hidden history of urban conservation" in and around San Francisco. As in New York, the first concern was water, and San Franciscans in the latter half ninteenth century looked to protect reservoirs and watersheds such as Hetch Hetchy for purely utilitarian reasons. At the same time, San Francisco's "City Beautiful" movement drew inspiration, as have many others, from Olmsted and Central Park, and created first Golden Gate Park in the 1870s and subsequently many other green spaces to provide oases of open air amid the gray urban canyons. As the Bay Area boomed after World War II, rapid suburbanization led a new generation of "open-space" activists who campaigned first for growth limits and zoning restrictions. They were followed by yet another generation in the 1980s, which took up the cause of conserving biodiversity and natural habitats. Throughout all these eras, opponents of conservation and open space argued that land preservation would drive up home prices.

A 2010 study by Denning, Christensen, and TNC scientist Rob McDonald found that the issue is not that simple. Examining more than sixty years of housing data beginning with the end of the war, they found that conservation did not substantially affect the housing supply. One explanation may be the tendency to protect land that is too hilly or wet for dense development. Another is that much of the land that would have been developed had it not been protected is near areas of high-end, single-family homes, so building there would add little to the overall supply of housing. Whatever the precise cause, conservation is just one of many factors that shape how cities grow, including the location of roads, jobs, and land that is dry most of the time. This is one trade-off city dwellers will not have to face. They do not always need to trade nature for housing, or economic growth and development. Livable cities in fact require not making that particularly bad deal.

In many cities, particularly older ones, the quality of the water is a major component of livability. Yet water from the tap is not the only concern; the water that falls as rain can be just as worrisome, and an even bigger concern if it does not fall at all.

How a City Can Be More Like a Forest

One defining characteristic of a city is that it is full of hard surfaces. Streets, sidewalks, buildings, and bridges shed water when it rains. All that water has to go somewhere, and it usually gets there fast. So for a city to function more like a forest or a field, step one is to slow down the water.

The issue is becoming more urgent. According to the Natural Resources Defense Council (NRDC), a leading New York–based policy, science, and advocacy organization, over the past fifty years the number of days with heavy precipitation events has increased more than 50 percent. If this trend continues, as climate models suggest it will, flash floods will pose an ever greater risk both to people and to the infrastructure built over decades—even centuries, in some places—to handle stormwater. On the flip side, droughts elsewhere will put drinking water supplies under greater stress and increase conflicts among agricultural, industrial, and residential water users.

The systems that deliver water are literally crumbling beneath our feet. In 2009, the American Society of Civil Engineers, the same group that gave the nation's levees a D- gave the same lousy grade to US wastewater facilities. For example, as of 2010, the budget for Washington, DC's water department, funded entirely from residents' water bills, was so low and the water mains and other infrastructure in such disrepair that replacing the entire aging system would take 300 years.

One estimate says that at least an annual investment of $180 billion is necessary for urban water infrastructure to deal with rapid population growth. If even 10 percent of this investment could be made in green infrastructure, that would represent a figure greater than the combined annual budgets of the major conservation NGOs, greatly enhancing the goals of conservation while providing necessary water to people.

The role of water is so important to green infrastructure that some experts speak of blue-green or turquoise infrastructure. The reason is clear: in natural conditions, rocks, soil, plants, and trees keep water where it falls, or slow water down on its way into wetlands, streams, and rivers. As a result, only 10 percent of rain becomes runoff, half gets absorbed, and the rest goes back into the air as water vapor. The páramo in Ecuador is a great example; a giant sponge that soaks up water where it falls. When the ground cannot absorb rain—whether because cattle have pounded it solid or because people have built office towers, apartment complexes, roads, and parking lots on it—nearly all the rain washes away, carrying pollution with it, and with increasing frequency overrunning stormwater systems.

NRDC says that even though just 3 percent of the United States is classified as urban, urban stormwater runoff pollutes water far beyond city limits. In the restrained bureaucratese of the EPA, an "impaired" river, lake, or estuary is so polluted that it cannot support current or desired uses. In these terms, stormwater runoff from cities is responsible, at a minimum, for 3 percent of all impaired river miles, 18 percent of impaired lake acres, and 32 percent of impaired square miles of estuaries.

These polluted waters harm fish and wildlife populations, kill native vegetation, contribute to stream bank erosion, foul drinking water supplies, and make recreational areas unsafe and unpleasant. Pollution makes people sick and those illnesses in turn become a further drag on the economy.

Landscape architects and engineers have devised a variety of techniques for making cities more porous or capturing rainwater where it falls. For example, rain barrels at the end of a gutter downspout catch water from rooftops, and rain gardens along sidewalks keep water out of sewer drains. Gravel driveways and parking lots, paving stones, and high-tech materials such as pervious concrete allow water to soak into the ground, significantly reducing runoff. Planting sod and other vegetation on rooftops not only slows the flow of water into storm sewers but also provides habitat for birds, cools and cleans the air, and by adding a layer of insulation saves on heating and cooling.

Making cities more like natural landscapes with green roofs and rain gardens may seem tiny solutions to massive problems. Indeed, one big hurdle in dealing with anything related to climate change is getting past the overwhelming feeling that anything less ambitious than continental-scale projects will fail to make any difference. Enough green infrastructure in enough places, however, will matter. In 2009, researchers from NRDC and the University of California, Santa Barbara found that building green infrastructure at new and redeveloped residential and commercial properties in Southern California and the San Francisco Bay area could increase local water supplies annually by up to 405,000 acre-feet—more than 130 billion gallons—by 2030. This represents roughly two-thirds of the volume of water used by the entire city of Los Angeles each year. Because more plentiful local water reduces the need for energy-intensive imported water, these savings translate into electricity savings of up to 1,225,500 megawatt-hours—decreasing the release of carbon dioxide into the atmosphere by as much as 535,500 metric tons per year. Perhaps most importantly, researchers say, these benefits would increase every year.

Green City, Clean Waters

Conservation of upstream forests that act as green infrastructure saves money for New York, Boston, and other cities. These efforts are largely invisible to most city residents, but green infrastructure right downtown, even more front and center than Staten Island's Bluebelt, will save money as well. In the United States, Philadelphia is a leader in this area.

Like many older cities, Philadelphia has one system of pipes and drains to handle both sewage and stormwater. The combined system serves three-quarters of the city's residents and underlies the oldest and most densely populated part of the city. On most days, the system works fine and transports water to a number of different wastewater treatment plants. In heavy rain or snow, however, the system cannot handle the volume, resulting in what engineers call a combined sewer overflow (CSO). Rather than suffer a catastrophic failure and widespread flooding, the city dumps millions of gallons of raw sewage into the Schuylkill and Delaware Rivers, which bracket the city to the west and east, as well as local creeks.

CSOs occur in dozens of other cities as well. Not only does this kind of dumping pour all manner of pollutants into the rivers and streams, the sheer volume of water scours riverbeds and strips vegetation off banks, leading to erosion and making it easier for nonnative species to become established. If this continues, urban waterways become smelly, chewed-up eyesores—just as Olmsted predicted for Boston's Muddy River.

In June 2011, the Pennsylvania Department of Environmental Protection approved Philadelphia's ambitious "Green City, Clean Waters" plan to reduce runoff over the next twenty-five years. The city plans to transform at least one-third of currently impervious surfaces into "greened acres," installing green roofs and rain gardens to capture the first inch of rainfall in any given storm. This could reduce runoff by 80 to 90 percent.

At the other end of the spectrum, cities that choose not to pursue environmentally friendly policies face considerable risks. The fact is, Philadelphia and other cities would have far less incentive to act if not for the hefty fines they face if they do not. The EPA has the authority, under the Clean Water Act, to levy fines or even bring the city to court on criminal charges, as it did in Pineville, Louisiana in 2011. City officials in Pineville knew that a pump was leaking hydraulic fluid but did nothing to repair it. When Pineville flooded in a hurricane in 2011, the fluid got into the nearby river and Bayou. The city itself—not the mayor, not the manager of the pumping station—pled guilty, received one year of probation, and had to, among other things, issue a formal apology.

Beyond the dark comedy of a city appearing in handcuffs before a judge and making a shamefaced apology, taking a city to court for environmental crimes is serious stuff. Philadelphia and others cities know the possible penalties and the Pineville story highlights the crucial role government must play in maintaining and protecting the benefits of nature. Even when economic benefits of nature are evident, regulation and enforcement are often required to bring various interests to the negotiating table.

Governments have generally been the builders of and investors in the infrastructure that society depends on. Accordingly, they should be the logical champions of natural infrastructure. Governments also provide regulation, the vital underpinning of all aspects of business and markets, and need to do the same with environmental assets as well. If companies can pollute the environment without charge or penalty, less enlightened companies will certainly pollute. The notion of natural capital and its important values should motivate cross sections of society to come together and advocate for well-designed environmental regulations.

Motivated by the threat of fines from the EPA under the Clean Water Act and by a desire to be as frugal as possible, Philadelphia now seeks to reduce the amount of sewage dumped into its rivers each year by nearly 8 billion gallons, with much of that reduction coming from green infrastructure. As of August 2011, Philadelphia's water department had completed or was in the process of designing a roster of improvements that reveals the project's gritty practicality: ninety-one stormwater tree trenches, thirty-three downspout planters, twenty-four rain gardens, twelve porous paving projects, nine stormwater bump-outs, nine swales, seven stormwater planters, six infiltration/storage trenches, three stormwater wetlands, and one stormwater basin. The water department also plans stream-corridor restoration projects to complement the green infrastructure efforts. Philadelphia considers its green infrastructure efforts part of a broader strategy to provide "more equitable access to healthy neighborhoods" for its residents and to make Philadelphia the "greenest city in America."

Philadelphia city officials estimate that an all-gray approach to reducing overflows would have cost billions more than the green infrastructure plan that will achieve comparable results. The green infrastructure plan includes at least $1.67 billion of investments in greened acres and $345 million in expanded sewage treatment plant capacity.

Over time, Philadelphia will almost certainly see a positive return on its green infrastructure investment. This return combines the full range of economic, social, and environmental benefits of the plan with all the costs avoided—air pollution emissions from gray-infrastructure manufacturing, installation, and runoff pumping and treatment. A 2009 analysis of Philadelphia's efforts focused on those "fringe benefits": additional recreational user days in the city's waterways, reduction of premature deaths and asthma attacks from air pollution and excessive heat, increased property values in greened neighborhoods, the ecosystem values of restored or created wetlands, poverty reduction from new local green jobs, and energy savings from the shading, cooling, and insulating effects of vegetation. The study found that over forty years the total value of the green infrastructure would be nearly $3 billion.

NOT EVERYONE HAS TAKEN PHILADELPHIA'S APPROACH. WASHINGTON, DC, for example, in 2011 began building a pipeline around the city to deal with its stormwater problems, at a cost of nearly $3 billion. The city also elected to spend a mere pittance, perhaps as little at $10 million, to investigate green infrastructure solutions.

Washington's decision reveals an important challenge for green infrastructure. The experiences of many other cities show that investing in nature works financially, environmentally, and socially, yet each year $250 billion in private capital is invested in gray infrastructure instead. This is partially because few government agencies or financial institutions make the effort to link the benefits of natural infrastructure with financing these projects. Changing this situation requires creative financing expertise—expertise too rarely used on environmental projects.

The private capital necessary to create green infrastructure that will have a far-reaching impact will not flow until savvy investors are satisfied on their own terms that it will be worthwhile. To that end, NRDC, TNC, and the investment firm EKO Asset Management Partners in 2011 created the Natural Infrastructure Innovative Financing Lab, whose goal is to shift a substantial portion of the billions in annual private capital investment in traditional infrastructure from gray to green solutions.

Green infrastructure works. Any city can become cleaner and healthier and can save money at the same time by investing in nature. This is about far more than stormwater. Hurricane Sandy almost immediately prompted city officials in New York City and elsewhere to begin thinking about how wetlands, reefs, and other green infrastructure can be part of the effort to prepare for the next big flood. And climate change practically guarantees there will be another.

Nearly 3 billion additional people will live in cities by 2050. More than four-fifths of all Americans currently live in cities of 50,000 people or more, and many of these cities, such as Houston or Jacksonville, Florida, sprawl across the landscape, gobbling up farms and fields with few zoning laws. What happens in cities will determine the pace and extent of environmental change, locally and globally. Such changes do not necessarily spell doom for nature and natural habitats.

Thinking about how cities will look several decades from now is essential to urban conservation. This seems counterintuitive, given the urgency of so many environmental challenges facing cities such as Philadelphia. We should not underestimate the value of efforts that offer real short-term payoffs, such as Philadelphia's initiative, which will make a real difference almost immediately.

Urban conservation is not without risk. The biggest risk may be transforming conservation into something people support only when they are its direct beneficiaries. If this were to happen, then conservation would become a far narrower and desiccated version of itself.

We have a moral imperative to place the interests of those creatures that are at the mercy of humankind above our own narrow self-interest. To abandon that imperative would be a great loss to conservation. Thus, urban conservation must broaden its support base not by preaching utilitarianism, but instead by demonstrating its widespread benefits. Cities offer the opportunity to demonstrate the value of nature writ large.

9

The Business Case for Nature

If working in cities seems foreign to many environmentalists, working with global corporations may seem even more so. People sometimes ask me why environmental organizations should collaborate with corporations such as The Dow Chemical Company, Shell Oil, or mining giant Rio Tinto. These companies have huge environmental footprints—why work with them? My response is always the same: shouldn't we try? The bigger the company's footprint, the bigger the opportunity for the company to reduce its impact on the environment by changing its behavior.

One of my scientists likens global corporations to keystone species. Keystone species have a disproportionately large effect on their ecosystems—analogous to a keystone in an arch. A good example is sea otters in the northeastern Pacific. Sea otters have enormous appetites and consume prodigious quantities of shellfish. Fishermen often view otters suspiciously, fearing the otters compete with them for the same abalone, clams, and crabs. However, when people hunt otters and their populations decline, their absence cascades throughout the ecosystem. Sea urchins—another species otters love to eat—soar in number. Sea urchins eat kelp, and without otters around to keep the urchin population in check, urchins tend to eat kelp beds absolutely bare. Kelp in turn is critical habitat for fish, shellfish, and other sea creatures. So, while fishermen might expect to benefit by eliminating a potential competitor, fewer otters actually means fewer shellfish, too.

By the same logic, certain companies serve as corporate analogs to such keystone species. Timber companies, for example, manage huge amounts of land, and their actions can dramatically transform entire landscapes. Remove these companies, or change how they work, and the results can be dramatic. Ecologists who manage fisheries or grasslands or forests make sure they understand the role of keystone species like sea otters and build management plans around them. Likewise, conservation organizations should be able to achieve important goals by working with public corporations such as Plum Creek Timber or Dow or BP, private companies like agribusiness giant Cargill and India's Tata, and state-owned enterprises from China to Brazil.

In many of the places conservationists want to protect, the underlying threat is human demand for food, energy, space, and water. Companies are the agents for this demand. Customer demand pushes companies to build more roads and other infrastructure, expand agricultural lands, and extract more minerals, oil, and natural gas. Simply ignoring these trends would only put the planet in greater peril. Likewise, just saying no to these companies and their customers is unlikely to be a successful strategy.

But what if instead of saying no, environmentalists ask "how"? How might these companies change their practices to achieve better environmental and business outcomes? How might government create incentives for companies to invest in and protect nature rather than degrade it? Asking *how* can change the way people think in important ways and deserves to be thoroughly explored.

Of course, some CEOs may superficially support environmental causes simply to achieve good PR—a practice called "greenwashing." But in today's ever more transparent world, that should be easy to avoid. Watchdog organizations are helpful, too: their criticism keeps everyone honest.

Even if some greenwashing continues, most business leaders increasingly understand that the main drivers of environmental action go far deeper than good PR, regulatory compliance, or even a desire to "do the right thing." Sustainability is moving from a fringe concern to a core focus of business decision-making. Conservation helps companies manage risks to their supply chains, keep costs down, identify new market opportunities, and protect essential business assets. Likewise, employees and customers today strongly prefer companies whose values align with theirs. Smart environmental strategies are an essential way to achieve such alignment.

The breakthrough insight is when companies recognize that the services they rely on from nature but heretofore took for granted and got for free, such as clean water and flood protection, will be neither guaranteed nor free in the coming years.

For example, in 2011 Dow's CEO, Andrew N. Liveris, challenged TNC to help the company apply the concept of natural capital to his company's business decisions and operations. He and his team wanted to answer the following questions, again focused on *how*: How do Dow's operations both affect and depend on nature's services? How would the natural assets that generate such services be accounted for on the company's balance sheet? How vulnerable are those services, and what might Dow do about those vulnerabilities— either on their own or by joining with other stakeholders to influence natural resource policy? How do such services also benefit the community? Would Dow's engagement in these issues have a ripple effect on other companies? The project that will attempt to answer these questions, now well underway and described later in this chapter, is a promising example of how the concept of natural capital can help change the way business is done.

Collaboration does not mean that companies should expect a free pass from environmentalists. Even companies leading the way on sustainability still have a long way to go. Some honest attempts between environmentalists and companies to collaborate will no doubt prove disappointing. When that happens we should tell that story as well.

Helping companies that have big footprints and enormous influence in the market to make better decisions and understand the value of nature has the potential to create real conservation gains. The proof that this approach works is not yet in, but it is still early. The time to experiment, and to be scrupulous in assessing the results, is now.

Staking Your Career on a Wetland

In 1996, regulatory pressure at a chemical plant in Seadrift, Texas dictated a need to increase the facility's water treatment capacity. Engineers usually design such operations conventionally. For engineers the first, second, and third options all generally involve pouring large amounts of concrete. So in Seadrift, the company assumed that it would build a water treatment plant, at a cost of about $40 million.

One engineer at Seadrift had other ideas. Perhaps he knew how New York had saved millions on water treatment; perhaps he had kept up with the academic literature on green infrastructure; perhaps he was simply clever. Whatever the reason, something prompted this engineer to make a bold move. He staked his career on an unconventional solution: constructing a wetland.

Rather than pour the concrete, the company built a wetland next to the manufacturing plant. The engineer's colleagues likely thought him nuts at first. But instead of spending $40 million on a conventional treatment system, the company spent $1.4 million on an unconventional one. Now the wetland treats 5 million gallons of water per day, meets all regulatory standards, and—a bonus for nature—provides habitat for a variety of wildlife.

The basic principles at work in Seadrift are familiar: consider the value of both green and gray infrastructure and invest appropriately. But there are two big differences here. The first is the company involved. This was no ordinary chemical manufacturer: the company that owns the Seadrift plant is Dow, the second largest chemical manufacturer in the world, operating in more than 160 countries with $60 billion in sales in 2011.

The second difference is that plant management did not base the project decision on a law or regulation; or out of a desire to avoid a particular risk, such as a flood; or because the company depended on a particular resource, such as water; or because the company wanted good PR. Simply put, the engineer's decision was just good business. He weighed the options, examined the pluses and minuses, and decided to invest in nature.

The consequences of that decision are far from simple. Dow's products, ubiquitous but largely unseen by consumers, are ingredients in everything from building materials to pet food. Dow's facilities consume vast quantities of water, so it owns large amounts of land along rivers and on coasts. The company makes dozens of products that would be toxic or otherwise harmful to people, the environment, or both if accidentally spilled or released.

In short, Dow has an enormous environmental footprint. It also has enormous market share and a global brand. Those factors combine to make Dow a promising partner for conservation. Companies pay attention to one another, particularly their competitors within industrial sectors. If a large and globally recognized company like Dow changes its environmental behavior and improves its business as a result, other companies are likely to follow Dow's lead.

Corporations benefit when they understand their dependence on nature. Many forward-thinking companies, among them 3M, DuPont,

General Mills, Caterpillar, and Dow, already know this. The depth of the change in perspective this entails should not be underestimated; it is fundamental. For generations, economists assumed that manufacturers could run down natural capital as much as they wanted, so long as the economy overall created enough man-made capital to replace it. When the scale of economic activity remained small in comparison to the scale of the planet itself, this may have been a workable assumption — but not anymore.

As companies begin to better understand this dynamic, they are seeing opportunities for new products and markets. A clearer vision of the importance of nature to businesses also points to ways to decrease environmental, legal, and social risks. But most importantly, the real payoff comes when corporations include the value of nature in all of their business decisions. Then, billions of dollars in economic activity can become an engine for the conservation of nature rather than its destruction.

Responsible Corporations

Suspicion of global corporations runs deep in the environmental community. Many of these companies have a long history of disregard for public and environmental health. For some environmentalists, that history is definitive: once a polluter, always a polluter.

A fuller telling of the story is less clear-cut, but one milestone was painfully obvious. In 1989, the *Exxon Valdez* ran aground in Alaska's Prince William Sound, spilling at least 11 million gallons of oil. Six months after the spill, a group of investors, public pension trustees, nongovernmental environmental organizations, foundations, public interest organizations, and labor unions founded the Coalition for Environmentally Responsible Economies (CERES). Its first task was to draft a set of principles for corporate environmental conduct, including biosphere protection, sustainable use of resources, and environmental restoration. This marked the first broad, public effort to get corporations to commit to reporting on and reducing their environmental impacts.

One businessman in particular saw an opportunity for real change. In 1990, Swiss industrialist Stephan Schmidheiny founded the Business Council for Sustainable Development. Preparations for the first world environment summit, to be held in Rio de Janeiro in June 1992, were already underway. Intended to ensure that world leaders at Rio heard from the business community, the council included the CEOs of forty-eight major corporations, including Royal Dutch Shell, Chevron, DuPont, and Dow.

Negotiations for the treaties that governments expected to sign at the Earth Summit, as it was called (the formal name was the United Nations Conference on Environment and Development), involved thousands of people from government agencies, nongovernmental organizations, academia, and business. The prospect of national governments making economically significant, binding commitments on climate change, biodiversity conservation, and desertification got the attention of business leaders. Many of the companies that signed on to the Council or various spinoffs likely did so for the PR benefits of being seen as green. Without a doubt, some businesses resisted making hard changes in their operations and tried to make do with better rhetoric. In the mid-1990s, not even the most committed among them fully understood the value of nature to their business as a whole. Some companies sought to avoid regulation; others began to value nature in specific contexts, as Coke now values water.

The CERES Principles, the Business Council for Sustainable Development, and the Earth Summit accelerated new thinking about the relationship between business and the environment. Attitudes inside and outside companies such as Dow, DuPont, and SC Johnson began to shift.

The gospel spread, and by the late 1990s, more companies saw the importance of reducing the impact of business on the environment.

Enormous momentum began to build behind what had come to be called Corporate Social Responsibility. In an early effort, EDF teamed up with McDonald's in 1990 to reduce the company's solid waste—a successful campaign that led to the demise of the polystyrene clamshell container, and one reason why nearly all fast-food restaurants now wrap their sandwiches in paper, significantly increasing the use of recycled materials.

Public demand for greater transparency on how company actions affect the environment grew so fast that companies and NGOs produced reams of reports. Investors increasingly scour such reports for clues about the future of the companies and the risks they may face from shortages of necessary resources and materials, natural disasters, and the like.

A Recovering Plunderer

The explosion of these sustainability reports provided institutional credibility for companies, and helped companies, investors, regulators, and public watchdogs to assess progress toward a more sustainable economy. Yet these efforts remained largely invisible to the general public. To the limited extent that they penetrated the media, they consisted of lists of corporate logos on a press release or a webpage.

It fell, almost by accident, to a mild-mannered carpet executive from Georgia to give substance to corporate promises about changing their environmental ways. The most visible and visionary leader of the business community's new focus was Ray Anderson, the CEO of Interface, the world's largest manufacturer of carpet tile.

In 1994, at age sixty, Anderson had run his company for more than two decades. He had, by his own admission, considered the environment only when government regulations forced him to do so. That same year he read *The Ecology of Commerce*, written by the business leader Paul Hawken. Hawken decried the paltry environmental efforts of most businesses, including his own firm, the gardening company

Smith & Hawken. Ecosystems were in decline, wrote Hawken, while a minority of people reaped huge benefits from nature:

> Since business in its myriad forms is primarily responsible for this plunder, it is appropriate that a growing number of companies ask themselves, how do we conduct business honorably in the latter days of industrialism and the beginning of an ecological age?

Anderson described the experience of reading Hawken's book as being hit with a "spear in the chest." He wept. The book did not simply castigate business and industry for their environmental misdeeds, but pointed out that those same companies could be a powerful force for positive change. From that moment on, Anderson began to describe himself as a "recovering plunderer" and set out to change his company—and indeed all companies.

Interface set a bold goal: zero waste, zero impact, and zero footprint by 2020. What the company called "Mission Zero," said Anderson, meant "eventually operating our petroleum-intensive company in such a way as to take from the earth only what can be renewed by the earth naturally and rapidly, not another fresh drop of oil, and to do no harm to the biosphere. Take nothing. Do no harm."

That kind of change means reimagining industrial processes from the beginning. It is, in the words of architect and designer William McDonough and the chemist Michael Braungart, about "remaking the way we make things." That suggests a revolution in business and economics—a revolution that we are closer to now than almost anyone could have imagined even a decade ago.

One element of Anderson's seven-point model of sustainability for Interface includes focusing on "the services their products provide, in lieu of the products themselves." Part of that means developing a carpet the company could collect from customers when it was worn out and use as the raw material for a new carpet. This is not just recycling, which usually means creating a lesser-quality product, like newsprint made from new printer paper, but a closed loop in which no additional inputs are needed.

Reimagining a carpet company as providing a service—covering your floor—instead of a product that would eventually end up in a landfill seemed a leap a decade ago, but others have followed suit. For many modern companies, material goods are no longer seen as ends in themselves; instead, companies make money by helping customers achieve their goals while using less product. The idea of separating a company's revenue from its material input is part of a larger effort to create a "circular" economy: an industrial system that reuses materials, eliminates waste, and reduces the use of toxic chemicals.

Like Interface, Xerox has an aggressive program to help customers buy less of its products, in this case paper and copying machines. Writer and consultant Andrew Winston calls this way of doing business "the big heresy." On its surface, this strategy seems counterintuitive. Yet Xerox knows that one way or another, its customers will become more efficient and will use fewer resources.

Another measure of companies' growing recognition of resource and other environmental challenges is the increasing number of chief sustainability officers. While in the past these roles sometimes had nice-sounding titles with little real influence in the company, that is no longer the case. Chief sustainability officers at companies like Wal-Mart, Unilever, and Coke work closely with their CEOs and are responsible for truly game-changing corporate initiatives. Chief sustainability officers are now also more likely to come to the job with real commercial credibility at the company. As CEO of Goldman Sachs, Henry M. Paulson chose me to head the firm's environmental efforts because I had run successful business ventures at the bank, not because I had an environmental track record. At Coke, Muhtar Kent chose Beatrice Perez to take the job after high-profile success as the company's chief marketing officer. The whole concept of corporate sustainability is going mainstream. A 2009 *Harvard Business Review* article touted sustainability as a driver of innovation in terms that would have been unheard of in business circles not long ago:

> [T]he current economic system has placed enormous pressure on the planet while catering to the needs of only about a quarter of the people on it, but over the next decade twice that number will become consumers and producers. Traditional approaches to business will collapse, and companies will need to develop innovative solutions.

This language comes not from fringe environmentalism, but instead from the measured voice of the business establishment. The verdict is clear: sustainability and profitability go together.

Some skeptics have long claimed that adopting social and environmental policies hurts business results, but many studies conclude the opposite. One study looked at companies over an eighteen-year period and found that the companies with strong policies on sustainability dramatically outperformed those without, whether performance was measured in terms of stock prices or profitability. The authors of the study—Robert G. Eccles and George Serafeim of Harvard Business School, and Ioannis Ioannou of London Business School—wrote:

> Failure to have a culture of sustainability is quickly becoming a source of competitive disadvantage. The argument about sustainability is over. It is the key to creating value for shareholders and all other stakeholders over the long term, thus ensuring the sustainability of the company itself.

The Millennium Assessment

Much of the foundation for this new thinking about corporate sustainability was established in 2005 with the release of the groundbreaking

Millennium Ecosystem Assessment. It was highly influential, for example, at Goldman Sachs when I worked on the firm's initial environmental forays. The study provided solid evidence to back our
hypothesis that nature was an essential business asset. Walt Reid,
the director of the study, was a key advisor to Goldman Sachs as we
formulated our initial environmental plans.

The Millennium Ecosystem Assessment was an ambitious global
effort to assess degradations to the world's ecosystems and the conse-
quent impact on human well-being. It was the first comprehensive
effort to apply economic thinking to the value of biodiversity and the
various services nature provides.

The principal result of the study was disturbing: people are degrading or using up nearly two-thirds of natural capital worldwide.
That includes the green infrastructure that provides basic necessities
such as fresh water, arable soil, productive fisheries, clean air and water, as well as the regulation of regional and local climate, natural
hazards, and pests.

The Millennium Assessment had a broad influence on governments and businesses and spawned numerous follow-up studies. One
study in particular took the ideas of the Millennium Assessment and
tried to make them relevant for how companies value nature. The
Economics of Ecosystems and Biodiversity (TEEB) study, led by the
United Nations Environment Program, got its start in 2007 when environment ministers from the governments of the world's leading and
emerging economies agreed to initiate the process of analyzing the
benefits and costs of biological diversity and its conservation.

TEEB provides both a theoretical and an empirical framework for
valuing these benefits and costs. The study also includes an economic
analysis of factors affecting ecosystems and biological diversity—an important step given new evidence about environmental degradation and
its potential impact on human welfare. The TEEB Report strongly endorsed the idea of making conservation a key business priority.

The analysis of TEEB builds on the Millennium Assessment. Together they show how individuals, businesses, and governments can recognize the values of nature, make shrewd investments in nature, and understand when it is or is not appropriate to capture those values for human benefit. Both efforts offer tools for rethinking economic assumptions that allow people to overlook—sometimes willfully, but more often out of necessity or ignorance—our dependence on nature.

Dow's Effort to Value Nature

The evolution of Dow's approach to these issues shows how far the corporate world has come. The company's first set of ten-year environmental goals in 1995, while admirable in many ways, mostly looked inward and focused on improving the company's environmental, safety, and health performance. No real surprise there. This was an incremental step, not a revolutionary leap of the kind Ray Anderson had made.

With its next set of the ten-year goals in 2005, Dow began to look beyond its walls to see how it could contribute to solving bigger problems than its own safety and environmental record. In 2010, halfway through its latest ten-year goals, Andrew Liveris asked Neil Hawkins, who began at the company as an engineer and rose to become vice president of its sustainability efforts, to review the goals and identify the biggest gaps. Hawkins—showing how a bold corporate sustainability officer can make big changes—concluded that the company, which had an admirable conservation ethic around its facilities, had not taken many steps beyond its own concerns to give tangible form to its stated value of protecting the planet.

That brought Hawkins and Dow to a crucial moment. How would the company move forward and embed environmental values into changing the way it made decisions? Scientific evidence on the value of nature to a company such as Dow may be clear and the economic arguments compelling. However, that evidence and those arguments will not carry the day until they serve as the basis for useful business tools, strategies, and policies. That is the challenge for Dow, for other corporations, and for the conservation community.

Whither the Brazos?

Dow Chemical was born in Michigan and still keeps its corporate headquarters there. The heart of its global operations, however, lies in Texas, and the success of those operations depend to a considerable degree on a single resource: the Brazos River.

The Brazos River rises in north-central Texas, about 200 miles northwest of Dallas. From there, it flows north toward Oklahoma before turning back to the Gulf of Mexico. More than 800 miles long, the Brazos is the longest river in Texas. It may also be the most endangered.

People have worried about the fate of the Brazos River since the 1950s, when the state and the Corps of Engineers began planning construction of a series of nine dams on the river over the next thirty years. In 1957, author John Graves canoed a stretch of the Brazos and wrote his elegiac *Goodbye to a River*, fearing the dams would transform the river beyond recognition.

Although only one dam was built, concerns over the river have only deepened. The city of Houston continues to grow and demands ever-increasing amounts of water from the Brazos. Other cities use its water as well. Farms for cotton and rice—water-intensive crops, propped up by heavy subsidies—and various industrial facilities also have claims on the river. Ironically, one of the more senior water rights holders happens to be the one farthest from the river's source. Just where the Brazos enters the Gulf, near the city of Freeport, is Dow's oldest site, one of the largest chemical facilities in the world.

Dow began building its Freeport complex in 1940. The site was perfect: right on the river, near a fine harbor, with natural gas reserves and salt domes nearby. Freeport is now the company's largest manufacturing facility, with more than sixty-five production plants on more than 7,000 acres and employing some 8,000 people. Freeport accounts for more than one-fifth of Dow's global production.

As the Freeport site grew, so did its appetite for freshwater—75,000 gallons per minute. Dow purchased senior rights to water from the Brazos, but that claim will mean little if no water remains in the river by time it gets to Freeport. That is no idle fear: the Brazos nearly ran dry during the horrific Texas drought of 2010–11. Climate change may bring even worse droughts in the years ahead, along with increasingly severe storms in the Gulf of Mexico.

Dow now sees that it has to address the larger landscape context for Freeport and indeed all its operations. Water is vital to Freeport and Freeport is vital to the company, so obviously the future of the Brazos is a major concern. However, addressing that problem is not enough: the company wants to know how to account for the value of that water, and indeed all of nature.

DOW NEEDS TO LOOK NO FURTHER THAN ITS OWN HISTORY FOR A model of how accounting for nature might work. Several decades ago, Dow made worker safety a top corporate priority, something every employee was aware of every day, through training programs and constant reinforcement from middle managers up to top executives. In this the company might have been a bit too successful; the joke in Midland, Michigan, where Dow is headquartered, is that you can tell which houses are owned by Dow employees because they are the folks mowing their lawns wearing earplugs and safety glasses. The focus on safety has become so pervasive that even visitors to Dow facilities quickly become uncomfortable using the stairs without holding onto a handrail.

One can imagine that protecting nature will become as deeply embedded in the corporate culture, and that will be a major milestone. In 2011, Dow became the first Fortune 50 company to try to provide a broad-based program to get there, through a five-year collaboration with

TNC. The collaboration is investigating linkages between business operations and the environment, with the goal of making sure that Dow can value nature and its services in everything the company does. With the help of conservation scientists and economists, Dow seeks to incorporate the value of nature into its company-wide goals, strategies, and objectives, and to develop tools so that other companies can do the same.

In short, the idea is to make what the plant managers in Seadrift did a regular part of business. Companies such as Dow are working to take heroism out of the process and to make explicitly considering the environment a routine part of how they decide where to build new facilities and manage land and water, and how these decisions affect other communities, both human and natural.

Groups like TNC do not seek to be consulting firms to all of the corporate world, but they do seek to demonstrate the possibilities that arise when leading companies ambitiously pursue environmental goals. So whether it is Dow incorporating the value of nature in specific business decisions, or Coke investing in and protecting specific watersheds, or Rio Tinto offsetting the impact of mines by creating protected areas, conservation and business together can show a new and better way to move forward.

The testable hypothesis is that, once businesses can quantify a broad range of services they depend on from nature, they will see a bottom-line payoff from investing in the natural assets that generate those services. If proven right, a straightforward business calculation will cause them to change their practices to favor nature. Those changes can ripple across entire industries. This is new. Some 400 of the Fortune 500 companies issue sustainability reports, but none specifically address nature's services in the language of a chief financial officer. Many companies have made commitments to reduce or even mitigate and offset their impacts on nature—a positive development to be sure—but no company has figured out how to comprehensively incorporate nature in its routine business decisions.

Building the value of nature into business requires strategic and cultural changes across every company. This transformation ranges from developing new business and sustainability goals, to identifying the types of decisions that should include evaluating nature, to specifying the factors that CFOs and other senior executives should consider when evaluating new sites, site changes, and new products and services. Companies must move from asking the question of why nature matters to business to more practical questions of how they need to change their business goals and processes.

Freeport

The initial focus of the collaboration between Dow and TNC is on the Freeport facility. Here the company and conservation scientists can review Dow's core business functions and work within the conditions of a site with longstanding methods and operations. The first time that Dow's engineers sat down with the ecologists and other experts they found themselves talking past each other. Working through that will be an ongoing process over the five years of the collaboration. There will also be other pilots, including one in Brazil. The idea is to study a variety of business models, supply chains, and other aspects of Dow's business to ensure a comprehensive analysis.

The biggest challenge will be putting dollar values on the goods and services Dow gets from nature. As a start, Dow is looking at three aspects of natural capital in Freeport: the Brazos River, coastal marshes and wetlands, and an area of forest known as the Columbia Bottomlands.

In the Brazos River, on one level, the math is easy enough: demand for water is going up and supply is going down. Dow would lose millions if it has to shut down the Freeport plants because of a lack of water. Such tidy equations hide a great deal of complexity. For example, what exactly is driving the anticipated drop in water supply? Data and climate models to date are not promising. Human demand for water is forecast to continue growing, while climate change may bring a greater likelihood of both drought and catastrophic storms and floods.

Water quantity is also not the sole concern. Water quality, particularly salinity, is another major issue for Dow. Saltwater and manufacturing equipment do not mix. Saltwater needs to be treated before it can be used, and such treatment increases costs. During periods of drought and low river flow, saltwater from the Gulf of Mexico migrates as far as forty-two miles up the Brazos River. Since Dow's major water intake is in the Harris Reservoir at mile forty-four, the location of the "salt wedge" is getting uncomfortably close.

As Dow understands the value of water to its business, this understanding can guide it on how much to invest in securing future supplies. Not long ago, a company like Dow might have addressed this challenge with brute force: bring in the engineers and build another pipeline, another reservoir, another dam. But today the company understands the need to think big, to see water as more than simply an input to production, and to situate its operations in the context of the broader landscape.

Scientists working with Dow have developed daily forecasts of how river flow in the Brazos will change under various climate-change scenarios. That is particularly important now. The severe drought in Texas sent a clear message and led to the development of an innovative, statewide fifty-year water plan. Few other states have been as aggressive in coordinating water use and conservation across broad regions. That process may help Dow and other users of the Brazos River determine where it is possible to increase the water supply in the basin. In the same way as Southern California cities pay farmers to conserve water, so a company like Dow may find the most cost-effective approach may be to work with upriver farmers or communities to change how they use water. Alternatively, the company may instead decide that the best investment is in green infrastructure—a marsh, for example. The methods developed here could be applied in other river basins to analyze water shortages in the face of climate change and increasing demand.

The Brazos situation raises an even broader issue. In one sense, water is the easiest resource to address because its benefits to a private company are so clear. It should be easy to persuade self-interested companies to invest in water conservation. However, water represents just one narrow slice of the values of nature. TNC and Dow are also trying to assess the full range of benefits that nature provides to the public. Some of these other values may not be as clear to a company as water or timber, but they can affect a company's position in indirect ways, by shaping the company's reputation and its relationship with local communities, and even its effects on staff members who live in the region. All these values of nature matter. The challenge now is to provide data and tools that companies can use as factors in decision-making alongside more traditional business costs and benefits.

Forests, Marshes, and Business

The seemingly inexorable growth of Houston and its suburbs means more than just a risk to the Brazos River. Residents depend heavily on their cars to get around. Add to that all the coal-fired power plants and heavy industry in and around the city and you have a recipe for significant air pollution concerns. No surprise that Houston has consistently exceeded the levels of pollution deemed acceptable by the Clean Air Act since 1979.

Ozone at ground level causes respiratory problems and damages trees and other vegetation (and miles up in the atmosphere it blocks ultraviolet radiation, but that's another story). For years, the EPA worked with the state government to reduce ozone levels in the eight counties around Houston, including Brazoria County, which includes Freeport. But in 2012, after more than thirty years of trying, the region still exceeds legal limits for ozone.

Court battles and regulatory wrangling had run their course, so the EPA finally threatened to start imposing huge fines on major industries, including Dow. That action reemphasizes that the question of how to value nature is not just for companies and conservation organizations. Government must play a role by crafting policies that offer incentives for Dow and other companies to make a proper accounting, and impose penalties if they do otherwise.

One way out of this mess may be to plant more trees. Freeport was once in the middle of a thousand square miles of floodplain forest called the Columbia Bottomlands. Nearly 75 percent of the forest has been lost to development, with the biggest remaining pieces protected in two national wildlife refuges—San Bernard just west of the city, and Brazoria bordering it to the east.

Replanting the green ash, sugarberry, elms, and other trees that made up the Columbia Bottomlands would have obvious conservation benefits. The forests provide critical habitat for migratory birds and many other species. From a business perspective, the more important benefits would be the amount of pollution the trees remove from the air.

The EPA lists tree planting as one step states can take to reduce ozone. But no one has tried it yet so many questions remain unanswered. For Dow, the central unknown factor is if the benefits of tree planting can be measured in dollars. If large-scale tree planting has a measurable effect on air quality in the region, then it could reduce the amount Dow needs to pay to meet environmental obligations. Conservationists, on the other hand, want to know what other benefits those trees might provide in terms of habitat, slowing climate change by absorbing carbon, and the like.

As scientists and economists parse the details, the results may demonstrate that tree planting can be an effective new business strategy. Making this business case for conservation would in turn generate more interest among other businesses in Texas and beyond. A successful emissions mitigation project by Dow could set the stage for other companies to do the same, leading to substantially improved air quality in the area. If reforestation costs less than or as much as typical engineering options, Dow and others are likely to incorporate reforestation into their strategies. The results and methodology will be made freely available, allowing other states and companies to consider reforestation an essential part of doing business.

THE TWO WILDLIFE REFUGES THAT BRACKET DOW'S FREEPORT FACILITY contain more than just the last remaining pieces of the Columbia Bottomland forest. Much of the refuges consist of marshes that extend into the Gulf, providing habitat for birds and nurseries for Gulf fish and shrimp. These marshes are also important to reducing the damage from storm-driven waves and flooding. Considering how frequently hurricanes and tropical storms hit Texas—ten direct hits since 2000—and how vulnerable it is to sea-level rise, these marshes are obviously of no small value to Dow.

Yet until now, the company has not considered the role that an intact, healthy marsh plays in reducing the potential damage from storms, focusing instead on typical man-made solutions such as levees and floodwalls. In order to test the hypothesis that preserving or restoring these coastal habitats makes good business sense and benefits conservation, Dow and TNC are developing methods to evaluate green infrastructure solutions alongside gray ones in their coastal natural hazard mitigation planning.

Measuring the value of the marshes in dollars will be as challenging as measuring the value of forests for pollution control. Dow typically did not consider the positive contribution of marshes as dynamic, living parts of the environment. Worse yet, standard flood insurance models treat marshland no differently than a parking lot.

The people responsible for making decisions about things like whether or not to build a particular levee in front of a particular plant to withstand a particular storm need to be as comfortable with noisy data about the performance and reliability of the marsh as they now are with the clean spreadsheets and project plans filled with labor and materials and insurance. If they do not reach this level of comfort, they risk building expensive facilities when nature could do the job as well or better, or getting the design of levee systems wrong because they fail to understand how healthy coastal habitats help levees do their job.

DOW'S STRATEGY IS NOT RISK FREE FROM A CONSERVATION PERSPECTIVE. After looking at the costs and benefits of all options and taking account of the values of nature, the company may decide that a standard engineering solution fits their bottom line best. There are no guarantees. But even if several decisions go against conservation interests, building nature into all of Dow's decisions across all of its facilities is almost certainly an important step in the right direction.

Some environmentalists are unwilling to work with corporations like Dow on projects like this. But that can be a good thing, too. Some of these organizations—take Greenpeace or Rainforest Action Network, for example—play the crucial role of environmental watchdogs. The watchdogs keep a close eye on collaborations like the one between TNC and Dow in order to ensure that they genuinely pursue positive results. If projects go awry, if transparency is lacking, or if environmental organizations are naive or make mistakes, they indeed need to be called out. This kind of criticism ultimately leads to progress; better strategies, savvier NGOs, more successful approaches to protect nature. In the broad ecosystem that makes up the environmental movement, there is a constructive role for a variety of organizational strategies.

For example, in 2009, Greenpeace published a report with the rather inflammatory title *Carbon Scam*. The report was critical of a forest carbon project in Bolivia that had been led by TNC with the support of General Motors and American Electric Power. TNC was proud of the environmental accomplishments of the deal—including the fact it represented the first time that an independent third party had identified the carbon benefits of protecting a forest. Greenpeace, however, raised some tough questions about whether the project fulfilled its commitments to the local people who depended on the forest for their livelihoods. What resulted from Greenpeace's report, once everyone got past the initial mistrust, was constructive thinking about how to make such projects work even better in future.

This kind of dialogue between environmental organizations—even when it leads to tough criticism—is an essential part of the effort to scale up environmental progress. But it should not discourage attempts to try new partnerships or innovative strategies. Environmentalists should take full advantage of the opportunity that partnerships with forward-thinking companies provide.

Imagine a future in which global corporations routinely neglect the importance of nature to their enterprise—in which they fail to see that their investments will be undermined if certain thresholds are crossed and ecosystems are so injured that degraded water, depleted soils, and extreme weather create a world that is hostile to business productivity. No one concerned with the natural world should allow that to happen.

Conclusion

THE VALUE OF NATURE CAN BE FOUND IN ALL SORTS OF LANDSCAPES
and in all sorts of people. Consider, for example, a remarkable young
man named Joshua Carrera.

Joshua Carrera hit bottom in 2005, when he was fifteen-years-old.
He was living in Brooklyn with his mother and sister, but his mother
had lost her job because of an injury. Public assistance ran out, and
they were evicted from their apartment. The family ended up in a
homeless shelter in the Bushwick section of Brooklyn.

Joshua did not have any particular interest in environmental issues,
but he enrolled in the High School for Environmental Studies, in Manhattan, because it got him out of Brooklyn and had good science
courses. The school, founded in 1992 and the first environmentally
themed high school in the country, offered something else even more
enticing: a chance to get out of New York altogether in the summer
through an internship program with TNC called LEAF—Leaders in
Environmental Action for the Future.

The first time Joshua applied to the program, he did not get one of the few slots available—another summer in the shelter. He got in the next year, and off he went to Vermont. He spent the summer pulling invasive weeds such as buckthorn and Japanese barberry from nature preserves near Lake Champlain. Toiling in the woods of a hot and humid Vermont summer, working in close contact with conservation scientists studying the preserves, Joshua got close to nature for the first time. He was living on his own for the first time, too, in a dorm at Green Mountain College in Poultney. By summer's end he had also visited the University of Vermont in Burlington, and decided he wanted to go there once he graduated from high school.

Joshua was accepted to the University where he majored in environmental studies and minored in wildlife biology. He soon began even more far-flung conservation efforts. He volunteered on a preserve in Montana, and by summer 2010 was working in the páramo in Ecuador, helping a local NGO track margay, an Andean species of wild cat. Although Joshua's mother was born in Ecuador, he'd had little connection to his roots there, and the country's remarkable natural diversity, including the Galápagos Islands. Now, he says, the Galápagos is where he belongs.

Getting kids out of the city and into nature, giving them hands-on experience in the work that scientists do, produces more science students than any other known intervention. This is crucial, for society faces twin challenges: the global economy increasingly depends on sophisticated technologies, and the need for even more dramatic innovation will only grow over the coming decades. We will see an ever-greater demand for workers trained in science, math, and engineering. At the same time, environmental degradation threatens the very foundation of modern, technologically advanced economies. Thus, the next generation will need to be both adept at technology and environmentally aware.

As Joshua shows, both of those issues can be addressed in a straightforward way: take people, especially young people, out of the city and give them an opportunity to connect with nature. Practical experience and modern science both confirm that these experiences can be transformative.

The national average for college students choosing life sciences as their major is 6 percent and 82 percent of these students are white. Among the 500-plus LEAF program graduates, the average is 34 percent and 80 percent are not white. Nationwide, about 70 percent of high-school graduates go straight to college; among LEAF alumni, more than 96 percent go straight to college. Not all of these results can be ascribed directly to nature, but it is also no coincidence: nature makes a big difference. Getting kids outdoors and engaged with nature produces the science students our society needs.

Biophilia

The values of nature that Joshua Carrera absorbed far from Bushwick can also be found in more mundane places as well — in real estate listings, for example.

As anyone who has tried to rent an apartment in Manhattan can tell you, the closer you get to Central Park, the higher the prices. Every realtor and every resident knows this pattern, which holds outside cities as well: houses with views of streams or forests sell for more than those without, and those near protected areas of one sort or another get the same premium as those on Central Park West and Fifth Avenue, some of the most expensive real estate in the world.

The effect goes well beyond real-estate prices. People in hospital rooms with views of trees recuperate more quickly than those whose windows look onto brick walls, and infirmaries dating to the Middle Ages had restorative gardens and natural areas. So pervasive a phenomenon must have deep roots in our cultures and in ourselves. But what, exactly, are those roots? The answer to that question lies in a fuller understanding of the value of nature.

Part of the explanation may lie in our biology. In 1984, E. O. Wilson coined the term *biophilia* to describe our innate and emotional connection to other living things. Human beings spent millennia living in forests and savannas, at least 100,000 generations of evolution during which each individual's life was spent almost entirely in nature — sensitive to, responding to, and stimulated by the surprises and sensory input that only nature can provide. Only now do most people on earth live in cities. Humanity cannot simply leave that evolutionary history behind and assume it will seamlessly adapt to environments that in planetary terms arrived only moments ago.

In that evolutionary sense, at least, cities are unnatural. The understanding that people thrive when connected to nature dates at least back to the Romans, who scattered deer parks throughout their empire, and perhaps even earlier. The notion that humans must play the role of managers or, less prosaically, gardeners of the planet finds echoes in the work of many decades of landscape designers, beginning with Frederick Law Olmsted.

The lives of Olmsted and Joshua Carrera display the broad value of nature: as refuge and as the wellspring of healthy cities, a source of both inspiration and tangible services people rely on every day. The inherent, spiritual value of nature has long been the focus of the modern conservation movement and will remain vital. However, balancing human needs with those of all the other species on the planet now can only be achieved when people learn how to value nature closer to home, in our businesses, in our cities, and in the value it provides every time someone draws a clean breath or turns on the tap to get a glass of water.

NOT ONLY DOES CONSERVATION NEED TO WORK IN MORE DIVERSE places than ever before, it needs to find allies among more diverse communities, too. The diversity of the participants in LEAF stands in distinct contrast to the typical supporters of mainstream conservation organizations: white, college-educated, and affluent. The prominent perception of conservation as something that concerns only a narrow and elite segment of the population is potentially devastating.

The typical supporter of conservation usually spent time outdoors backpacking or hiking when they were young, and that experience led them, a decade or more later, to begin supporting conservation organizations. But the number of people participating in those sorts of outdoor activities has been dropping. Unstructured outdoor activity is down by half from the previous generation. Children in the United States average just thirty minutes a week of unregulated time outdoors. Their weekly electronic media exposure, on the other hand, is almost forty-five hours a week.

In his book *Last Child in the Woods*, Richard Luov called this phenomenon "nature deficit disorder." That name gets at another essential value of nature: more and more studies show that spending time in nature is good for our health.

Recent experiments suggest that living in cities has a measurable impact on the way people think and react to stress. In one study, researchers asked people living in big cities, towns, and rural areas to do something stressful: they took a difficult, timed math test. They reacted as would any middle-schooler, with increased heart rate and blood pressure, but also with increased activity in specific parts of the brain known to be related to stress. The people from rural areas showed the least stress, the people who lived in big cities responded with the highest stress levels and those who had been born and raised in those cities responded worst of all.

So as a native habitat, a city may be at odds with the way our brains are hardwired. This research suggests that getting children into nature more often may be vitally important, even more important than the evidence from the LEAF program has shown. Such efforts are sometimes couched in terms of the need to save nature, but they may be just as important in saving the children.

Environmental psychology has several theories for the restorative potential of nature, centering on reduction of overall stress and providing a respite from having to focus our attention on so many things at once. The precise mechanism of nature's ability to reduce stress remains to be described, but this is not just fodder for academic speculation. Individuals, businesses, and governments have real money at stake. Getting adults into nature reduces stress, and reducing stress is among the best ways to stay healthy. While politicians tie themselves in knots over the high cost of healthcare, part of the solution may literally be right outside our doors.

The United States spends more on healthcare per person than any other nation in the world—nearly $9,000 per person per year. This is big business and a huge financial burden for many companies. In response, some corporations have saved themselves money—and improved the lives of their employees—by encouraging healthy lifestyles. For example, Johnson & Johnson started a "Live for Life" health promotion program for its employees more than twenty-five years ago, and as a result now saves itself at least $500 per employee per year in healthcare costs.

In addition to reducing stress, nature may play other roles in lowering healthcare costs. Outdoor recreation and nature recreation reduce obesity, which is quickly becoming one of the greatest health problems in the world. Now that medicine has largely eliminated infectious diseases as a hazard, future health challenges will revolve around quality of life and lifestyle diseases.

Businesses that provide opportunities for their employees to enjoy nature will end up with a healthier workforce and lower healthcare costs. This connection between nature and health is at the cutting edge of biological research and will take some time to filter into common practice. But by 2030, businesses that aim to be among the best places to work may invest in nature and access to nature just as they currently invest in onsite exercise facilities.

The prospect of cutting healthcare costs by connecting employees to nature may seem New-Age hokum, and on that basis some of the more conservative elements of the business community may dismiss the idea. However, to the corporate executives who are paying attention, the value of nature is front and center.

Resilience

Twin articles of faith have long guided our behavior as individuals, businesses, and nations: society will always have the resources it needs, and if anything runs short, then creative businesses can simply replace it with something else that is not so scarce. For the first time in human history, these assumptions are open to serious question at a global scale.

No pragmatist can fail to appreciate the implications of these facts. The wreckage of civilizations that ignored them litters human history. Huge improvements in agriculture and technology convinced many people that somehow the idea of limits no longer holds and has allowed the past several centuries to play out on a natural stage so reliable in terms of resources that it seemingly became inconsequential.

The assumption that there will always be enough water to drink, good land to grow crops and graze animals, and enough fish to fill our nets will be hard to displace. So will our faith in the human ability to find some clever technological solution, not realizing that at some point those solutions run up against the immutable laws of physics.

Our challenges will only grow. Not only will global population likely soar to 9 billion-plus people by 2050, but the world's middle class will also grow by an even larger amount. This is a positive development in most respects; it is wonderful to see people lifted from poverty. Yet all those additional people—with growing consumer appetites—will translate to soaring demand for food, water, energy, and land.

As if that is not enough of a challenge, climate change will make these issues still more complicated. As the planet inevitably warms, presently good arable land will dry up and lose its agricultural value. Likewise, water scarcity will grow more acute, sea levels will rise, and damaging storms will become more frequent.

Nature remains resilient. When people do the right thing, nature can recover some or all of its former glory. But we are really pushing our luck.

As I said in the Introduction, I am an optimist. I think good things will happen if humankind makes the right investments in nature, right now. But I am also a realist, grounded in science.

Science tells us that assumptions of never-ending plenty held as long as human populations and our economies were small relative to the scale of the systems we were exploiting. But now the scale of human activities is no longer dwarfed by the planet itself; the planet has limits, and we are nearing them and in places exceeding them. Every farmer knows you should not eat your seed corn, and every banker knows you should not spend your principal. Yet that is exactly what we are doing.

People have typically valued nature either sentimentally, or else as a bunch of commodities—raw materials—whose value is based on what it costs to extract them and what price they ultimately bring on the market. Now, everyone from farmers and fishermen to bankers and financiers are waking up to two vital facts: we depend on nature in far more complex ways than we knew, and natural capital is not inexhaustible.

Conservation and business need a more sophisticated and nuanced calculation, one based on sound financial principles and a deeper appreciation for how nature contributes to economic and ecological well-being. When conventional economics leaves natural capital out of the equation, both ecosystems and the economies built upon them are imperiled.

The good news: investing in nature is a great deal. Even if you set aside the benefits to nature and take a steely-eyed look at the bottom line, the opportunities are too good to pass up. The case for investing in nature is inspiring and ultimately optimistic.

More good news: investing in nature transforms the way people see their place in it. Time after time, people—farmers in Iowa, sugarcane growers in Colombia, jet-setting corporate executives—who absolutely do not think of themselves as environmentalists have come to realize that their lives and livelihoods depend on healthy natural systems. They are attracted to a particular investment in nature for the specific, practical returns they hope to receive from it. When the investment pans out, as it usually does and will do more and more as investors become more sophisticated, the result is a whole new outlook.

How we all best move forward together is also important. We want everyone to be engaged in the environmental movement. There will be some bad actors, but personal experience tells me that most people—no matter what their background or their political leanings—who are exposed to the values and wonders of nature will choose to do everything they can to protect the environment.

What about the various debates and controversies that sometimes get in the way of environmental progress? As environmentalists we should be humble about our strategies; the point is to make credible progress toward a diverse and sustainable plant, not score ideological points. So we should welcome constructive criticism and new ideas, and commit to finding objective measures of our progress. I recommend that we heed the advice of Yale's William Nordhaus—one of academia's most pre-eminent thought leaders on environmental challenges: "We need to approach the issues with a cool head and a warm heart. And with respect for sound logic and good science."

A new valuation of nature, one that integrates conservation values and human development, science and economics means seeing things whole; if we want a successful business, a livable city, a green, diverse, and vibrant planet, we have to take nature into account, and recognize the real value of the services nature provides.

An age of limits and scarcity does not necessarily mean an age of want. It does, however, mean an age of care, of stewardship. All our action must heed and respect nature. As stewards of the land have long known, with care even badly damaged places can be renewed, perhaps not as exact replicas of what they were, but vibrant and life-sustaining nonetheless. The continued resilience of many threatened ecosystems gives us hope. That too is a value of nature.

Afterword

Since first publishing *Nature's Fortune* in 2013, I have talked with many people about the book's message. I've learned that the idea of investing in nature resonates with people from different backgrounds, including those who do not view themselves as environmentalists. It is clear that valuing nature can be a strong foundation for broadening support and making progress on the key environmental challenges we face.

The conservation movement has a lot to be proud of—from expanded protected areas to the establishment of crucial government policies and regulations. Conservation successes during the past several years have reinforced that view. There are even tentative signs that the economy can grow without a corresponding increase in carbon dioxide emissions. That said, all the things we want more of—forests, fisheries, top soil, intact watersheds, coral reefs, biodiversity—continue to decline. And all the things we want less of, such as carbon dioxide in the atmosphere, continue to increase. We need to accelerate and scale up our efforts. But how?

First, we need more people on our side. As much as we love our supporters and depend on their passion, there are simply not enough of us, by ourselves, to create change at a scale that matters. A single trip to Capitol Hill should be enough to convince anyone of that. At this point, too few members of Congress believe the environment is a top priority for their constituents.

Where will we find new supporters—people who will advocate for conservation not just on Capitol Hill but in boardrooms, in classrooms, in kitchens, and at town hall meetings? While talking to people about the book, I've discovered that one key to finding these new supporters is getting people to think about nature as an investment opportunity.

One dramatic example stems from the tragedy of Hurricane Sandy, which hit the East Coast just as I finished writing the book. Shortly afterward, I was invited to join New York Governor Andrew Cuomo's commission to find ways to strengthen infrastructure in the face of natural disasters. Although I was pleased to see TNC's recommendations included in the commission's report, I never anticipated just how completely New York would embrace the role of natural infrastructure in protecting coastal communities from the impacts of future storms and climate change.

Take, for example, Howard Beach in Queens, which was hit by a ten-foot storm surge when Sandy raged ashore. To test natural infrastructure as a solution, the Federal Emergency Management Agency (FEMA) granted the state $50 million to restore 55 acres of salt marsh next to Howard Beach. The restoration would help protect the community from sea level rise, storm surges, and coastal flooding. A study found that a mix of built and natural defenses, such as the salt marshes, could save Howard Beach up to $466 million in avoided losses from a future one-in-one hundred-year storm event.

This idea is taking hold far beyond New York. FEMA is inviting cities across the country to propose projects that use natural infrastructure. One year after Sandy, President Barack Obama issued an executive order paving the way for nature-based climate solutions.

And looking beyond disaster readiness, TNC recently co-wrote a report that found one-in-four cities would see a positive return from investing in watershed conservation. As people see the concrete benefits of investing in nature through projects taking root across the country, the message is becoming increasingly clear: Conservation, far from a luxury, is an investment opportunity we cannot afford to miss.

But first, we must overcome an existing hurdle. Investing in nature will remain an abstract notion unless we find more money to actually invest. The conservation community relies on philanthropic gifts and grants from governments and other institutions, and we will continue to do so for many of our initiatives. However, there are limits to that support.

The good news is that more and more people are viewing nature as a great investment opportunity. *Impact investing*—investments intended to return principal and generate profit while driving positive societal impacts—is booming. Impact investing for conservation projects is still emerging, but already its potential is obvious. A recent TNC study found that the total market for conservation impact investments could increase to some $37 billion in the next five years.

That's a lot of capital for conservation. But unlocking this new source of funding will require a robust pipeline of investment opportunities. Projects must satisfy hard-headed investors by proving they offer adequate risk-return ratios, and they must be run by seasoned management teams. Investors look for solid track records and measurable impacts—two areas of improvement for many conservation projects. So, we need to lay the foundation first. That's why TNC joined with JPMorgan Chase to launch NatureVest, a new entity that puts money to work for conservation, acting much like a bank for nature.

NatureVest bridges the gap between conservation projects and potential investors. In the rangelands of northern Kenya, for example, overgrazing has become a serious issue, threatening both local communities and wildlife. The solution: Invest in cattle-herding communities who agree to improve their grazing practices. Through a $13-million investment (a combination of debt, equity, and in-kind

contributions) NatureVest and its partners are scaling up a program
that buys cattle directly from these local communities at reasonable
prices, then fattens and slaughters the cattle to sell to the Nairobi market at higher prices. These transactions generate positive financial, social, and conservation outcomes, and both the herding communities
and the investors reap benefits.

Government investment in nature is another area with huge potential. China is now in the process of establishing a network of conservation zones that restrict development in areas providing critical
ecosystem services, such as water resources and natural infrastructure
that protects against floods and sandstorms. These areas now span
about 35 percent of the country and are expected to expand to 45 percent by mid-2015.

China's top leaders also announced plans to track natural capital and ecosystem services through a new metric, Gross Ecosystem
Product (GEP), which they will report alongside wealth and income
figures in national economic accounts. Whether GEP will influence
decision-making as much as GDP remains to be seen, but China is
the first nation to officially factor in the nature-based underpinnings
of wealth and well-being.

In the Gulf of Mexico, the RESTORE Act will fund conservation
projects through billions of dollars in damages and fines from the
companies responsible for the 2010 Deepwater Horizon oil spill. It's
encouraging that many projects seeking RESTORE Act funding involve reconstructing marshland, barrier beaches and islands, oyster
reefs, coastal forests, and living shorelines—all natural elements that
provide multiple benefits, including shoreline protection.

Some of the money from the RESTORE Act will go to Gulf states
and counties to use as they see fit, and other funds will go to tourism development and conventional infrastructure, such as roads and
bridges. In Florida's Monroe County, government officials chose the
Florida Keys' coral reef as the most important contributor to tourism and community safety. They will spend more than half of their
$1-million allocation, working with TNC, to reconstruct portions of

the reef, which will support the county's fisheries and tourism industry while helping protect the islands from wave-driven erosion and floods.

Scientists and economists also are finding better ways to demonstrate nature's value. One study, conducted as part of TNC's work with Dow Chemical (Chapter 9), shows that forests can help improve air quality. The study provides the first hard evidence that large-scale forest restoration surrounding an urban area can cost-effectively reduce air pollution. Based on these results, a company investing in forest restoration should qualify for pollution mitigation credits from the government.

If these results are corroborated through future research, then planting trees may join the list of conventional engineering solutions for combatting air pollution. Forest restoration comes at a similar upfront cost, but the long-term benefits far outweigh typical pollution reduction methods: Forests sequester carbon, mitigate climate change, cool air temperatures, improve water quality, and reduce flood risk, as well as provide wildlife habitat and recreation sites.

Corporations are beginning to see that nature is good for business. Reinsurance giant Swiss Re now puts oyster reefs and salt marshes on the same cost curve as sandbags and break walls when calculating storm insurance prices. Shell Oil is looking into applications of natural infrastructure—restoration of marshes, oyster reefs, and hydrology—to help protect its pipelines from erosion. If it works, Shell's small pilot effort could be scaled up for other sites.

In the Amazon, TNC's work with Cargill to stop soy farmers from cutting new areas of forest (Chapter 5) is now expanding to cattle ranchers. This is a tougher challenge, but early signs are encouraging. The same is true for efforts to halt the expansion of palm oil plantations, which are a major cause of deforestation in Asia, particularly Indonesia.

These are things that no one sector—governments, industries, conservation groups—can do on its own. We must get out of our silos and work together.

That leads me to the most important thing I have learned from talking with people about the book: We need to change the dialogue about conservation. Talking about nature as an investment does just that. I have seen firsthand how ideas such as water funds (Chapter 2) transform contentious debates into collaborative problem-solving.

Renewable energy, another great example, shows we can even change the dialogue about climate change—without a doubt the most divisive environmental issue we face. Solar power is taking off around the country, and many people jumping onboard would never identify themselves as liberals or environmentalists. In San Diego, surveys found that while liberals invested in solar because it's good for the planet, conservatives did so because it reduced their electricity bills. Any way you look at it, more people using solar energy is great news. But instead of tapping into these diverse reasons for investing in solar, sometimes we righteously lecture people about why they should change their behaviors. Time and again, research has shown this confrontational approach does not work. In fact, it often prompts people to rebel and act in the opposite manner, even if it's not in their best interests.

There is an important lesson here: The way we talk about things matters. For instance, critics often mock those who doubt climate change. But that doesn't get us very far. We don't get anywhere by assuming people with whom we disagree are evil or uneducated. Most likely, they are neither, and thinking so only makes it impossible to find commonalities and work together. Establishing common ground with diverse parties is not easy. In fact, it may be the hardest thing we have to do—but it might just be the most important.

Collaboration is difficult for environmentalists because we sometimes get too set on the good-versus-evil mentality. Too often, in a knee-jerk response, we say that business is bad, conservatives are wrong, or people with doubts about climate are "deniers." But these are the very people and organizations with whom we need to work. And when we collaborate, progress accelerates and breakthrough innovation occurs.

Nobody is against the environment, and nobody is against nature — that would be crazy. But we've gotten emotionally over-loaded. We need to calm down, lower the temperature, and get on to collaborative problem-solving.

The changes we need to make are well within our reach. There is room in this effort for a diverse set of players—activists and business people, liberals and conservatives, people who love nature for its own sake and those who view it as the foundation of a sustainable economy.

You might think those unlikely allies will never come together as an effective force for change. I don't believe that. Bringing people together is not just the way to advance our conservation goals. It is also a rewarding—in fact, a joyous—way to live life. I'm constantly encouraged by stories I hear of people and organizations putting aside their differences, finding common ground and working together to make substantial progress on some of the world's most pressing issues. It is not true that all important things come with a fight. In fact, I believe it's just the opposite. I'm pleased to be part of the progress that humanity has made over the centuries—working together to solve the problems that we know without a doubt must be solved.

Acknowledgments

I HAVE HAD MANY COLLABORATORS SINCE I JOINED TNC. LEADERS of the environmental community welcomed me and offered advice whenever I asked. For all their help I thank Bruce Babbitt, Frances Beinecke, Michael Brune, Eileen Claussen, Brett Jenks, Thomas Kiernan, Fred Krupp, Jonathan Lash, Thomas E. Lovejoy, Bill McKibben, Molly McUsic, Timothy Profeta, Kent Redford, William K. Reilly, Carter S. Roberts, Cristián Samper, Steven E. Sanderson, Larry J. Schweiger, Peter A. Seligman, Philip R. Sharp, James Gustave Speth, Tensie Whelan, Timothy E. Wirth, and David Yarnold.

I was also fortunate to have special mentors as I transitioned into the conservation community: John Holdren, Hank Paulson, Wendy Paulson, Walt Reid, Matt Arnold, and my predecessor as CEO of TNC, Steve McCormick. I thank as well my colleagues at Goldman Sachs who helped get our environmental effort underway: Brad Abelow, Abby Joseph Cohen, Megan Guy, Larry Linden, Kyung-Ah Park, John Rogers, Sonal Shah, and Tracy Wolstencroft. Let me also recognize and thank the following good friends for their encouragement and support: Marshall Goldsmith, Claudia Madrazo, Susan McCaw, Tashia Morgridge, Christine M. Morse, Ginger Sall, Gene Sykes, Ted Turner, Hansjorg Wyss, and Robert W. Wilson.

Some friends and colleagues went beyond the call of duty and read the full draft of this book with enormous vigor and energy: Gretchen Daily, Peter Kareiva, Guilio Boccalletti, Jimmie Powell, Jeremy Grantham, and Amy Tercek. M. Sanjayan, Glenn Prickett, Zoe Kant, Jonathan Foley, and Karin Paque also took on the full draft in its early and rougher stages.

The Board of Directors of TNC was instrumental in this project, giving me crucial support to take on this task in addition to my role as CEO. I thank the TNC's board members who served during my tenure to date for their service and wise counsel: Teresa Beck, David Blood, Shona L. Brown, Joel E. Cohen, Gordon Crawford, Gretchen C. Daily, Steven A. Denning, Joseph H. Gleberman, Jeremy Grantham, Harry Groome, Frank E. Loy, Jack Ma, Craig O. McCaw, Thomas J. Meredith, Thomas S. Middleton, Roger Milliken Jr., James C. Morgan, John P. Morgridge, William W. Murdoch, Stephen Polasky, Roberto Hernández Ramírez, James E. Rogers, Mary H. Ruckelshaus, John P. Sall, Cristian Samper, Muneer A. Satter, Christine M. Scott, Thomas J. Tierney, Moses Tsang, Frances A. Ulmer, P. Roy Vagelos, Georgia C. Welles, Margaret C. Whitman, and Shirley Young. The book's contents and recommendations are my own and do not constitute endorsement by The Nature Conservancy's staff, senior managers, or Board of Directors.

For their hospitality in Louisiana, I thank Keith Ouchley, Seth Blitch, Jim Bergan, Jean Landry, Chris Rice, and Dan Weber.

My agent, Lisa Adams of the Garamond Agency, was instrumental in getting this project off the ground and helping steer it along the way. My editor, TJ Kelleher, sharpened the arguments and made the book something that people would enjoy reading.

Heartfelt thanks to the following people who offered their time and expertise to make this book better: All of the scholars, scientists, advocates, and activists who I asked for help gave it willingly and unstintingly, and they corrected numerous errors of fact or interpretation. Any errors that remain are my own.

Ricardo Bayon

Mike Beck

Michael Bell

Bob Bendick

Silvia Benitez

Eron Bloomgarden

Justine Browne

Tim Boucher

Cindy Brown

Rob Brumbaugh

Mark Bryer

Teresa Duran

David Cleary

Chuck Cook

Greg Fishbein

Edward Game

Brigitte Griswold

Craig Groves

Judy Haner

Neil Hawkins

Zoe Kant

Robert Lalasz

Craig Leisher

Frank Lowenstein

Peter Malik

Rob McDonald

Jen Molnar

Jensen Montambault

Jeff Opperman

Aurelio Ramos

Brian Richter

Bill Raynor

Mary Ruckelshaus

Jason Scott

Jeff Seabright

Heather Tallis

Jerry Touval

Ronnie Ulmer

Joni Ward

Sheila Walsh

Janine Wilkin

I am inspired daily by the dedication of the enormously talented and mission-driven team at TNC. They have taught me so much I don't know where to start in thanking them. Likewise, I am grateful to TNC's passionate trustees, members, and supporters, as well as our many partners, some but not all of whom are mentioned in this book. Thanks to all of you: you are the reason TNC is making great progress as we pursue our mission of saving the lands and waters on which all life depends.

Works Cited

All URL addresses herein are accessible as of December 2012.

Chapter 1: Maybe It's Not *Chinatown* After All

Aldaya, M. M., and A. Y. Hoekstra. "The Water Needed for Italians to Eat Pasta and Pizza." *Agricultural Systems* 103 (2010): 351–60.

Bratman, G. N., J. P. Hamilton, and G. C. Daily. "The Impacts of Nature Experience on Human Cognitive Function and Mental Health." *Annals of the New York Academy of Sciences* 1249 (2012): 118–36.

"Case against Coca-Cola Kerala State: India. The Rights to Water and Sanitation." www.righttowater.info/ways-to-influence/legal-approaches/case -against-coca-cola-kerala-state-india.

"Coca-Cola on the Yangtze: A Corporate Campaign for Clean Water in China." *Law and Public Policy*, August 18, 2010, knowledge.wharton.upenn .edu/article.cfm?articleid=2568.

Cohen, R., B. Nelson, and G. Wolff. *Energy Down the Drain: The Hidden Costs of California's Water Supply.* New York: Natural Resources Defense Council, 2004. www.nrdc.org/water/conservation/edrain/edrain.pdf.

Congressional Budget Office. "Future Investment in Drinking Water and Wastewater Infrastructure." 2002. www.cbo.gov/doc.cfm?index=3983 &type=0&sequence=7.

Dellapenna, J. W. "The Importance of Getting Names Right: The Myth of Markets for Water." *William and Mary Environmental Law and Policy Review* 25 (2000): 317–77. smartech.gatech.edu/jspui/bitstream/1853/43445/3/DellapennaJ-01.pdf.

Denning, C. A., R. I. McDonald, and J. Christensen. "Did Land Protection in Silicon Valley Reduce the Housing Stock?" *Biological Conservation* 143 (2010): 1087–93.

Dunn, A. D. 2010. "Siting Green Infrastructure: Legal and Policy Solutions to Alleviate Urban Poverty and Promote Healthy Communities." *Environmental Affairs* 37 (2010): 41–66. digitalcommons.pace.edu/lawfaculty/559.

Fishman, C. *The Big Thirst: The Secret Life and Turbulent Future of Water.* New York: Free Press, 2011.

Fuller, R. A., K. N. Irvine, P. Devine-Wright, P. H. Warren, and K. J. Gaston. "Psychological Benefits of Greenspace Increase with Biodiversity." *Biology Letters* 3 (2007): 390–94.

Gardiner, B. "Beverage Industry Works to Cap Its Water Use." *New York Times*, March 21, 2011. www.nytimes.com/2011/03/22/business/energy-environment/22iht-rbog-beverage-22.html?pagewanted=all.

Garrison, N., and K. Hobbs. *Rooftops to Rivers II: Green Strategies for Controlling Stormwater and Combined Sewer Overflows.* New York: Natural Resources Defense Council, 2011. www.nrdc.org/water/pollution/rooftopsii/files/rooftopstoriversII.pdf.

Garrison, N., R. C. Wilkinson, and R. Horner. *A Clear Blue Future: How Greening California Cities Can Address Water Resources and Climate Challenges in the 21st Century.* Seattle: Natural Resources Defense Council, 2009. www.nrdc.org/water/lid/files/lid_hi.pdf.

Gill, S. E., J. F. Handley, A. R. Ennos, and S. Pauleit. "Adapting Cities for Climate Change: The Role of the Green Infrastructure." *Built Environment* 33 (2007): 115–33. tinyurl.com/936q5lv.

Jones, P. "Corporate Giants Back WRI." *Environmental Finance*, August 18, 2011. www.environmental-finance.com/news/view/1923 (subscription necessary).

Kloss, C., and C. Calarusse. *Rooftops to Rivers: Green Strategies for Controlling Stormwater and Combined Sewer Overflows.* Washington: Natural Resources Defense Council, 2006. www.nrdc.org/water/pollution/rooftops/rooftops.pdf.

Laurence, C. "US Farmers Fear the Return of the Dust Bowl." *The Telegraph*, March 7, 2011. www.telegraph.co.uk/earth/8359076/US-farmers-fear-the-return-of-the-Dust-Bowl.html.

Lederbogen, F., P. Kirsch, L. Haddad, F. Streit, H. Tost, P. Schuch, S. Wüst, J. C. Pruessner, M. Rietschel, M. Deuschle, and A. Meyer-Lindenberg. "City Living and Urban Upbringing Affect Neural Social Stress Processing in Humans." *Nature* 474 (2011): 498–501.

Mildenberg, D. "Pickens Water-to-Riches Dream Fizzles as Texas Cities Buy Rights." *Bloomberg Businessweek*, July 14, 2011. www.businessweek.com/news/2011-07-14/pickens-water-to-riches-dream-fizzles-as-texas-cities-buy-rights.html.

Nidumolu, R., C. K. Prahalad, and M. R. Rangaswami. "Why Sustainability Is Now the Key Driver of Innovation." *Harvard Business Review*, September 2009. hbr.org/2009/09/why-sustainability-is-now-the-key-driver-of-innovation/es.

Olmsted, F. L. "The Value and Care of Parks." Report to the Congress of the State of California, 1865. Reprinted in *The American Environment*, ed. R. Nash, 18–24. Reading, MA: Addison-Wesley Pub. Co., 1976.

———. "Yosemite and the Mariposa Grove: A Preliminary Report, 1865." www.yosemite.ca.us/library/olmsted/report.html.

Penn, I. "The Profits on Water Are Huge, but the Raw Material Is Free." *Tampa Bay Times*, March 16, 2008. www.tampabay.com/news/environmentwater/article418793.ece.

Raucher, R. S. "A Triple Bottom Line Assessment of Traditional and Green Infrastructure Options for Controlling CSO Events in Philadelphia's Watersheds: Final Report," August 24, 2009. Boulder, CO: Stratus Consulting Inc. www.michigan.gov/documents/dnr/TBL.AssessmentGreenvsTraditionalStormwaterMgt_293337_7.pdf.

Welch, K. "Authority Seals Water Deal with Pickens." *Amarillo Globe-News*, December 30, 2011. tinyurl.com/9xh57al.

Zimmerman, E. "Hiring in Hydrology Resists the Slump." *New York Times*, March 7, 2009. www.nytimes.com/2009/03/08/jobs/08start.html?_r=1&ref=earth.

Chapter 2: Not a Drop to Drink

Appleton, A. F. "How New York City Used an Ecosystem Services Strategy Carried Out Through an Urban-Rural Partnership to Preserve the Pristine

Quality of Its Drinking Water and Save Billions of Dollars." New York: Forest Trends—Tokyo, 2002. moderncms.ecosystemmarketplace.com/repository /moderncms_documents/NYC_H2O_Ecosystem_Services.pdf.

Asquith, N., and S. Wunder, eds. *Payments for Watershed Services: The Bellagio Conversations.* Santa Cruz de la Sierra: Fundación Natura Bolivia, 2008. tinyurl.com/8c9bhtf.

Bratman, G. N., J. P. Hamilton, and G. C. Daily. "The Impacts of Nature Experience on Human Cognitive Function and Mental Health." *Annals of the New York Academy of Sciences* 1249 (2012): 118–36.

Brauman, K. A., G. C. Daily, T. K. Duarte, and H. A. Mooney. "The Nature and Value of Ecosystem Services: An Overview Highlighting Hydrologic Services." *Annual Review of Environment and Resources* 32 (2007): 67–98.

"Coca-Cola on the Yangtze: A Corporate Campaign for Clean Water in China." *Law and Public Policy,* August 18, 2010, knowledge.wharton.upenn .edu/article.cfm?articleid=2568.

Daily, G. C., and P. Matson. "Ecosystem Services: From Theory to Implementation." *Proceedings of the National Academy of Sciences of the United States of America* 105 (2008): 9455–56. tinyurl.com/9o2svx7.

Denning, C. A., R. I. McDonald, and J. Christensen. "Did Land Protection in Silicon Valley Reduce the Housing Stock?" *Biological Conservation* 143 (2010): 1087–93.

Dunn, A. D. "Siting Green Infrastructure: Legal and Policy Solutions to Alleviate Urban Poverty and Promote Healthy Communities." *Environmental Affairs* 37 (2010): 41–66. digitalcommons.pace.edu/lawfaculty/559.

Fishman, C. "Why GE, Coca-Cola, and IBM Are Getting into the Water Business." *Fast Company* 154, April 11, 2011. www.fastcompany.com /magazine/154/a-sea-of-dollars.html.

———. *The Big Thirst: The Secret Life and Turbulent Future of Water.* New York: Free Press, 2011.

Fuller, R. A., K. N. Irvine, P. Devine-Wright, P. H. Warren, and K. J. Gaston. "Psychological Benefits of Greenspace Increase with Biodiversity." *Biology Letters* 3 (2007): 390–94.

Gardiner, B. "Beverage Industry Works to Cap Its Water Use." *New York Times,* March 21, 2011. www.nytimes.com/2011/03/22/business/energy -environment/22iht-rbog-beverage-22.html?pagewanted=all.

Garrison, N., and K. Hobbs. *Rooftops to Rivers II: Green Strategies for Controlling Stormwater and Combined Sewer Overflows.* New York: Natural

Resources Defense Council, 2011. www.nrdc.org/water/pollution/rooftopsii
/files/rooftopstoriversII.pdf.

Garrison, N., R. C. Wilkinson, and R. Horner. *A Clear Blue Future:
How Greening California Cities Can Address Water Resources and Climate
Challenges in the 21st Century*. Seattle: Natural Resources Defense Coun-
cil, 2009. www.nrdc.org/water/lid/files/lid_hi.pdf.

Gill, S. E., J. F. Handley, A. R. Ennos, and S. Pauleit. "Adapting Cities
for Climate Change: The Role of the Green Infrastructure." *Built Environment* 33 (2007): 115–33. tinyurl.com/936q5lv.

Goldman, R. L., H. Tallis, P. Kareiva, and G. C. Daily. "Field Evidence
That Ecosystem Service Projects Support Biodiversity and Diversify Options." *Proceedings of the National Academy of Sciences of the United States
of America* 105 (2008): 9445–48.

Goldstein, E. "New York State Authorizes 105,000-Acre NYC Watershed Land Acquisition Program to Safeguard Downstate Water Supply and
Region's Economy." NRDC *Switchboard*, February 16, 2011. switchboard
.nrdc.org/blogs/egoldstein/new_york_state_authorizes_1050.html.

Jones, P. "Corporate Giants Back WRI." *Environmental Finance*, August
18, 2011. www.environmental-finance.com/news/view/1923 (subscription
necessary).

Kenny, A. 2006. "Ecosystem Services in the New York City Watershed."
Ecosystem Marketplace, February 10, 2006. www.ecosystemmarketplace
.com/pages/dynamic/article.page.php?page_id=4130&section=home.

Kloss, C., and C. Calarusse. *Rooftops to Rivers: Green Strategies for Controlling Stormwater and Combined Sewer Overflows*. Washington: Natural
Resources Defense Council, 2006. www.nrdc.org/water/pollution/rooftops
/rooftops.pdf.

Lederbogen, F., P. Kirsch, L. Haddad, F. Streit, H. Tost, P. Schuch, S.
Wüst, J. C. Pruessner, M. Rietschel, M. Deuschle, and A. Meyer-Lindenberg.
"City Living and Urban Upbringing Affect Neural Social Stress Processing
in Humans." *Nature* 474 (2011): 498–501.

Marx, E. "Water Resources Briefing Part 1: Water Scarcity—Draining
Away." *Ethical Corporation*, October 3, 2011. www.ethicalcorp.com
/environment/water-resources-briefing-part-1-water-scarcity-draining-away.

Olmsted, F. L. "The Value and Care of Parks." Report to the Congress
of the State of California, 1865. Reprinted in *The American Environment*,
ed. R. Nash, 18–24. Reading, MA: Addison-Wesley Pub. Co., 1976.

Perrot-Maître, D. "The Vittel Payments for Ecosystem Services: A 'Perfect' PES Case?" London, UK: International Institute for Environment and Development (IIED), 2006. pubs.iied.org/pdfs/G00388.pdf.

Raucher, R. S. "A Triple Bottom Line Assessment of Traditional and Green Infrastructure Options for Controlling CSO Events in Philadelphia's Watersheds: Final Report," August 24, 2009. Boulder, CO: Stratus Consulting Inc. findit.library.jhu.edu/link_router/index/65979491.

Salzman, J. "Creating Markets for Ecosystem Services: Notes from the Field." *New York University Law Review* 80 (2005): 870–961.

Tallis, H., R. Goldman, M. Uhl, and B. Brosi. "Integrating Conservation and Development in the Field: Implementing Ecosystem Service Projects." *Frontiers in Ecology and the Environment* 7 (2009): 12–20. www.esajournals.org/doi/pdf/10.1890/080012.

Warne, D. S. "New York City's Watershed Protection Program." Undated presentation by David S. Warne, Assistant Commissioner, New York City Department of Environmental Protection. wren.palwv.org/documents/WarneWatershedProtectionforPA-four.pdf.

Chapter 3: Let Floodplains Be Floodplains

Barry, J. M. *Rising Tide: The Great Mississippi Flood of 1927 and How It Changed America.* New York: Simon & Schuster, 1997.

BBC News. "Colombia Flooding Continues with Thousands Homeless." December 16, 2010. www.bbc.co.uk/news/world-latin-america-12006568.

Chapman, S. S., B. A. Kleiss, J. M. Omernik, T. L. Foti, and E. O. Murray. "Ecoregions of the Mississippi Alluvial Plain." Color poster with map, descriptive text, summary tables, and photographs; map scale 1:1,150,000. Reston, VA: US Geological Survey, 2004. www.epa.gov/wed/pages/ecoregions/map_eco.htm.

Criss, R. E., and W. E. Winston. "Public Safety and Faulty Flood Statistics." *Environmental Health Perspectives* 116 (2008): A516. www.ncbi.nlm.nih.gov/pmc/articles/PMC2599774/.

Goldenberg, S. "Americans Take a Gamble with the Mississippi Floods." *The Guardian*, May 22, 2011. www.guardian.co.uk/world/2011/may/22/americans-gamble-mississippi-floods.

Hilburn, G. "Levee Breached." *The News-Star* (Monroe, LA), May 25, 2009, A-1.

Jenkins, W. A., B. C. Murray, R. A. Kramer, and S. P. Faulkner. "Valuing

Ecosystem Services from Wetlands Restoration in the Mississippi Alluvial Valley." *Ecological Economics* 69 (2010): 1051–61. tinyurl.com/8omwj57.

Newbold, R. "Project Will Take Ouachita Back to Its Origins." *The Piney Woods Journal,* June 2009. www.thepineywoods.com/OuachitaJun09.htm.

Risk Management Solutions. "The 1927 Great Mississippi Flood: 80-Year Retrospective." RMS Special Report. Hoboken, NJ: Risk Management Solutions, 2007. www.rms.com/publications/1927_MississippiFlood.pdf.

Warner, A. J. J. Opperman, and R. Pietrowsky. "A Call to Enhance the Resiliency of the Nation's Water Management." *Journal of Water Resources Planning and Management* (ASCE) 137 (2011): 305–08. tinyurl.com/9hay5cv.

Chapter 4: The New Fishing

American Oceans Campaign v. Daley, 183 F. Supp. 2d 1 (US District Court, District of Columbia), September 2000. tinyurl.com/d2dmx2y.

Barringer, F. 2007. "Conservationists Experiment with a Legal Device to Protect Depleted Fisheries." *New York Times,* November 7, 2007. www.nytimes.com/2007/11/06/world/americas/06iht-rbogwater.1.8211949.html.

Beck, M. W., T. D. Marsh, S. E. Reisewitz, and M. L. Bortman. "New Tools for Marine Conservation: The Leasing and Ownership of Submerged Lands." *Conservation Biology* 18 (2004): 1214–23. tinyurl.com/cfdtk8k.

Bell, M. "Central Coast Groundfish Project: Use of Private Agreements." 2008. www.mcatoolkit.org/Field_Projects/Field_Projects_US_California_3_Trawler_Buyout.html.

Bettencourt, G. "New Rules Are Saving Fish and Helping Fishers." *Mercury News,* January 11, 2012.

Bilsky, E. A. "Conserving Marine Habitats." *Sustainable Development Law & Policy* (2006): 67–70, 84. tinyurl.com/9gz6pgr.

Clover, C. "Sea Change: Deal Saves California Fishing Industry." *The Telegraph,* June 5, 2009. www.telegraph.co.uk/earth/environment/conservation/5446093/Sea-change-deal-saves-California-fishing-industry.html.

Coastal Conservancy. "Morro Bay and Port San Luis: Commercial Fisheries Business Plan." San Luis Obispo, CA: Lisa Wise Consulting, Inc., 2008. tinyurl.com/9cynltm.

Cushman, J. 1994. "Commercial Fishing Halt Is Urged for Georges Bank." *New York Times.* October 27, 1994. Section B, page 14.

Dasgupta, P. *The Control of Resources.* Cambridge, MA: Harvard University Press, 1982.

Dunkel, T. "Blue's Ocean." *Nature Conservancy Magazine*, 2009.

Diamond, J. *Collapse: How Societies Choose to Fail or Succeed*. New York: Penguin Books, 2011.

Fields, L. L. *The Entangling Net: Alaska's Commercial Fishing Women Tell Their Lives*. Urbana: University of Illinois Press, 1997.

Food and Agriculture Organization of the United Nations. "The State of World Fisheries and Aquaculture 2012." Rome: FAO Fisheries and Aquaculture Department, 2012. www.fao.org/docrep/016/i2727e/i2727e.pdf.

Gupta, S. 2010. "Pioneers for Sustainable Trawling." *New Scientist* 208:1.

Gutiérrez, N. L., R. Hilborn, and O. Defeo. "Leadership, Social Capital and Incentives Promote Successful Fisheries." *Nature* 470 (2011): 386–89. tinyurl.com/8bfsanm.

Huxley, T. H. "Inaugural Address for the Fisheries Exhibition, London (1833)." aleph0.clarku.edu/huxley/SM5/fish.html.

Jacobs, J. *The Nature of Economies*. New York: Modern Library, 2000.

Kura, Y., C. Revenga, E. Hoshino, and G. Mock. *Fishing for Answers: Making Sense of the Global Fish Crisis*. Washington, DC: World Resources Institute, 2004.

National Marine Fisheries Service. "Our Living Oceans: Report on the Status of US Living Marine Resources," 6th ed. Washington, DC: US Department of Commerce, 2009. tinyurl.com/9xz2ofh.

"New Fishery-Management Regime Pays Off with Less Waste." Editorial, *Seattle Times*, January 11, 2012. seattletimes.nwsource.com/html/editorials /2017210967_edit12boatquotas.html.

"New Fish Practice Seems to Work." Editorial, *Daily Astorian*, January 12, 2012. tinyurl.com/9xgdjxs.

Pacific Fishery Management Council. "Pacific Coast Groundfish Fishery Management Plan for the California, Oregon, and Washington Groundfish Fishery." Portland, OR: Pacific Fishery Management Council, 2011. tinyurl.com/8fjosqt.

Pew Oceans Commission. "Socioeconomic Perspectives on Marine Fisheries in the United States." Arlington, VA: Pew Oceans Commission, 2003. tinyurl.com/8l9ublh.

Shewchuk, B. "Men, Women, and Fishers." *CBC News Online*, August 24, 2000. www.cbc.ca/news/indepth/words/fishermen.html.

Sims, D. W., and A. J. Southward. "Dwindling Fish Numbers Already of Concern in 1883." *Nature* 439 (2006): 660.

Tercek, M. 2011. "Keeping More Fish in the Ocean: Good for People, Good for Nature." *Huffington Post*, March 22, 2011. www.huffingtonpost .com/mark-tercek/keeping-more-fish-in-the-_b_838679.html.

Wilber, C. D. "The Great Valleys and Prairies of Nebraska and the Northwest." Omaha, NB: Daily Republican Print, 1881. tinyurl.com/9pou9jy.

Worm, B., E. B. Barbier, N. Beaumont, E. Duffy, C. Folke, B. S. Halpern, J. B. C. Jackson, H. K. Lotze, F. Micheli, S. R. Palumbi, E. Sala, K. A. Selkoe, J. J. Stachowicz, and R. Watson. "Impacts of Biodiversity Loss on Ocean Ecosystem Services." *Science* 314 (2006): 787–90.

———. "Response to Comments on 'Impacts of Biodiversity Loss on Ocean Ecosystem Services.'" *Science* 316 (2007): 1285.

Chapter 5: Feeding the World—and Saving It

Assunção, J., C. C. e Gandour, and R. Rocha. "Deforestation Slowdown in the Legal Amazon: Prices or Policies?" Climate Policy Initiative / PUC-Rio. Rio de Janeiro: Climate Policy Initiative, 2012. tinyurl.com/9u5dxcg.

Brown, D. "The 'Recipe for Disaster' That Killed 80 and Left a £5bn Bill." *The Telegraph*, October 27, 2000. www.telegraph.co.uk/news/uknews /1371964/The-recipe-for-disaster-that-killed-80-and-left-a-5bn-bill.html.

Campos, M. T., and D. C. Nepstad. 2006. "Smallholders, the Amazon's new Conservationists." *Conservation Biology* 20 (2006): 1553–56. tinyurl .com/9nwucml.

Chomitz, K. M. "At Loggerheads? Agricultural Expansion, Poverty Reduction, and Environment in the Tropical Forests." Washington, DC: The World Bank, 2007. tinyurl.com/9zzbxq3.

Cleary, D. "What Should We Do About Beef from the Amazon?" *Cool Green Science: The Conservation Blog of the Nature Conservancy*, July 20, 2009. blog.nature.org/2009/07/beef-amazon-deforestation-david-cleary/.

Dobbs, R., J. Oppenheim, F. Thompson, M. Brinkman, and M. Zornes. "Resource Revolution: Meeting the World's Energy, Materials, Food, and Water Needs." McKinsey Global Institute and McKinsey Sustainability & Resource Productivity Practice, 2011. tinyurl.com/8qjdhbn.

Ewers, R. M., J. P. W. Scharlemann, A. Balmford, and R. E. Green. "Do Increases in Agricultural Yield Spare Land for Nature?" *Global Change Biology* 15 (2009): 1716–26. tinyurl.com/8egpoyt.

Foley, J. A. "Can We Feed the World and Sustain the Planet?" *Scientific American* 305 (2011): 60–65.

Foley, J. A., G. P. Asner, M. H. Costa, M. T. Coe, R. DeFries, H. K. Gibbs, E. A. Howard, S. Olson, J. Patz, N. Ramankutty, and P. Snyder. "Amazonia Revealed: Forest Degradation and Loss of Ecosystem Goods and Services in the Amazon Basin." *Frontiers in Ecology and the Environment* 5 (2007): 25–32. tinyurl.com/9bhhzb2.

Foley, J. A., R. DeFries, G. P. Asner, C. Barford, G. Bonan, S. R. Carpenter, F. S. Chapin, M. T. Coe, G. C. Daily, H. K. Gibbs, J. H. Helkowski, T. Holloway, E. A. Howard, C. J. Kucharik, C. Monfreda, J. A. Patz, I. C. Prentice, N. Ramankutty, and P. K. Snyder. "Global Consequences of Land Use." *Science* 309 (2005): 570–74.

Foley, J. A., N. Ramankutty, K. A. Brauman, E. S. Cassidy, J. S. Gerber, M. Johnston, N. D. Mueller, C. O'Connell, D. K. Ray, P. C. West, C. Balzer, E. M. Bennett, S. R. Carpenter, J. Hill, C. Monfreda, S. Polasky, J. Rockstrom, J. Sheehan, S. Siebert, D. Tilman, and D. P. M. Zaks. "Solutions for a Cultivated Planet." *Nature* 478 (2011): 337–42.

Godfray, H. J. Charles, J. Beddington, I. R. Crute, L. Haddad, D. Lawrence, J. F. Muir, J. Pretty, S. Robinson, S. M. Thomas, and C. Toulmin. "Food Security: The Challenge of Feeding 9 Billion People." *Science* 327 (2010): 812–18. www.sciencemag.org/content/327/5967/812.full.

Kaufman, M. "New Allies on the Amazon." *Washington Post*, April 24, 2007. www.washingtonpost.com/wp-dyn/content/article/2007/04/23/AR2007042301903.html.

Lambin, E. F., and P. Meyfroidt. "Global Land Use Change, Economic Globalization, and the Looming Land Scarcity." *Proceedings of the National Academy of Sciences of the United States of America* 108 (2011): 3465–72. www.pnas.org/content/108/9/3465.full.pdf+html.

Macedo, M. N., R. S. DeFries, D. C. Morton, C. M. Stickler, G. L. Galford, and Y. E. Shimabukuro. "Decoupling of Deforestation and Soy Production in the Southern Amazon During the Late 2000s." *Proceedings of the National Academy of Sciences of the United States of America* 109 (2012): 1341–46. www.pnas.org/content/109/4/1341.full.pdf.

Morton, D. C., R. S. DeFries, Y. E. Shimabukoro, L. O. Anderson, E. Arai, F. del Bon Espirito-Santo, R. Freitas, and J. Morisette. "Cropland Expansion Changes Deforestation Dynamics in the Southern Brazilian Amazon." *Proceedings of the National Academy of Sciences of the United States of America* 103 (2006): 14637–41. www.pnas.org/content/103/39/14637.full.pdf+html.

National CJD Surveillance Unit. "Creutzfeldt-Jakob Disease Surveil-

lance in the UK." Eighteenth Annual Report. www.cjd.ed.ac.uk/documents
/report18.pdf.

National Creutzfeldt-Jakob Disease Research & Surveillance Unit
(NCJDRSU). "Variant Creutzfeldt-Jakob Disease Current Data (August
2012)."

Nepstad, D. C., D. G. McGrath, and B. Soares-Filho. "Systemic Conservation, REDD, and the Future of the Amazon Basin." *Conservation Biology* 25 (2011): 1113–16.

Nepstad, D. C., C. M. Stickler, B. Soares-Filho, and F. Merry. "Interac-
tion among Amazon Land Use, Forests and Climate: Prospects for a Near-
Term Forest Tipping Point." *Philosophical Transactions of the Royal Society*
B 363 (2007): 1737–46.

Nepstad, D., B. S. Soares-Filho, F. Merry, A. Lima, P. Moutinho, J.
Carter, M. Bowman, A. Cattaneo, H. Rodrigues, S. Schwartzman, D. G.
McGrath, C. M. Stickler, R. Lubowski, P. Piris-Cabezas, S. Rivero, A. Alen-
car, O. Almeida, and O. Stella. "The End of Deforestation in the Brazilian
Amazon." *Science* 326 (2009): 1350–51. www.lerf.esalq.usp.br/divulgacao
/recomendados/artigos/nepstad2009.pdf.

Nepstad, D. C., C. M. Stickler, and O. T. Almeida. "Globalization of
the Amazon Soy and Beef Industries: Opportunities for Conservation." *Conservation Biology* 20 (2006): 1595–603.

Owen, D. *The Conundrum: How Scientific Innovation, Increased Efficiency, and Good Intentions Can Make Our Energy and Climate Problems
Worse*. New York: Riverhead Books, 2012.

Rudorff, B. F. M., M. Adami, D. Alves Aguiar, M. A. Moreira, M. P.
Mello, L. Fabiani, D. F. Amaral, and B. M. Pires. "The Soy Moratorium in
the Amazon Biome Monitored by Remote Sensing Images." *Remote Sensing*
3 (2011): 185–202. www.mdpi.com/2072-4292/3/1/185/pdf.

Tercek, M. "Feeding the World Through Smarter Agriculture." *Cool
Green Science: The Conservation Blog of the Nature Conservancy*, April 27,
2012. blog.nature.org/2012/04/feeding-the-world-without-destroying-our
-planet/.

———."How to Feed 7 Billion and Counting." *Huffington Post*, November 11, 2011. www.huffingtonpost.com/mark-tercek/how-to-feed-7-billion
-and_b_1069666.html.

Thurow, R., and S. Kilman. *Enough: Why the World's Poorest Starve in
an Age of Plenty*. New York: PublicAffairs, 2009.

Tscharntke, T., Y. Clough, T. C. Wanger, L. Jackson, I. Motzke, I. Perfecto, J. Vandermeer, and A. Whitbread. "Global Food Security, Biodiversity Conservation, and the Future of Agricultural Intensification." *Biological Conservation* 151 (2012): 53–59. www.sciencedirect.com/science/article/pii/S0006320712000821#.

World Organisation for Animal Health. "Number of Cases of Bovine Spongiform Encephalopathy (BSE) Reported in the United Kingdom." Chart. Paris: OIE, 2012. www.oie.int/en/animal-health-in-the-world/bse-specific-data/number-of-cases-in-the-united-kingdom/.

Chapter 6: The Million-Dollar Mile

Agardy, T., G. N. di Sciara, and P. Christie. "Mind the Gap: Addressing the Shortcomings of Marine Protected Areas Through Large Scale Marine Spatial Planning." *Marine Policy* 35 (2011): 226–32.

Cressey, D. "Plans for Marine Protection Highlight Science Gap." *Nature* 469 (2011): 146. www.nature.com/news/2011/110110/full/469146a.html.

Gell, F. R., and C. M. Roberts. "Benefits Beyond Boundaries: The Fishery Effects of Marine Reserves and Fishery Closures." *Trends in Ecology and Evolution* 18 (2003): 448–55.

Hamilton R. J., T. Potuku, and J. R. Montambault. "Community-Based Conservation Results in the Recovery of Reef Fish Spawning Aggregations in the Coral Triangle." *Biological Conservation* 144 (2011): 1850–58.

IUCN World Commission on Protected Areas. "Establishing Resilient Marine Protected Area Networks—Making It Happen." Washington, DC: IUCN-WCPA, NOAA, and TNC, 2008. tinyurl.com/9d8o44n.

Leisher, C., P. van Beukering, and L. M. Scherl. "Nature's Investment Bank: How Marine Protected Areas Contribute to Poverty Reduction." Arlington, VA: TNC, 2007. tinyurl.com/9mgt8xy.

Lubchenco, J., and L. E. Petes. "The Interconnected Biosphere: Science at the Ocean's Tipping Points." *Oceanography* 23 (2010): 115–29. www.tos.org/oceanography/archive/23-2_lubchenco.pdf.

Partnership for Interdisciplinary Studies of Coastal Oceans (PISCO). "The Science of Marine Reserves," 2nd ed., International Version. www.piscoweb.org/files/images/pdf/SMR_Intl_LowRes.pdf.

Russ, G. R. and A. C. Alcala. "Enhanced Biodiversity beyond Marine

Reserve Boundaries: The Cup Spillith Over." *Ecological Applications* 21 (2011): 241–50.

United Nations Development Programme, UN Environment Programme, the World Bank, and WRI. "World Resources 2005—The Wealth of the Poor." Washington, DC: WRI, 2005. pdf.wri.org/wrr05_full_hires.pdf.

Weeks, R., G. R. Russ, A. C. Alcala, and A. T. White. "Effectiveness of Marine Protected Areas in the Philippines for Biodiversity Conservation." *Conservation Biology* 24 (2010): 531–40.

World Bank Group. *Attacking Poverty: The World Bank Development Report 2000/2001*. New York: Oxford University Press, 2000.

Chapter 7: Investing in the Future in the Face of Climate Change

Aldy, J. E., and R. N. Stavins. "The Promise and Problems of Pricing Carbon: Theory and Practice." Harvard Kennedy School Faculty Research Series RWP11–041, 2011. web.hks.harvard.edu/publications/getFile.aspx?Id=734.

Angelsen, A. "Forest Cover Change in Space and Time: Combining the von Thünen and Forest Transition Theories." World Bank Policy Research Working Paper WPS 4117. Washington, DC: World Bank, 2007. tinyurl .com/8tryoaz.

———, ed. *Moving Ahead with REDD: Issues, Options and Implications*. Bogor, Indonesia: CIFOR, 2008. tinyurl.com/8knycvm.

"Better REDD Than Dead: A Special Report on Forests." *The Economist*, September 23, 2010. www.economist.com/node/17062737.

Boucher, D. *Out of the Woods: A Realistic Role for Tropical Forests in Curbing Global Warming*. Cambridge, MA: Union of Concerned Scientists, 2008. www.ucsusa.org/assets/documents/global_warming/UCS-REDD -Boucher-report.pdf.

Bowen, A. "The Case for Carbon Pricing." London: Grantham Institute on Climate Change and the Environment, 2011. www2.lse.ac.uk/Grantham Institute/publications/Policy/docs/PB_case-carbon-pricing_Bowen.pdf.

Busch, J., F. Godoy, W. R. Turner, and C. A. Harvey. "Biodiversity Co-Benefits of Reducing Emissions from Deforestation under Alternative Reference Levels and Levels of Finance." *Conservation Letters* 4 (2011): 101–15.

Cleetus, R. "Finding Common Ground in the Debate Between Carbon Tax and Cap-and-Trade Policies." *Bulletin of the Atomic Scientists* 67 (2011): 19–27.

Danielsen, F., M. K. Sorensen, M. F. Olwig, V. Selvam, F. Parish, N. D. Burgess, T. Hiraishi, V. M. Karunagaran, M. S. Rasmussen, L. B. Hansen, A. Quarto, and N. Suryadiputra. "The Asian Tsunami: A Protective Role for Coastal Vegetation." *Science* 310 (2005): 643.

Elias, P., and K. Lininger. "The Plus Side: Promoting Sustainable Carbon Sequestration in Tropical Forests." Cambridge, MA: Union of Concerned Scientists, 2010. www.ucsusa.org/assets/documents/global_warming/The-Plus-Side.pdf.

Environmental Justice Foundation. "Mangroves: Nature's Defence against Tsunamis—A Report on the Impact of Mangrove Loss and Shrimp Farm Development on Coastal Defences." London, UK: Environmental Justice Foundation, 2006. www.pacificdisaster.net/pdnadmin/data/documents/2604.html.

Gilman E. L., J. Ellison, N. C. Duke, and C. Field. "Threats to Mangroves from Climate Change and Adaptation Options." *Aquatic Botany* 89 (2008): 237–50.

Gricsom, B., P. Ellis, F. Putz, and J. Halperin. "Emissions and Potential Emissions Reductions from Logging Concessions of East Kalimantan, Indonesia." Washington, DC: USAID, 2011. tinyurl.com/9x7br2t.

Hamilton, K., R. Bayon, G. Turner, and D. Higgins. "State of the Voluntary Carbon Markets 2007: Picking Up Steam." Washington, DC: Ecosystem Marketplace, 2007. ecosystemmarketplace.com/documents/acrobat/StateoftheVoluntaryCarbonMarket18July_Final.pdf.

Hansen, J., M. Sato, and R. Ruedy. "Perception of Climate Change." *Proceedings of the National Academy of Sciences of the United States of America*, August 6, 2012. www.pnas.org/content/109/37/E2415.full.pdf+htm.

Harris, N. L., S. Brown, S. C. Hagen, S. S. Saatchi, S. Petrova, W. Salas, M. C. Hansen, P. V. Potapov, and A. Lotsch. "Baseline Map of Carbon Emissions from Deforestation in Tropical Regions." *Science* 336 (2012):1573–76.

Hoffman, A. J. "Getting Ahead of the Curve: Corporate Strategies That Address Climate Change." Ann Arbor, MI: Pew Center on Global Climate Change, 2006. www.c2es.org/docUploads/PEW_CorpStrategies.pdf.

Informal Working Group on Interim Finance for REDD. Discussion Document. October 27, 2009. www.theredddesk.org/sites/default/files/resources/pdf/2010/Report_of_the_Informal_Working_Group_on_Interim_Finance_for_REDD_IWG_IFR__October_2009.pdf.

Kanninen M, D. Murdiyarso, F. Seymour, A. Angelsen, S. Wunder, and

L. German. "Do Trees Grow on Money? The Implications of Deforestation Research for Policies to Promote REDD." Bogor, Indonesia: CIFOR, 2007. www.cifor.org/publications/pdf_files/Books/BKanninen0701.pdf.

Kindermann G., M. Obersteiner, B. Sohngen, J. Sathaye, K. Andrasko, E. Rametsteiner, B. Schlamadinger, S. Wunder, and R. Beach. "Global Cost Estimates of Reducing Carbon Emissions Through Avoided Deforestation." *Proceedings of the National Academy of Sciences of the United States of America* 105 (2008): 10302–07. www.pnas.org/content/105/30 /10302.full.

Kodas, M. 2012. "Life on the Edge (of Wildfire)." *OnEarth*, August 7, 2012. www.onearth.org/article/life-on-the-edge-of-wildfire.

Madsen, T., and N. Willcox. "When It Rains, It Pours: Global Warming and the Increase in Extreme Precipitation from 1948 to 2011." Washington, DC: Environment America Research & Policy Center, 2012. www.environmentamerica.org/sites/environment/files/reports/When%20It %20Rains%2C%20It%20Pours%20vUS.pdf.

Matthews, J. H., B. A. J. Wickel, and S. Freeman. "Converging Currents in Climate-Relevant Conservation: Water, Infrastructure, and Institutions." PLOS *Biology* 9 (2011): e1001159. doi:10.1371/journal.pbio.1001159.

Nepstad, D., B. Soares-Filho, F. Merry, P. Moutinho, H. Oliveira Rodrigues, M. Bowman, S. Schwartzman, O. Almeida, and S. Rivero. "The Costs and Benefits of Reducing Carbon Emissions from Deforestation and Forest Degradation in the Brazilian Amazon." Falmouth, MA: The Woods Hole Research Center, 2007. www.whrc.org/policy/pdf/cop13/WHRC _Amazon_REDD.pdf.

Nordhaus, W. D. "The Architecture of Climate Economics: Designing a Global Agreement on Global Warming." *Bulletin of the Atomic Scientists* 67 (2011): 9–18.

———. "Economic Aspects of Global Warming in a Post-Copenhagen Environment." *Proceedings of the National Academy of Sciences of the United States of America* 107 (2010): 11721–26. nordhaus.econ.yale.edu /documents/Copen_020310.pdf.

———. *A Question of Balance: Weighing the Options on Global Warming Policies.* New Haven, CT: Yale University Press, 2008.

Peters-Stanley, M., and K. Hamilton. "Developing Dimension: State of the Voluntary Carbon Markets 2012." A Report by Ecosystem Marketplace & Bloomberg New Energy Finance, 2012. www.forest-trends.org/documents /files/doc_3164.pdf.

Powell, N., M. Osbeck, S. B. Tan, and V. C. Toan. "World Resources Report Case Study. Mangrove Restoration and Rehabilitation for Climate Change Adaptation in Vietnam." World Resources Report, Washington DC. http://www.worldresourcesreport.org/files/wrr/wrr_case_study_mangrove _restoration_vietnam.pdf.

Putz, F. E., P. A. Zuidema, T. Synnott, M. Peña-Claros, M. A. Pinard, D. Sheil, J. K. Vanclay, P. Sist, S. Gourlet-Fleury, B. Griscom, J. Palmer, and R. Zagt. "Sustaining Conservation Values in Selectively Logged Tropical Forests: The Attained and the Attainable." *Conservation Letters* 5 (2012): 296–303.

Royal Academy of Engineering. "Infrastructure, Engineering and Climate Change Adaptation—Ensuring Services in an Uncertain Future." London, UK: The Royal Academy of Engineering on behalf of *Engineering the Future*, 2011. www.raeng.org.uk/adaptation.

Sathirathai, S., and E. B. Barbier. "Valuing Mangrove Conservation in Southern Thailand." *Contemporary Economic Policy* 19 (2001): 109–22. tinyurl.com/8lgpmpw.

Siikamäki, J., J. N. Sanchirico, and S. L. Jardine. "Global Economic Potential for Reducing Carbon Dioxide Emissions from Mangrove Loss." *Proceedings of the National Academy of Sciences of the United States of America*, July 2012. www.pnas.org/cgi/doi/10.1073/pnas.1200519109.

Stavins, R. N., and K. R. Richards. "The Cost of US Forest-Based Carbon Sequestration." Arlington, VA: Pew Center on Global Climate Change, 2005. www.c2es.org/docUploads/Sequest_Final.pdf.

Williams, N. "Tsunami Insight to Mangrove Value." *Current Biology* 15 (2005). tinyurl.com/8ka7lg3.

Zarin, D. J. "Carbon from Tropical Deforestation." *Science* 336 (2012): 1518–19.

Chapter 8: Town and Country

American Water Intelligence. *DC Water Chief: Right Place, Right Time*. Vol. 3(3): 22–23. December, 2010.

Bratman, G. N., J. P. Hamilton, and G. C. Daily. "The Impacts of Nature Experience on Human Cognitive Function and Mental Health." *Annals of the New York Academy of Sciences* 1249 (2012): 118–36.

"Coca-Cola on the Yangtze: A Corporate Campaign for Clean Water in China." *Law and Public Policy*, August 18, 2010, knowledge.wharton.upenn .edu/article.cfm?articleid=2568.

Cohen, R., B. Nelson, and G. Wolff. *Energy Down the Drain: The Hidden Costs of California's Water Supply*. New York: Natural Resources Defense Council, 2004. www.nrdc.org/water/conservation/edrain/edrain .pdf.

Denning, C. A., R. I. McDonald, and J. Christensen. "Did Land Protection in Silicon Valley Reduce the Housing Stock?" *Biological Conservation* 143 (2010): 1087–93.

Dunn, A. D. 2010. "Siting Green Infrastructure: Legal and Policy Solutions to Alleviate Urban Poverty and Promote Healthy Communities." *Environmental Affairs* 37 (2010): 41–66. digitalcommons.pace.edu/lawfaculty /559.

Fishman, C. "Why GE, Coca-Cola, and IBM Are Getting into the Water Business." *Fast Company* 154, April 11, 2011. www.fastcompany.com /magazine/154/a-sea-of-dollars.html.

———. *The Big Thirst: The Secret Life and Turbulent Future of Water*. New York: Free Press, 2011.

Fuller, R. A., K. N. Irvine, P. Devine-Wright, P. H. Warren, and K. J. Gaston. "Psychological Benefits of Greenspace Increase with Biodiversity." *Biology Letters* 3 (2007): 390–94.

Gardiner, B. "Beverage Industry Works to Cap Its Water Use." *New York Times*, March 21, 2011. www.nytimes.com/2011/03/22/business/energy -environment/22iht-rbog-beverage-22.html?pagewanted=all.

Garrison, N., and K. Hobbs. 2011. *Rooftops to Rivers II: Green Strategies for Controlling Stormwater and Combined Sewer Overflows*. New York: Natural Resources Defense Council, 2011. www.nrdc.org/water/pollution/rooftopsii /files/rooftopstoriversII.pdf.

Garrison, N., R. C. Wilkinson, and R. Horner. *A Clear Blue Future: How Greening California Cities Can Address Water Resources and Climate Challenges in the 21st Century*. Seattle: Natural Resources Defense Council, 2009. www.nrdc.org/water/lid/files/lid_hi.pdf.

Gill, S. E., J. F. Handley, A. R. Ennos, and S. Pauleit. "Adapting Cities for Climate Change: The Role of the Green Infrastructure." *Built Environment* 33 (2007): 115–33. tinyurl.com/936q5lv.

Jones, P. "Corporate Giants Back WRI." *Environmental Finance*, August 18, 2011. www.environmental-finance.com/news/view/1923 (subscription necessary).

Kloss, C., and C. Calarusse. *Rooftops to Rivers: Green Strategies for Controlling Stormwater and Combined Sewer Overflows*. Washington: Natural

Resources Defense Council, 2006. www.nrdc.org/water/pollution/rooftops
/rooftops.pdf.

Land Trust Alliance. 2010 National Land Trust Census Report. www
.landtrustalliance.org/land-trusts/land-trust-census/national-land-trust-census
-2010/2010-final-report.

Lederbogen, F., P. Kirsch, L. Haddad, F. Streit, H. Tost, P. Schuch, S.
Wüst, J. C. Pruessner, M. Rietschel, M. Deuschle, and A. Meyer-Lindenberg.
"City Living and Urban Upbringing Affect Neural Social Stress Processing in
Humans." *Nature* 474 (2011): 498–501.

Mell, I. "Green Infrastructure: Concepts and Planning." *FORUM
Ejournal* 8 (2008): 69–80.

Nidumolu, R., C. K. Prahalad, and M. R. Rangaswami. "Why Sustainability Is Now the Key Driver of Innovation." *Harvard Business Review*, September 2009.

Olmsted, F. L. "The Value and Care of Parks." Report to the Congress
of the State of California, 1865. Reprinted in *The American Environment*,
ed. R. Nash, 18–24. Reading, MA: Addison-Wesley Pub. Co., 1976.

———. "Yosemite and the Mariposa Grove: A Preliminary Report, 1865."
www.yosemite.ca.us/library/olmsted/report.html.

Raucher, R. S. "A Triple Bottom Line Assessment of Traditional and
Green Infrastructure Options for Controlling CSO Events in Philadel-
phia's Watersheds: Final Report," August 24, 2009. Boulder, CO: Stratus
Consulting Inc. www.michigan.gov/documents/dnr/TBL.AssessmentGreen
VsTraditionalStormwaterMgt_293337_7.pdf.

Rybczynski, W. *A Clearing in the Distance: Frederick Law Olmsted and
America in the Nineteenth Century.* New York: Scribner, 1999.

Chapter 9: The Business Case for Nature

Eccles, R. G., I. Ioannou, and G. Serafeim. "The Impact of a Corporate
Culture of Sustainability on Corporate Behavior and Performance." Harvard
Business School Working Paper 12–035, May 9, 2012. www.hbs.edu
/research/pdf/12–035.pdf

Nidumolu, R., C. K. Prahalad, and M. R. Rangaswami. "Why Sustainability Is Now the Key Driver of Innovation." *Harvard Business Review*, September 2009.

Tercek, M. "Rio+20: Leadership from New Directions." *Cool Green*

Science: The Conservation Blog of the Nature Conservancy, June 27, 2012. blog.nature.org/2012/06/rio-20-leadership-new-directions-mark-tercek/.

———. "Making the Business Case for Conservation." *Cool Green Science: The Conservation Blog of the Nature Conservancy*, January 27, 2012. blog.nature.org/2012/01/making-the-business-case-for-conservation/.

Walsh, S. "Science in the TNC-Dow Collaboration Analysis #2: Preserving or Restoring Coastal Habitats & Coastal Risk Mitigation." *Science Chronicles*, April 16, 2012. www.conservationgateway.org/News/Pages/science-tnc-dow-collaboraaspx16.aspx.

White, A. "Sustainability and the Accountable Corporation." *Environment* 41 (1999): 30–43.

Conclusion

Nordhaus, W. D. "Why the Global Warming Skeptics Are Wrong." *New York Review of Books*, February 22, 2012.

Index